Pomp and Circumstance

Noël Coward was born in 1899 in Teddington, Middlesex. He made his name as a playwright with *The Vortex* (1924), in which he also appeared. His numerous other successful plays included *Fallen Angels* (1925), *Hay Fever* (1925), *Private Lives* (1933), *Design for Living* (1933), and *Blithe Spirit* (1941). During the war he wrote screenplays such as *Brief Encounter* (1944) and *This Happy Breed* (1942). In the fifties he began a new career as a cabaret entertainer. He published volumes of verse and a novel (*Pomp and Circumstance*, 1960), two volumes of autobiography and four volumes of short stories: *To Step Aside* (1939), *Star Quality* (1951), *Pretty Polly Barlow* (1964) and *Bon Voyage* (1967). He was knighted in 1970 and died three years later in Jamaica.

Noël Coward

POMP AND CIRCUMSTANCE

A novel

METHUEN

1 3 5 7 9 10 8 6 4 2

This edition published in 1999 by Methuen Publishing Limited
215 Vauxhall Bridge Road, London SW1V 1EJ

Peribo Pty Limited, 58 Beaumont Road, Mount Kuring-Gai,
NSW 2080, Australia, ACN 002 273 761
(for Australia and New Zealand)

Pomp and Circumstance first published in the United Kingdom
in 1960 by William Heinemann Ltd
First published by Methuen London Ltd in 1983

Methuen Publishing Limited Reg. No. 3543167

ISBN 0 413 56370 7

A CIP catalogue record for this book is
available from the British Library

Papers used by Methuen Publishing Limited are natural,
recyclable products made from wood grown in sustainable forests.
The manufacturing processes conform to environmental
regulations of the country of origin.

ONE

There's no use pretending that Government House architecturally has anything to recommend it at all because it hasn't; it is quite agreeable inside with nice airy rooms and deep-set verandahs, but outside it is unequivocally hideous. Viewed from any aspect it looks like a gargantuan mauve blancmange. It was built in the early nineteen hundreds after the old one had burned down, and nobody knows why it should have been painted mauve in the first place or why it should always have been repainted mauve since. It has domes and towers and buttresses and a few bastard Norman windows and, underneath, a series of thick stone arches forming a sort of catacomb. Actually this eccentricity has been satisfactorily explained—it is a refuge for the inmates to retire to when menaced by acts of God such as typhoons and earthquakes, although I cannot feel it would be much of a comfort in a flood. When Lady Alexandra first saw it leering out at her from its grove of poincianas she laughed so much that she choked and was unable to get out of the car when it arrived at the door until someone had brought her a glass of water. Lady A. is gay and charming and H.E. (Sir George Shotter) is just right. He is nice-looking without being wildly distinguished; solid in the right sort of way and with a quizzical gleam in his eye. Actually he takes a bit of knowing, because he is shy and not a cheerful extrovert like she is, but if you persevere and prod about a bit you get the quizzical gleam and then you know you're home.

As a matter of fact she and I are old comrades in arms because we were in the M.T.C. together at the beginning of the war and used to drill in Lowndes Square and call our superior officers "Madam," and later on, when we considered ourselves officers and

9

had paid for some very snappy uniforms, we used to be called "Madam" ourselves and drive important Brass Hats to and from airports and stations and, on Sundays, to Boulters Lock with their secretaries.

Later still, during the blitzes, we had more gruesome assignments and had to remain tight-lipped and coldly efficient while we dragged people out of bombed houses and took them off to hospitals. Sandra was absolutely wonderful throughout, and we used to giggle a lot, not when we were dragging the bodies out, naturally, but at other times. She was still Lady Alexandra Haven then and hadn't married anybody, although she had been walking out with dear George since nineteen thirty-nine. He was a rather left-wing politician and had been furious about Munich, which endeared him to me from the start.

However, as she was also walking out with several other suitors at the time, nobody thought that she would marry George, but she did, in nineteen forty-three, and they had a fairly eccentric honeymoon darting about the Middle East trying to locate his regiment, which had suddenly been sent there.

By then of course she had left the M.T.C. and I had too, with great relief, I must admit. It was all very fine at the beginning when we were upheld by splendid patriotism and felt sort of dedicated, but after a bit the overweening femaleness of the whole setup began to get us down. I know it is a shameful confession, but to me there is always something vaguely hilarious about women in uniform. I know the A.T.S. were wonderful, and the W.A.A.F.s were wonderful and the W.R.N.S. gallant and efficient to the last lanyard; but it's when they march and drill and their busts wobble that it makes me want to laugh. This was one of the things that Sandra and I used to giggle about most. In fact we still do when we have time to have a gossip and those curious days come winging back to us out of the past.

Anyhow now she's our governor's lady, and it's lovely having them here and makes going to G.H. something to look forward to, which it certainly wasn't when the poor Blaises were here. Not that they weren't perfectly nice and well disposed and did all they had to do affably and conscientiously, but they were both dim and a bit dessicated and lacked vitality to such a degree that one felt oxygen should be served after the fish. Poor Lady Blaise suffered, uncomplainingly, from some obscure malaise called dia-something-or-other. It wasn't "betes" or "rrhoea," but whatever it was it dimmed her down more than ever and she gave you the impression that she was swimming languidly through the years in her own personal aquarium.

He, Sir Hilary, was just straight out of Madame Tussaud's, pale he was through and through, his eyes were pale, his skin was pale and his hair was pale and when he reviewed troops or stood about on public platforms he looked as if he had been arranged there and set in position with an unseen iron bar behind him to keep him from falling on his face.

Now everything has changed including, thank God, the chintzes. The whole house has taken on a lightness that it certainly never had before.

It isn't that Sandra possesses much domestic virtuosity. She occasionally has ideas about the food and bouts of sudden enthusiasm during which she sends to New York and Paris for exotic cookery books, but by the time they arrive she has forgotten all about it and pecks away at trifles and *rissoles* without even noticing them. What she has infused into the dry bones of that pompous old Gothic mausoleum, is personality.

Nevertheless she nips away from it whenever she can find an opportunity and comes up to our plantation and kicks her shoes off and just lies about. The children adore her because she treats them casually as adults and doesn't suddenly put on a treacly indulgent voice and ask them what they want to be when they grow up and whether they like being at school. Simon, the eldest, is seven and a half and the twins, Janet and Cokey, are six. Cokey's real name is Sarah-Ellen, but one day when she was tiny and she and Janet were lying in their pram in the garden, a coconut,—a small one, fortunately—fell from the tree, missed her head by an inch, and gave her a nasty bruise on the shoulder. Although startled, she didn't shriek or make a scene, she merely stretched out a pudgy hand and patted it reprovingly and said "Naughty Cokey," and if that isn't a nauseating echo of babyhood I should like to know what is. Anyhow "Cokey" stuck, and that's the end of that rather dull little explanation.

On a blazing afternoon last March, Sandra arrived, unexpectedly as usual, in the G.H. station wagon. She looked cool and ravishing in a green linen suit, but there was a hectic gleam in her eye. I was lying on the back verandah trying to get interested in one of those contemporary overintrospective novels which I knew I ought to read but didn't really want to. This one was written by a hysterical character who, after an absolutely beastly childhood in Frankfurt, became a member of "the party" and went to the Ukraine with a high-powered revolutionary called Irma who had level brows, smouldering eyes, and was given to sudden outbursts of tigerish sensuality in course of which she would pull down the author's head onto her mouth, giving hoarse inarticulate cries while her disengaged hand fumbled with the buttons of her tunic. It was just at the moment when, sensibly, I think, he had decided to renounce communism, that Sandra appeared.

She kicked off her shoes as usual, flung herself down on the swing seat which creaked violently, and said, "Thank God you're in; I couldn't have borne it if you hadn't been."

I asked her if she wanted a cold drink, and she replied that she didn't want a cold drink or tea or anything except to lie down flat and merge herself into a stream of universal consciousness where time ceased to exist and she hadn't got to concentrate on anything in the least specific. Lunch, she went on to say, had been undiluted misery from the avocado pears right on through the curry to the lemon meringue pie and the coffee. There had been an Anglican bishop with an ear-splitting cough, an American senator and his wife, and a fierce aluminium tycoon from Pittsburgh. Added to this, Cuckoo Honey, the colonial secretary's wife, had been at her worst, which was saying a good deal, and had mortally offended the American senator by embarking on a quite gratuitous dissertation on the Negro problem, about which she obviously knew less than nothing.

"The dreadful thing about poor Cuckoo is her complete unawareness of her own insensate conceit." Sandra stretched herself out and groaned. "She has examined herself minutely from every angle and been unable to find a flaw. She is neither cruel, unkind, nor malignant but she manages, time and again, to give the impression of being all three. She blurts out whatever happens to be whirling through her idiotic head without pausing to consider for a split second the feelings of whoever she's talking to. It would have been perfectly obvious to a drunken child of three that the senator was a real old Deep Southern die-hard who had been weaned on mint juleps and been taken to lynchings as a birthday treat, and of course she had to choose him of all people to let fly at with all her inaccurate, woolly humanitarianism. Naturally the whole atmosphere shuddered with embarrassment, the senator went purple in the face, and I murmured something inept about racial discrimination being too complex a subject for a gay, informal luncheon, but she disregarded this completely and ploughed on through a jungle of clichés with her voice getting higher and higher until finally I was forced to jump up quite suddenly like a jack-in-the-box and sweep her and the senator's wife onto the verandah where they sat tight-lipped and glowering at each other."

Sandra gave a deep sigh and fumbled in her bag for a cigarette. "Then, when at long last they had all cleared off and I had flown at her and sent her home in tears, George appeared shaking like a leaf and told me in sepulchral tones the 'Great News'!"

"What on earth do you mean?" I said, throwing her a box of matches.

"It's absolutely top secret." She lit her cigarette and threw the matches back to me. "He made me swear not to mention it to a living soul, even you, but I said that was nonsense and I always told you everything, so he gave in on condition that I made you promise on your solemn word of honour to keep your trap shut until the official announcement is made."

"Official announcement of what?"

"They're coming here in June."

"Who's coming here in June?"

"The Queen of course," said Sandra. "And Prince Philip. They're arriving in a warship on the twenty-first and going to spend three days. Three whole days and three whole nights, and long long before those three whole days and nights I shall be led away in a strait jacket like that poor beast in *Streetcar Named Desire*."

"Well!" I murmured rather inadequately. "What an excitement!"

"Can you imagine," cried Sandra tragically, "what's going to happen to all of us between now and June? Can you visualize the heart-burnings, the squabbles, the planning committees, the entertainment committees, the awful, degrading jockeyings for position that will go on? It will be a nightmare."

"There's no sense in working yourself up into a frizz," I said soothingly. "I expect quite a lot of it will be great fun, and anyhow it will be a wonderful thing for the island. The Samolans will be terribly proud and thrilled."

"I know all that," said Sandra. "I *know* it will be wonderful for the island *and* for the dear Samolans. I know it is a splendid thing for George that it should happen during his term of governorship. I know it will give a terrific boost to the Samolan tourist trade and that it will be wonderful for all the hotels and all the native arts and crafts and all the university students and the local scouts and the Women's Federation. There is only one lonely, quivering creature for whom it will not be so wonderful and that is the wretched governor's wife upon whose frail, stooping shoulders the crushing brunt of the whole carry-on will fall."

"Cheer up, dear," I said, "you'll probably enjoy every minute of it and boss everybody about and have the whale of a time."

"I had hoped," said Sandra, "that you would be sympathetic and understanding and stand by me in my hour of tribulation, but I see now that those hopes were based on shifting sand. I can already see a glint of awful suburban royal snobbery in your eye. You will probably be worse than anyone in the colony; you'll keep on rushing up to them and bobbing up and down like a cork."

"It's no good attacking me for being a royal snob," I replied. "It's the way I've been brought up, and it's too late to change me now. I have a lovely schoolgirl sentimental excitement bubbling up in me already. I have even, while you were moaning and growling, been planning a fascinating new evening dress and wondering whether there will be time for Jeannie to get my tiara out of Barclay's Bank and have it sent out to me. It's actually rather a gloomy little affair which was left to me by Aunt Cordelia, but it has a certain frowsy distinction."

Sandra sighed. "I think I would like some tea after all," she said.

I rang the bell for Tahali to bring tea. The governor's lady had stretched out flat on her back again and had closed her eyes: every now and then she put her left foot down and rocked the swing seat and each time she did this it creaked complainingly and I wondered if there was any oil in the house and if so whether or not I should be able to get it into the hinges without ruining the loose cover. I have never, alas, been any good at doing those handy little domestic chores which are essential to the smooth running of a gracious home, and in this gracious home there is always something a little wrong somewhere. At the very moment that I write there are two rings broken on Robin's shower curtain which I have been meaning to see to for weeks, and the seat in the downstairs loo won't stay up when you want it to. This of course doesn't affect female visitors but is tricky for the men who have to get themselves into an unnatural sideways position and prop it up with one knee.

Apparently nothing can be done about it without taking the whole caboodle to pieces and putting it together again and this means sending for Mr. Pana-Oti, the plumber, which I dread. But with the Great Occasion pending, definite action would certainly have to be taken before June. Not that I expected the royal visitors to spend much time in my downstairs loo, but you never know and Prince Philip just *might* have a flat tyre on his way to the golf course and somebody or other just *might* say, "Sir, the Craigie plantation is only a stone's throw away and if, Sir, you would care for a nice cool drink and a wash and brush-up I'm sure they'd be honoured and delighted. They're awfully nice people although *she's* a bit erratic . . ." Then in they'd all troop and I should hear that awful crash and be forever mortified.

Sandra opened one eye and looked at me. "You look harassed. What are you thinking about?"

"The Duke of Edinburgh," I replied.

"I might have known it," she said crossly and shut it again.

Tahali appeared with the tea tray which he placed carefully on the banana-mesh table which is native-made, very attractive and atmospheric, but inclined to wobble. After he had deposited it he made a beautiful bow to Sandra and went back into the house. Tahali is a treasure and the light of my life. When Robin first brought me here just after we were married Tahali was sixteen and was a sort of odd-job boy about the place. A year later, as he was outstandingly efficient, cheerful, and decorative, we promoted him to houseboy and for the last two years he has been major-domo, butler, and chauffeur combined and runs the whole place and I couldn't get through a day without him. He is tall and handsome and, like most Samolans, happily free from a sense of sin. He has a wife and three children in his home village on the other side of the island whom he visits reluctantly twice a year,

15

and some intimate friends and several other children here in Pendarla whom he visits more frequently. Every so often he has a lapse and gets very drunk indeed on Kala-Kala and staggers back to the house in the early hours and appears with breakfast looking bleary and hang-dog and altogether dreadful.

On these occasions he is either lectured by Robin and bursts into tears, or reasoned with, solemnly, by me, which usually ends in gay, uninhibited laughter. This is because he knows instinctively that there isn't an ounce of moral conviction behind my words and that in my deep heart I couldn't care less if he gets fried as a coot every now and then providing he doesn't do it too often and let it interfere with his work and upset the other servants.

I am aware that this *laissez-faire* attitude of mine to accepted moral standards is most unsuitable in a respectable British matron: I am also aware that as a professed Christian living on an island which has only sketchily been reclaimed from cheerful paganism that it is my bounden duty to stamp out evil whenever I see it rearing its ugly head and set a stern example to those lesser breeds about me. But I am no good at that sort of thing on account of having my own personal views about what is evil and what isn't.

If I caught Tahali being cruel to a child or wilfully hurting an animal I should beat him out of the house with my bare hands, but if he wants to get drunk occasionally and pop into bed with some of his friends I can see no earthly reason why he shouldn't, and no spiritual reason either, for that matter. He's a young man, very good-looking and full of vitality, and I think he would be a fool not to seize every gay opportunity he can. Of course if he showed any signs of taking to drink seriously and becoming a sodden alcoholic I should do everything in my power to stop him because it would ruin his looks and snuff out his charm and make him foolish and useless to himself and to everyone else. But there is little likelihood of that happening, because Samolans seldom become alcoholics, in fact they never do anything to excess like we do on our superior Western plane, I suppose because they're not neurotic and we are. There are no dope addicts or nymphomaniacs or dypsomaniacs or pathological sex murderers in Samolo. There is a great deal of sex which goes on all the time with a winsome disregard of gender, but there are very few "sex crimes." In England

16

we know that no little girl can hope to get across Wandsworth Common after dark without being "interfered with," whereas here she could prattle her way across the whole length and breadth of the island without anything happening to her at all beyond possibly being stuffed with guavas and mangoes by kindly villagers and given indigestion.

Sandra sat up on the swing seat and patted her hair into place. "You ought to do something about this creaking," she said. "It's ear-splitting."

"I know, it's been driving me mad for months."

"It needs oiling."

"I know it does. I've been meaning to have it done, but somehow I've never got round to it."

"If there's an oil can in the house I could do it for you myself in two minutes."

"You won't do any such thing," I said. "You'd get it all over yourself and your dress, and anyhow it's no use trying to impress me with your Camp Fire Girl efficiency. You were worse than I was in the M.T.C."

"Oh no I wasn't," she replied, buttering a cassava cake and putting a dollop of jam on it. "I once changed a tire in ten minutes on the Esher By-Pass in the pouring rain. The old boy I was driving was most impressed."

"Didn't he offer to help?"

"Of course he did, but I wouldn't let him. He was very old anyhow and blazing with medals, and it would have been terribly infra-dig if anyone had passed and seen him scrambling about with me on the macadam getting soaked to skin. Also he might have had a heart attack."

"What was he blazing with medals for on the Esher By-Pass?"

"I don't know." Sandra looked vaguely out over the ravine to the hills on the other side; the banana leaves were a shiny blue-green in the late afternoon sunlight. "I'd picked him up in Portsmouth and was taking him to some sort of function at the Dorchester. Have those bananas been newly sprayed or is there something the matter with them? They look strangely blue to me."

"Sprayed," I said. "All that crop was done this morning. They'd be wonderful to paint, wouldn't they? Except that nobody would believe it."

"I don't think that matters. Look at Gauguin with all those pink mountains and brown ladies with short legs and no bones. Nobody could believe those for a minute. Oh dear!" she sighed and began to put on her shoes. "I shall have to go home, and I don't want to a bit because it's so lovely and peaceful here in spite of that awful creaking. You swear not to breathe a word about the *great news* to a living soul. You'd better come to lunch tomorrow and we can go to my sitting room afterwards and start making lists."

"What sort of lists?"

"All sorts of lists," she said firmly and rose to her feet. "I don't think there's anyone particularly gruesome lunching tomorrow. At least you'll be spared Cuckoo because I don't intend to invite her to anything for two weeks just to teach her a sharp lesson, and the most awful thing about it is that she'll really mind. Isn't that extraordinary? I'd be only too relieved if it were me." We strolled through the house and out onto the front verandah. "She loves officialdom," Sandra went on. "She wraps it round her like a fur coat and snuggles down into it. Can you imagine what she'll be like when poor Edward finally gets made into a governor of somewhere or other? Which I suppose eventually he will be. She'll be a fiend incarnate, insult people right and left and run the A.D.C.s ragged and all with the best intentions. I expect a lot of that anaemic *folie de grandeur* comes from being born and brought up on that bloody hill station in India. She must have been a perfect pig of a girl galloping about in jodhpurs and romping with all those hot subalterns. Oh God!" She kissed me absently and climbed into the station wagon.

"You're working yourself up into another state," I said, "which will get you nowhere and merely upset your acids, and in any case you have far more important problems to think about than Cuckoo Honey."

"Thank you, darling, for reminding." She gave a slight giggle. "One o'clock on the dot and thanks for the cassava cakes, which I know have put on at least two pounds." She waved her hand, and the car turned under the eucalyptus tree and disappeared down the drive.

I returned thoughtfully to the back verandah and poured myself out another cup of tea. The sun was not far from setting and Nanny, who had gone off in the Austin to shop in the town and fetch the children from school, would be back with them at any minute. There was no time to start doing anything like the *Times* crossword or oiling the swing seat, and I couldn't bear the thought of returning to that humourless Communist and his uninspired, conscience-stricken rationalizations, so I just sat down, lit a cigarette, and looked at the view which, as usual at this hour of the day, was carrying on like an impressionist exhibition.

There is no glimpse of the sea from this back verandah, only the plantation first going down to the river at the bottom of the ravine and then the mauvish rocks and feathery bamboos climbing up the hill, and behind this more hills rolling away into the distance where the high peaks of the Lailanu Mountains stick up like blue fingers into the vivid sky.

TWO

In due course Nanny and the children arrived and the peace of
the evening was rent into a thousand fragments. They flew out
of the car and came whooping into the house; Cokey fell down
immediately and had to be picked up and comforted; Simon had
a lump on his forehead the size of a cricket ball which was the
outcome of a fight with Dickie Chalmers, who had hit him with a
ruler; the dogs appeared suddenly from the kitchen quarters and
barked enthusiastically and jumped up at everybody and knocked
over a small table with rather a sullen photograph of Robin's sister
on it which I didn't mind about really because it always irritated
me every time I looked at it. It isn't that I don't like Helen; we've
got on perfectly well on the few occasions when we've had to, but
she has a dour personality and always gives me the impression
that she is about to accuse me of doing something wrong. She lives
in a cold grey house in Perthshire filled with antlers and stuffed
pike, and I live in perpetual fear that she and Hamish will suddenly decide to come out and stay with us.

When the general pandemonium had subsided and the children
and dogs had mercifully disappeared into the garden, Nanny
came out onto the verandah and sat down purposefully. She had
taken her hat off, frizzed out her hair, and seemed all set for a
cosy little chat. Nanny, I think, calls for a little explanation. In
the first place she isn't a Nanny at all in the accepted sense of the
word. Her real name is Vera Longman and she came out to Samolo with her mother, who apparently was a brute of the first
water, one of those bridge-playing, ambulant English widows who
travel about the world on a small income, trailing clouds of Cheltenham and quarrelling with hotel managers. Anyhow she died of

a heart attack in the Beach Grove Guest House in nineteen fifty and left the wretched Vera, who had devoted her life to her, without a penny. Everyone was very kind and rallied round, Lady Blaise started a secret fund to which we all subscribed anonymously so that Vera shouldn't feel humiliated when she came face to face with any of us socially, and Siggy Rubia got her a temporary job in the travel bureau in the Royal Samolan which only lasted for the winter season but at least gave her breathing space and time to look round.

She came to us two years ago because she said she was good with children, and it's really been a great success on the whole. She *is* good with the children, firm and sensible and quite kind, and although I cannot say that they absolutely dote on her, they accept her philosophically and, as a rule, do what she tells them.

Robin can't stand her: her ineradicable refinement irritates him, and he says that she goes through life aching to be insulted. Personally I like her all right in an arid sort of way but she discourages intimacy, and although on occasion I have tried to break through her cast-iron rectitude and make her let down her hair a bit, I have never really succeeded. I like to think, in my more sentimental moments, that her heart has been frozen by a disastrous love affair and that one day she will meet the man of her dreams and blossom like a rose, but I don't hold out any great hopes of this. Her ego has been permanently squeezed out of shape by her horrible old mother, and even if she has a man of her dreams, which I strongly doubt, her bright, prim little laugh and her unparalleled gift for clichés would probably scare him off before he got to first base.

I asked her if she wanted any tea, but she said she had already had tea with Mrs. Turling, whom she had met in Rodrigues' store buying plain linen table napkins on which she proposed to paint sprays of flowers. Mrs. Turling is one of our local institutions. She and the admiral have lived here for years and are much loved. He is bright red and an established authority on weather conditions, and she is pale and pretty and indefatigable; she never stops painting and sewing and crocheting and contriving dainty little gifts for sales of work. He always refers to her as "Princess," and they are both well over seventy.

"Mrs. Turling told me something very interesting," said Nanny, lowering her voice and leaning forward as though she suspected there might be a microphone concealed in the vase of hibiscus. "Of course it may only be one of those rumours, but apparently the admiral had heard it at the club and came home in a state of great excitement."

"What sort of rumour?"

"I know I oughtn't to tell you because she swore me to secrecy, but I just can't keep it to myself." Nanny gave one of her little giggles which madden Robin so much, and looked furtively over her shoulder.

"Come on, Nanny," I said, leaning forward too so that our heads were only a couple of feet from one another. "You know how dearly I love a nice bit of island gossip."

"This isn't exactly gossip, it's much more important than that, I mean it's really something tremendously thrilling, that is, if it's true."

Nanny leaned still closer until I feared that she might topple forward into my lap. Of course I had guessed by then what she was going to tell me, but it would have been cruel to deflate her so I gave a little sigh of repressed excitement. "Go on," I said breathlessly. "Give. I'm on tenterhooks."

"The Queen," she said triumphantly. "The Queen and Prince Philip are coming here to pay an official visit in June!"

I fell back as though stunned and stared at her with flattering disbelief. "No," I said. "It can't be true!"

"The admiral seems to think it is. He said it was all over the club."

"But why hasn't it been announced in the papers?"

"It has to be kept a dead secret," said Nanny. "Until all the final arrangements are settled. At least that's what Mrs. Turling said. It will be wonderful, won't it? I mean if it is true. Think how thrilled the Samolans will be to see our lovely young Queen and her handsome husband, I mean it will be a frightfully *good* thing from every point of view, a sort of reminder of home and the mother country and that we all belong to one great big family. Mrs. Turling said she wouldn't be surprised if it didn't make an enormous difference to the elections and absolutely routed the Samolan Socialist Nationals. After all there's nothing so important as personal contact, is there? I mean the very fact that the natives will be able to see the Queen with their own eyes is bound to have a tremendous effect, isn't it?"

"It's a pity," I said, feeling that the atmosphere was becoming too highly charged, "that they should decide to come slap in the middle of the rainy season."

"Her Majesty won't mind that," said Nanny brightly. "In England she is always having to do all sorts of things in the pouring rain, and she never pays the faintest attention. Why, only the other day there was a picture of her in *The Reaper* at a racecourse somewhere or other standing there smiling in a positive sea of umbrellas. Besides, out here, even in the rainy season, it's only really bad for a few hours every day, I mean it's not like England when it goes on all the time."

At this moment we were interrupted by Tahali coming down to remove the tea tray. Nanny backed her chair away guiltily as though we had been discovered doing something shameful, and embarked, with what I presume she considered superb presence of mind, on an unconvincing tirade against the traffic congestion in the town.

"And the police really are hopeless," she said. "They motion you on with one hand and hold you back with the other."

"That's life in a nutshell," I said absently.

"How do you mean?" Nanny, arrested in mid-flight, looked puzzled.

"Well," I murmured uneasily, trying to collect my mind, which had wandered back to Aunt Cordelia's tiara. "It's one of the most tiresome aspects of democratic living, isn't it?"

Tahali, who, I suspect, knew that I was improvising, shot me a quick look that was almost a wink and disappeared with the tray.

"What is?" Nanny persisted, a small frown puckering her pale forehead.

"This awful business of being encouraged to do things at one moment and then prevented from doing them the next. Like buying a new car," I added rather wildly.

"But you haven't bought a new car, have you?"

"Of course I haven't. I was merely using that as an example. We are encouraged to buy new cars all the time because it's good for the motor trade and keeps everyone employed and every new car is keyed up to go much much faster than the old one did and you go whizzing off in it flushed with triumph and are immediately arrested for exceeding the speed limit."

"I'm afraid I don't quite understand."

"Never mind," I said desperately. "It really couldn't matter less. It was only when you said about the police motioning you on with one hand and holding you back with the other and I said 'That's life in a nutshell,' which didn't really mean much anyhow and sort of slipped out, and you not unnaturally asked me what I meant and I had to think of some way to justify it."

"Justify what?"

"Life in a nutshell." I put my head back and closed my eyes.

"You are funny sometimes, Mrs. Craigie, you really are," she said with a whinny. "I never know what you are going to say next."

"Neither do I," I replied with my eyes still closed.

"You haven't got a headache, have you?"

The solicitude in her voice forced me to look at her. She had risen to her feet and was staring at me anxiously with her head a little on one side as though she were trying to read someone else's paper in a railway carriage.

"As a matter of fact," I said, "I have got a little bit of a headache; it's been rather an oppressive afternoon and I foolishly had some sherry before lunch, which always goes gurgling down straight onto my liver."

"I *am* so sorry. Is there anything I can do?"

"Not a thing. If you'll go and cope with the children I'll pop upstairs and take a couple of aspirin and have a bath."

"Very well. I'll leave you to your own devices." She started down the steps into the garden and then turned. "You won't say anything about what I told you, will you? Mrs. Turling swore me to secrecy."

"Honour as a scout," I said, and away she went across the grass looking as though she'd been invented by Katherine Mansfield.

THREE

I went upstairs and absent-mindedly took two aspirin, remembering after I had swallowed them that I really hadn't a headache at all but had only pretended to have one in order to get rid of Nanny. Then I sat down rather hopelessly on the bed and looked round the room deciding, as I had decided a hundred times before, that I was sick to death of it as it was and that the time had come to have it repainted, change all the furniture around, and make it look entirely different. I knew that Robin would kick like a steer if I suggested this because he is a creature of habit and likes things to be well ordered and immutable and comfortably familiar, but ah me! I am not like that at all, too much sameness for too long gives me claustrophobia. I am possessed by unreasonable devils and am temperamentally allergic to leaving well alone. Once when I was very young I twisted my old straw hat into the shape of a boat and put it on back to front, and there was a terrible drama and I was smacked and not allowed to go to tea with the Verekers.

There was nothing actually wrong with our bedroom. It was light and charming and made no demands of any sort, but Maisie Coffrington had given me some of those lush American magazinès devoted exclusively to house decoration and filled with shiny coloured illustrations of patios in California, gracious living rooms in Florida, and exquisite, rough-luxury cabins in the Adirondacks with a lot of natural stone, scarlet carpets, vast square armchairs, and barbecues all over the place. Not that I wanted to have that sort of thing in our bedroom, but I did toy with the idea of deep bottle-green walls and an enormous white rug and two gay functional bedside tables specially designed with places for everything. I admit I quailed a bit when I thought of asking Tali-Lapa, our local carpenter, to make two functional bedside tables. Samolan craftsmen are industrious and enthusiastic to a man, but they have absolutely no eye and are congenitally incapable of making identical pairs of anything.

Dismissing the functional tables, bottle-green walls, and white rug for a moment I was just getting under way with a new idea of everything being a delicate shell pink with soft smoke-grey curtains and perhaps a touch of apple green somewhere, when Eulalie came in with the afternoon post. Eulalie is definitely beautiful and pure Gauguin except that she hasn't got short legs—she has very long, slow-moving legs. Everything about her is slow-moving and languorous. I have watched her sometimes tidying the verandah and marvelled that anyone could do anything at such a slow tempo without falling into a deep sleep. She moves from object to object like a weary odalisque after an unusually exhausting evening with the boys. Every now and then she stops moving altogether and just stands perfectly still gazing in front of her. If she did this because she was suddenly overcome by the beauty of the view or because she saw something peculiar going on in the garden it would be understandable, but she frequently does it when she is facing a blank wall.

Having lowered the salver with the letters on it to within my reach, she waited remotely while I gathered them up and then, with a languid smile, undulated slowly from the room.

There were three *Time and Tides*, two *Punches*, a few bills and circulars, and a letter from Mother. The familiar, copperplatish handwriting always gives me a slight pang, half of pleasure and half of apprehension: she is well over seventy and I am always dreading to hear that the doctors have found a sinister lump somewhere or other, or that she has fallen down and broken something. After a certain age I know that old ladies are rather given to falling down, and although Jeannie is never away from her side and looks after her devotedly, it is still a worry. In this instance, however, my fears were groundless because she was obviously in cracking spirits and full of wickedness.

My darling Grizel,

I received a letter from you only two days ago dated *December 7th* which means that it took more than a month to get here.

I *cannot* understand this unless you carried it about for ages and forgot to post it. If this is not so you had better complain to your Post Office and I will send Jeannie to make a protest at this end. It is all most tiresome and I was beginning to worry. There is no particular news except that the eldest Bletchley girl has run off again, this time if you please with one of those young men from the British Council who go about organizing art exhibitions in Scandinavia and Belgium and other ridiculous places. Poor Lilian Bletchley as you can imagine is in a *terrible* state. She came to luncheon with me on Tuesday last looking quite *demented* and Jeannie had to make her an egg nog. I'm sorry for her of course but it's all entirely her own fault for having brought up those wretched girls *unsuitably* from the very beginning. *Nothing* was good enough for them, they were spoiled within an *inch* of their lives and look at the result! Nothing but squabblings and judicial separations and vulgar lawsuits about money and now *this!* I always thought that Jill, the youngest, had more sense than the other three put together but now it appears that *she* also has kicked over the traces and is living with a married man in Aix-en-Provence. People really do behave in the most extraordinary manner these days. Jeannie says that it's the result of the war but I think it's pure selfishness. I cannot think of anything else interesting to tell you. I went with poor Grace Felstead (John is back in the London Clinic) to a matinee of one of those American musical plays and my dear we were *absolutely deafened!* The woman who acted the lead was quite hideous and had a voice like a corncrake and she kept on singing the same song over and over again until I could have strangled her. Our heads were splitting when we came out and instead of having tea at Gunter's I dropped Grace off at the Ladies Empire Club and came straight home and went to bed. Please give my love to Robin and the darling children. *How* I wish I could have just one glimpse of them. The snapshots you sent are lovely although the one with you in it standing on the steps upsets me a little—you look dreadfully pale and tired. I do hope you're not gadding about too much. I must really stop now because Jeannie is waiting to take this to the pillar-box. Take care of yourself my pet.

Your loving
Mother.

P.S. Fancy the Queen and Prince Philip coming out to visit Samolo in June! I expect there will be all sorts of high jinks.

I put the letter back into the envelope and went out onto our small private verandah. It was almost dark, the lights were coming up in the town, and the fireflies were shimmering in the hibiscus hedge. Mother's letters always made me a little sad, not a serious sadness but a sort of gentle nostalgia made up of homesickness and remembrance of things past and a sense of Time's wingèd chariot cracking along far too fast and whisking us all towards old age and rheumatics and the quiet grave.

I saw Mother clearly in her comfortable little flat in Eaton Square, sitting at the window and looking out at the lights of the cars through the trees; looking also perhaps back over the long years to when she was young and pretty and the future lay before her illimitably, shining with promise and with no presage of ultimate twilight. And there she was now, sixty years later, with the twilight settling round her, growing perceptibly a little darker with each scurrying day until soon, very soon, there would be no margin left and her story would be over and done with.

I was aware that Mother, unlike me, still held on tenuously to a few religious convictions. She was far from being a pious, churchgoing, hundred-per-cent believer, but what she had been taught so firmly as a child still lay at hand, ready to be reached out for should occasion warrant it. I am certain that death held out no fears for her, but whether this was because she was naturally courageous by temperament or upheld, in the secret recesses of her heart, by visions of an afterlife when she would encounter all her old friends again and live for all eternity in a cosy, compassionate vacuum, I had no idea. Personally I cling to no such ambiguous hopes. I have very definite feelings about an afterlife, and they are nearly all on the debit side. I find it difficult enough in this brief span to cope successfully with old friends who suddenly appear from the long ago, changed beyond all recognition and expecting that our relationship should be resumed on the same terms that it was before, quite regardless of the disrupting years between. The thought that immediately the last breath has left my body I shall be transported lock, stock, and barrel onto some nameless celestial plane and plumped down among a crowd of old chums whom I haven't thought of for years, fills me with dismay. Also, I do believe that when the time comes for me to die, providing I don't get bashed to death in an aeroplane or drowned or written off in some violent accident, that I shall be ready for it and quite reconciled to it. I envisage myself as a very old lady indeed with a certain wistful pleasure. I shall try my best not to be a nuisance to other people, although I am sure I shall snap a bit at moments just to keep my hand in. I shall, I trust, be less fidgety than I am now. Tranquil and ivory-coloured, I shall sit in a quiet room and wait, with a welcoming, tremulous smile, for the visits of my grandchildren and perhaps great-grandchildren. When they have gone and the room, bereft of their youth and vitality and high spirits, falls back into its accustomed dimness, I shall gently unwrap the presents they have brought me, for I sincerely hope that they will seldom visit me empty-handed, and, smiling indulgently, I shall shake my head—an ordinary shake, not a Parkinson's-disease one—and slip like a wraith into my bed and wait, just wait without emotion and without fear, for the Great Reaper to finish me off. Of course I am fully aware that it may not turn out like this at all. I may become a fractious old monster, deaf as a post and full of wind and ghastliness, or I might pack up, embittered and lonely and very cross indeed, in some awful boardinghouse in Folkestone. There is no knowing really, and it really isn't any good worrying about it or making plans. One must just face up to it when it does come, and square one's frail bent shoulders and try to be as dignified as possible.

I came in from the verandah, turned on the lights, and looked rather gloomily at the dresses hanging in my cupboard. Robin and I were dining with Bimbo and Lucy Chalmers, and I couldn't possibly wear my comfortable black again because I had worn it when they dined here last week and also when I went with them to the opening of the new Super-Cinema in the Madana Road. I was certainly glad of it then because it doesn't crease immediately like my blue "Victor Stiebel," and the dress-circle "divan" seats at the Super-Cinema are Super-Luxe like deep plush bathtubs and you practically have to lie in them.

I finally took my grey "Ordinary" off the hanger and laid it on the bed. It is noncommittal and has a good line. Although Robin says it makes me look like a wardress I am fond of it. While I was listlessly doing this and wishing I was a terrific film star with a wardrobe crammed with fascinating ensembles for every moment of the day, he came in looking preoccupied and clutching a whisky and soda.

"That bloody little Dickie Chalmers hit Simon with a ruler."

"I know he did."

"It's raised a hell of a bump on his forehead."

"I know it has," I said. "Simon seemed quite proud of it."

"He's two years older than Simon and much bigger. I'd like to give him a damned good thrashing."

"Why don't you?" I said. "We can be there in three quarters of an hour if we hurry, and you can go straight up to the nursery on arrival and beat the daylight out of him while I try to keep Lucy and Bimbo amused on the patio. I don't suppose they will be entirely pleased and it may start the evening off on rather an ugly note, but if you feel all that strongly about it——"

"I'm surprised at you, really I am." Robin looked at me reproachfully. "I should have thought that when your own son has been bullied and victimized you could at least show a little natural resentment."

"Don't be silly, darling," I said. "He hasn't really been all that bullied and victimized. He just got into a fight and Dickie batted him with a ruler. I expect it was six of one and half a dozen of the other anyhow. Simon's always getting into fights, and I'm sure you did too when you were his age; there's a pugnacious streak in you both."

"I'm not in the least pugnacious. I just happen to like fair play, and I don't consider it fair play for a great hulk like Dickie to attack a boy half his size with a ruler. Why couldn't he use his fists?"

"I can't see that that would have been much better; he might have knocked his teeth out."

At this moment the telephone rang. Robin silently lifted the receiver off and handed it to me. I took it and sat down on the bed. It was Lucy Chalmers and her voice sounded a little strained. "Listen, darling," she said, "there's a slight drama on and I thought I had better warn you about it before you and Robin get here. Bimbo's in the bath, but he'll be out in a minute so there isn't much time. Where's Robin?"

"Here," I replied. "About three feet away from me and just about to sit down on my grey dress."

Robin shot me a baleful look and mooched out onto the verandah.

"I'll talk quietly then," went on Lucy. "And you can make any replies you consider suitable without giving anything away."

"What on earth's happened?"

"I'm afraid it's your Pride and Joy darling, he really has made a beast of himself. He and Dickie got into a squabble during the lunch hour at school today. It started quite cheerfully apparently with both of them throwing pellets of plasticine at each other, then it got out of hand and Simon rushed at Dickie like a battering ram and knocked him backwards off a form——"

"Was this before or after Dickie had hit him with a ruler?" I enquired coldly.

"Before," said Lucy. "Dickie grabbed the ruler in self-defence because Simon was really quite out of control and carrying on like a maniac, then one of the other children tried to separate them and Simon broke away and kicked Dickie with all his force between the legs and now Dickie's in bed and we've had to send for Dr. Spears. Both the poor child's testicles are swollen and he's in agony."

"Oh dear." I dropped my voice because Robin came wandering in from the verandah. "I really am dreadfully sorry."

"I wouldn't have worried you about this normally," Lucy continued, "but Bimbo's in a tearing rage and snorting fire and brimstone and muttering a lot of old-school-tie nonsense about fair play and why hasn't Simon been brought up to use his fists——"

"Don't," I felt myself starting to laugh. "I've just been through all that two minutes ago."

"It isn't really a laughing matter," said Lucy dubiously, but I could discern a slight crack in her voice. "And at all costs warn Robin to try to keep his temper and let Bimbo have his say without flying into a rage, otherwise we shall end up with a high-powered feud on our hands and everybody will start cutting everybody and it will be hell."

"All right, I'll do my best. I really am sorry about Dickie."

"I must stop now," said Lucy. "Bimbo's out of the bath and beginning to roar again. Dinner at eightish, but you'd better come early and get the worst over."

I put the receiver back thoughtfully, took a cigarette out of the china box on the bed table and lit it. My impulse to laugh had faded, and I felt suddenly depressed. It was kind and friendly of Lucy to have telephoned and I was grateful to her but, at the same time, vaguely irritated by her conspiratorial attitude. I have never been a great upholder of the overworked theory that men are just great big overgrown schoolboys and that it is the natural duty of wives to pander whimsically to their husbands, indulge their tantrums with infinite understanding and superior intuition, and coax them back into sunny domesticity. I saw no real reason, if Bimbo was in a rage and flew at Robin, why Robin should be expected to be tactful and "let him have his say." Simon obviously had behaved very badly, but after all he was only seven and a half and Dickie was nearly ten.

I looked across the room at Robin, who was fiddling with the things on my dressing table. His shirt was creased and sweaty, he was wearing his filthy old khaki riding breeches, and his expression was still a bit sullen, but I had a sudden impulse to fling my arms round him and was overwhelmingly thankful that I was married to him and not to Bimbo. Bimbo was nice enough and I was quite fond of him, but he was a much heartier type than Robin and consequently a great deal less interesting. Bimbo's values were cut-and-dried and immutable, but Robin's, behind his perfectly normal facade, were more fluid and less conventionally predictable.

"What was all that about?" He stopped fidgeting at the dressing table and came over to me.

"It was Lucy. She's in rather a state. It appears that Simon wasn't quite as bullied and victimized as you thought he was."

"How do you mean?"

"Dickie is in bed and in considerable pain."

"Good." Robin sipped his whisky and soda. "That may teach him to hit people his own size."

"As far as fair play is concerned neither of the boys exactly abided by the Queensberry rules, and I'm afraid we must face the fact that Simon, to put it mildly, has behaved unethically."

"I don't suppose you were particularly ethical at the age of seven and a half."

"I'm sure I wasn't, but I was seven and a half a very long time ago and what we are discussing occurred today."

"What happened? What did Simon do? Or rather what did Lucy say he did?"

"He kicked Dickie very hard indeed between the legs."

"Serve him right," said Robin.

"Lucy says his testicles are badly swollen and they've had to send for Dr. Spears."

"Balls."

"It isn't balls, it's true."

"I didn't mean balls in that sense," said Robin. "I just can't abide the word 'testicles.' It's smug and refined like 'commence' and 'serviette' and 'haemorrhoids.' When in doubt, always turn to the good old honest Anglo-Saxon words. If you have piles, say so."

"Certainly," I said. "I'll tell everybody. I'll put an announcement in *The Reaper*."

"I should expect *Nanny* to say 'testicles.'"

"I doubt if she will. I don't think her mind runs on those lines."

"I bet it does," said Robin, taking another swig at his drink. "Her subconscious mind anyhow. I'll bet Nanny's subconscious mind is a welter of sex frustrations and lewd eroticism. Just you try giving her an anaesthetic and see what happens."

"I have no intention of trying to give Nanny an anaesthetic. Although I admit that there are moments when I should like to."

"A spate of the most appalling four-letter words would come tumbling out of her like an avalanche," Robin grinned. "It would be fascinating."

"If you're so interested," I said, "you can arrange for Dr. Bowman to give her a whiff of gas before lunch tomorrow. I shan't be here because I'm lunching at G.H., but you can have a few chums in and thoroughly enjoy yourselves. In the meantime, if you don't mind, I should like to get back to the subject in hand."

"Very well," said Robin cheerfully, his imaginative flights about Nanny having apparently dissipated his former irritation. "Fire away."

"It's an unpleasant situation, and we really must try to handle it as tactfully as possible."

33

"Did the doctor say it was serious?"

"I don't know because he hadn't arrived when Lucy telephoned. It must be fairly bad because she said that poor Dickie was in agony."

"I expect he is." Robin nodded his head sagely. "Things like that can be very painful. I was once hit in the crotch by a cricket ball and was laid up for three days. It was beastly while it lasted, but I got over it all right."

"I see you have, dear. But it really doesn't help us much at the present moment, does it?"

"I don't see what we can be expected to do about it anyway. It isn't our fault if Dickie Chalmers rushes at our son with a ruler and he is forced to defend himself to the best of his ability."

"The criticism that may be levelled against us is that we haven't sufficiently imbued our dear little son with the spirit of fair play. At least that's what Bimbo's going to say. He's apparently hopping mad."

"I don't care what Bimbo says. He's brought up those children like guttersnipes anyhow. The boy's always strutting about in that damned cowboy getup and showing off, and the girl's always snivelling."

"She isn't *always* snivelling, darling. She just happens to have a cold that she can't shake off."

"She must be bloody unhealthy if she can't shake off a cold in this climate."

"Perhaps she is," I said patiently. "She may have defective lungs, adenoids, and a grumbling appendix, for all I know. But whatever she has it's entirely irrelevant to this particular discussion."

"I'll give Bimbo 'fair play' if he starts any nonsense with me."

"That's exactly what I'm dreading." I moved over and slipped my arm coaxingly through his. "Please, please keep your temper and let him have his say however much he irritates you. After all the wretched Dickie did get the worst of it, and we really don't want to have a blazing row with the Chalmers with everybody taking sides and gossiping their heads off. This *is* a small island and we *are* old friends. Do be good and sympathetic and, even if sorely tempted, don't fight back. And incidentally," I added, "you'd better, I think, have a word or two with Simon. He's been a little too nonchalant over the whole thing."

"All right, love," he said, "don't fuss. I'll be a model of restraint. You'd better have your bath and I'll have mine, it's twenty past seven already. I'll give Simon a talking-to in the morning." He kissed me absently, put down his empty glass on my dressing table, and started to go out of the room when he turned. "By the way," he said, "I had rather an exciting piece of news for you, but this business put it right out of my head."

"What is it?"

"It'll keep. There's no time to go into it now. Anyhow it's top secret and must remain so for a week or two. I'll tell you later if you promise not to breathe a word to a living soul."

"I promise," I said with a giggle, and went into the bathroom.

FOUR

On the way to Bimbo and Lucy's, Robin broke the news to me about the royal visit and I expressed suitable amazement. "It will be a good thing for the island in one way," he said, "but our lives won't be worth living until it's all over."

"That's what Sandra said," I replied without thinking.

"Sandra? When?"

"She came over this afternoon," I said hurriedly. "And we were just gossiping about things in general and she said——"

"She told you about the Queen and Prince Philip coming?"

"Yes," I guiltily replied, realizing that the game was up. "But she swore me to the deadest secrecy."

"Then why the hell did you pretend to be so surprised when I told you just now?"

"I didn't want to spoil your fun. There's nothing more deflating than telling someone some exciting news and discovering that they already know it, and anyhow you were already in a rather gritty mood over the Simon and Dickie business and I thought——"

"Testicles!" said Robin laconically. "You were just being thoroughly sly and deceitful, and you ought to be ashamed of yourself."

"I am," I said meekly, "and I humbly apologize, so there."

"She had no right to tell you if it's supposed to be all that secret."

"I know she hadn't, dear, but after all you did, didn't you?"

"Well, you're my wife after all, and I don't approve of men having secrets from their wives."

"I'm delighted to hear it, and I hope you will cling like a leech

36

to that inspiring little axiom until you're a very very old gentleman."

"I make no promises." Robin negotiated the hairpin bend into the Chalmerses' drive with a muttered imprecation. "If my wife develops into a liar and a dissembler and a fawning sycophant I may be forced to change my attitude entirely and never tell her a single thing ever again."

"I said I was sorry so you needn't go on rubbing it in. It was only a well-intentioned little white lie anyhow."

"Sandra ought to be ashamed of herself too. She's the governor's lady and governor's ladies should be above gabbing to their friends and blurting out state secrets."

"Nanny blurted out the state secret too," I said. "She's heard it from the 'Princess.' And apparently everyone in England knows it because Mother put it in a postscript. She said she expected we should have high jinks!"

At this moment we arrived at the Chalmerses' front verandah and Lucy came tripping down the steps to greet us with rather overdone enthusiasm. Bimbo, who followed her, was less cordial. There was a definite strain in the atmosphere, but there was nothing to do but rise above it, so we all trooped through the house to the back patio and decided what we wanted to drink and made conversation. When Bimbo had given us martinis and the houseboy had wandered round with a dish of very hot little sausages on sticks which one was left with when one had eaten the sausage, I felt I couldn't bear the general air of unspoken reproach any longer and decided to come boldly out into the open.

"How is Dickie?" I asked firmly.

"He's dropped off to sleep," said Bimbo. "The doctor had to give him a sedative. The poor little chap's in great pain."

"It's a horrid thing to have happened," I said. "And I really couldn't be more sorry. Boys are sadistic little fiends sometimes, aren't they?"

"Some are," said Bimbo pointedly. "There's no doubt about that."

"Simon's got a bloody great lump on his forehead," said Robin. "He looked flushed and a bit feverish when we said good night to him, but that of course may be concussion."

The bland sincerity with which Robin told this flagrant lie shattered me so much that I swallowed the olive from my martini whole and choked. This fortunately caused a diversion and Lucy brought me a glass of water. While I was sipping it with the tears rolling down my face, Bimbo and Robin went out into the garden.

"Oh God!" said Lucy, looking after them with an agitated expression. "Now what are we to do?"

"Nothing at all," I said hoarsely. "Let them argue it out between them and get it off their chests. We can't spend the whole evening with them snarling and growling and walking round each other like bull terriers. Is Dickie really bad? The doctor didn't say it was anything serious, did he?"

"No, not anything actually serious, thank God, but naturally painful . . . the poor child's testicles are inflamed."

"Balls," I said automatically.

"I think it's very unfeeling of you to talk like that. Particularly as it was your little beast who is entirely responsible for the whole thing."

"I didn't mean to be unfeeling. It's only that Robin's been giving me a lecture about good old honest Anglo-Saxon words and balls happens to be one of them. And anyway my Simon's no more of a little beast than your Dickie is, really. They're both little beasts and you know it. And for us to quarrel about it would be absolutely idiotic. Let's make ourselves another martini with practically no Noilly Prat in it at all and get as high as a flag on the Fourth of July and not care what happens."

"Is it true about Simon having concussion?"

"Certainly it is," I said brightly, going over to the drink table. "His face was scarlet, his eyes were glittering unnaturally like jewels, and he kept on making dreadful little inarticulate sounds."

"That's a flaming lie if ever I heard one."

"Of course it was," I said, clattering some ice into the shaker. "I only said it to make you feel better about poor Dickie's what-do-you-call-'ems. Come over and cut some lemon peel and for God's sake don't let's go on about it any more."

Lucy sighed and came over to the table. "What are we going to do if they come to blows?"

"Throw a pail of cold water over them like you have to do with dogs when they get themselves into those awful sailors' knots."

"That never does any good with our dogs," said Lucy gloomily.

"I've tried it several times, and all that happens is that I get sopping wet and they go on dragging each other backwards and forwards across the lawn."

"God moves in mysterious ways."

"That sounds blasphemous."

"Nature, then," I said, pouring out two glasses of practically neat gin. "It's nature that's the trouble really. Nature makes a mock of our high endeavours and humiliates us all along the line. Almost every natural instinct we have leads us straight as a die to the most appalling indignities. I expect that's why all those dreary religious reformers carry on the way they do about sex being a sin and the life of the spirit being the thing to hang on to tooth and claw. It's probably because they have such an exaggerated social sense that they are mortified every time they go to the loo."

"This is pure dynamite," said Lucy. "I think we'd better go and sit down again, but bring the shaker over because in a few minutes' time we may not be able to get to it."

We moved over to the other side of the patio and settled ourselves comfortably on a luxurious swing seat which hadn't the vestige of a creak and rocked us soothingly backwards and forwards.

I am frequently saddened by a sudden awareness that other people's houses are more efficiently run than my own. This of course may be an illusion engendered by some deep-rooted and unexplained inferiority complex, and I certainly hope that this is true, but inferiority complex or no inferiority complex, there was no denying that Lucy's patio was a great deal more soigné and better kept than our own back verandah at home. It wasn't only that her swing seat didn't creak and ours did, it was the whole feeling of the place. There wasn't too much furniture and what there was was well placed, comfortable, and unobtrusive; the banana-mesh mats were the right size and not frayed at the edges, the covers were all spotless and the lighting discreet. I made a mental note to get rid of our horrible old Pareanda wood standard lamp the first thing in the morning. It wobbles when you touch it because it hasn't enough lead in its base, it falls over in the slightest breeze, its shade is bent out of shape and invariably crooked, and you get an electric shock whenever you turn it on. Then of course there was Lucy's garden. Whenever I thought of Lucy's garden my heart

sank. I knew as I stared out at it lying in the moonlight in front
of me that there wasn't a flower out of place, that the hibiscus
hedges were properly clipped and not straggling in all directions,
that the orange "Kalilani" creeper on the pergola by the swimming
pool was really *on* the pergola and not hanging down in untidy
loops ready to throttle you when you passed under it, and there
were no unsightly brown patches on the grass. Admittedly Lucy
has a green thumb and is an ardent gardener whereas I haven't and
am not, but even so there was no excuse, in this lush climate, to
have a garden that alternated between a Douanier Rousseau jungle and a disused football field.

I made another mental note to have another serious talk with
Jock after I had got rid of the standard lamp. Jock has been with
us for years and his real name is Pynalu Topoalani, which in Samolan means "friend from the mountain," but Robin decided this was
too much of a mouthful to say whenever you wanted some fresh
lettuce and so he has been Jock ever since and very proud of it he
is too. He is amiable and lazy and, when questioned about anything, pretends to be very knowledgeable about prevailing winds
and fertilizer and what will or won't grow in different places,
but actually I don't believe he knows any more about gardening
than I do.

"What do you do to keep your poinsettias so prim and tidy?"
I said abruptly. "Mine always grow very tall indeed and teeter
about."

"Prune them of course," said Lucy. "Be ruthless, cut them off
in their prime."

"I'm always afraid they'll die if I do that."

"They won't. They'll spread out sideways and flourish."

"It's difficult to believe, isn't it? I don't somehow feel that I
should spread sideways and flourish if people kept snipping little
bits of me. I should be absolutely miserable. Like that poor girl
in *Titus Andronicus*," I added.

"What happened to her?"

"She had her hands cut off and her tongue cut out and was
ravished."

"Oh dear, how horrid," said Lucy. "What on earth for?"

"I can't quite remember. I think it was to pay somebody out

for something. The whole play's about people paying each other out."

"Fancy!" Lucy replied politely. "Who wrote it?"

"Shakespeare of course. I should have thought everyone knew that."

"I didn't. I haven't really read much Shakespeare. *Romeo and Juliet* and *Julius Caesar* naturally because we had to do those at school. I played Mark Antony," Lucy giggled. "But I didn't understand a word of it."

"I'm still surprised you didn't know that Shakespeare wrote *Titus Andronicus*."

"I don't see why. It might just as easily have been one of those Greek dramatists. They were always writing about horrors and eyes being gouged out and incest."

"You ought to persevere with Shakespeare, darling, really you ought," I said earnestly. "It's tremendously well worth it. I know some of it's difficult and you keep having to turn back to find out who's fighting who, but if you press on you suddenly come to the most lovely bits."

"It's all those 'on'ts' and 'to'ts' and 'ho theres' that put me off," said Lucy. "They muddle me."

"What about the sonnets?"

"It's no use being cross with me, but I haven't read those either."

"Oh, Lucy!"

"Pour out the rest of the martini and stop looking disapproving. I'm not an intellectual type and I know it. I don't read every book that comes out like you do, and I couldn't do the *Times* crossword if you paid me a thousand pounds. I envy you with all my heart and soul sometimes, really I do. I should so love to be able to quote things at dinner parties and startle people with tremendously apt allusions, but I can't remember anything from one day to the next and it's no good pretending I can. All I'm fit for is to run the house and garden and look after Bimbo and the children," she sighed. "I'm really nothing but a drone, and at the moment"— she giggled again—"a rather drunk drone!"

"Drunk drone's wonderful!" I said. "Even Shakespeare couldn't do better than Drunk Drone—oh dear——" I started to laugh helplessly and, reaching for my bag, knocked the cocktail shaker onto the floor with a crash.

"There now!" said Lucy. "There's another wedding present gone and a jolly good thing too because martinis are much better when you make them in a glass jug anyhow." She began to laugh too, and we both got into one of those violent *fou rires* that are impossible to control, at which moment of course Robin and Bimbo reappeared from the garden and stared at us disapprovingly.

"What was that crash?" asked Bimbo.

"The cocktail shaker," said Lucy convulsively. "Grizel's broken it."

"What's so funny about that?" Bimbo picked it up and put it back on the drink table while Robin retrieved the lid which had rolled under the swing seat.

"It wasn't only that." Lucy made a gallant effort to pull herself together. "It was me being a drone and *Titus Andronicus* and a lot of other things. We'll be all right in a minute. Just leave us alone."

"Who the hell's *Titus Andronicus?*" said Bimbo irritably.

Lucy went off into a fresh gale of laughter. "Ask Grizel—she apparently knows him intimately."

"You're both tight as ticks," said Robin. "That's what's wrong with you."

"It's entirely your fault if we are," I said. "You both went stamping off into the garden and abandoned us and we thought you were going to have a blazing row about the children and ruin the whole evening and the strain of it all agitated us so much that we flew to the bottle. Is everything all right or are you both still 'horribly stuffed with epithets of war'?"

"What on earth are you talking about?" Bimbo looked so bewildered that I started to laugh again and buried my face in my handkerchief.

"Shakespeare," said Robin. "The old girl's certainly in a bad way."

At this moment dinner was announced and, as usual in that house, was delicious; beautifully cooked and swiftly and unobtrusively served and my inferiority complex reared its head again and tormented me. I glanced furtively at Laaina, Lucy's parlour maid, whisking the plates on and off the table with brisk efficiency, and thought gloomily of Eulalie ambling to and fro in slow motion like a dazed acolyte engaged in some obscure, interminable religious ritual, handing people the wrong things at the wrong moment and looking as if she were on the verge of diabetic coma. I also wondered sadly why, as rice was one of the most recurrent standbys in Samolan cooking, ours should always be moistly coagulated into unappetizing lumps, whereas everyone else's was invariably crisp and separate and done to a turn. There was, I reflected, a great deal to be said for being a drone, drunk or sober. Drones, although insensitive to the higher flights of classic poesy, were at least able to go into their own kitchens whenever they felt like it without fear of the cook giving notice and with, it must be admitted, the certain knowledge that they knew what they were talking about. My own cook is personally a dear and I am devoted to her, but the slightest, most veiled, criticism of any of her more mediocre achievements sends her off into a state of acute melancholia and she retires in tears to her quarters and has to be given aspirin.

She can occasionally be cajoled into temporary enthusiasm by a new recipe. Then all is excitement and bustle and God's in his Heaven and she hums little Samolan folk songs in a breathy contralto. But if the new dish doesn't turn out entirely successfully and I suggest tactfully that next time we try it with a little less pepper or a little more garlic, down we go again, the whole world darkens, and out comes the aspirin.

Towards the end of dinner, during which the conversation had been normal and cheerful and happily devoid of any references to our respective progeny, Bimbo suddenly put down his wineglass with an air of decision.

"I've got a fairly startling bit of news for you both," he said. "But you must really promise on your word of honour to keep it under your hats because it was told to me in the strictest confidence. Lucy knows of course because I told her, but apart from us nobody has an inkling."

I shot Robin a quick look, but he avoided my eye and said with the utmost blandness: "What on earth's happened?"

"It hasn't happened yet," said Bimbo enjoying himself. "But it's going to."

"You're not going to have another baby?" Robin was obviously enjoying himself too.

"Over my dead body," said Lucy fervently.

"Come on then—what is it?"

"You swear you'll keep it to yourselves?"

"Of course."

"Because it isn't apparently official yet, and from every point of view it would be bad for anyone to know about it until it is."

"All right, all right," Robin's impatience was beautifully convincing. "I promise that our lips shall be hermetically sealed. What is it?"

"We're going to have some visitors."

"So are we," said Robin. "The Frobishers are flying over from Noonaeo next week, children and all, and we're dreading it."

"Don't be tiresome, Robin," I said. "Come on, Bimbo, you've kept us on edge quite long enough."

"It's the Queen." Bimbo paused. "And Prince Philip and their secretaries and equerries and ladies in waiting and Uncle Tom Cobley and all."

"Good God!" cried Robin dramatically. "When?"

"In June, they're going to stay three whole days."

"How wonderful," I said, restraining an impulse to overdo it and clap my hands. "How tremendously exciting! And what a splendid thing it will be for the island!"

"Well, in one way it will and in another way it won't!" Bimbo's tone was portentous, as though he was privy to dire underhand plots. "It'll boost the tourist trade of course and the island will be overrun with trippers and newspaper reporters, but it might cause a bit of trouble politically."

"I don't see why, really," interposed Lucy. "All those scruffy old left-wingers in the S.S.N.P. will tidge themselves like mad and be livid if they're not invited to all the functions."

"What I was really thinking about was inflation," said Bimbo. "All the prices of everything will go rocketing up and then there'll be the inevitable anticlimax when it's all over and we shall be in the soup."

"That could be prevented all right with a little foresight and organization," said Robin.

"Anyhow it will be worth it," Lucy laughed. "Think of all the carry-on and the excitements. Think of old Mrs. Innes-Glendower! She'll be in an absolute frenzy. She once curtsied to the Queen when she was Princess Elizabeth, and her heel caught in the hem of her dress. She's lived on that poignant memory for years. Then of course there will be all the dreadful arguments about who is invited to the garden party and who to the dinner party. We shall be in a constant whirl and I can't wait."

"H.E.'s the one I'm sorry for," said Bimbo. "And Lady A. They're going to have a hell of a time."

"They'll take it in their stride, I expect," said Robin. "H.E. isn't the type to be easily flustered, and she has terrific vitality."

"I shall send home for my tiara," I said.

"Good Lord," Robin groaned. "I didn't know you'd got one. Why didn't you tell me?"

"It never occurred to me that you'd be interested. Anyhow one doesn't go about saying to people, 'I've got a tiara.' It would sound silly."

"I'm not people. I'm the man you married."

"It's only a very small one," I said meekly. "Aunt Cordelia left it to me in her will, and she must have had a head like a pea."

From then on the discussion of the royal visit continued with unabated enthusiasm until we left. Sometimes it was general and we all contributed our views at the top of our voices, and sometimes we paired off and Robin and Bimbo went on about the political and commercial implications of it while Lucy and I occupied ourselves with the more frivolous social aspects which certainly offered rich food for conjecture.

Samolan society, like most small, remote communities which flourish under the Union Jack, is divided into definite classified groups which in turn are subdivided into cliques which inevitably look down on or up at each other as the case might be. It is only on specific occasions like the winter and summer garden parties at Government House and the Ralstons' annual Christmas Eve cocktail scrum that all the groups and cliques mingle democratically and present a united front, and even then there are a number of unresolved feuds seething away below the surface which seldom erupt into open hostility but are there nevertheless, shadowing the proceedings with potential drama and adding a pleasurable spice of peril.

The presence of such august visitors on the island for three days would without doubt create terrific social tension; smouldering embers of long-cherished resentments would burst into flame;

inferiority complexes, far more basic and virulent than mine, would fatten and grow and become gorged with eagerly sought umbrage; anxiously awaited invitations would be mislaid in the post; infuriated ladies would arrive at functions wearing identical dresses; there would be a spate of angry letters to *The Reaper* criticizing the official arrangements and shrill protests from any given area in the island not included in the Queen's itinerary. In fact, if one allowed one's imagination full play, the possibilities were unlimited.

"Wouldn't it be awful if there was a typhoon?" said Lucy. "June's a tricky month."

"I don't suppose there will be, after all there hasn't been a really bad one since 1929."

"All the more reason for there to be one this year. We should all have to batten ourselves down and barricade ourselves in and the poor Queen and the Prince would have to sit under those hideous arches at Government House for hours and hours. It's really too appalling to think about."

"Don't then," I said. "Concentrate on perfect weather and everything going perfectly. People who permit their minds to be obsessed with the fear of disasters almost always attract them."

"I don't think I could really attract a typhoon however obsessed I was."

"Probably not all by yourself, but if everybody thought of nothing but typhoons day and night for long enough we might have one before we knew where we were. The power of collective thought is incalculable."

"You do use splendid words," said Lucy admiringly. "I should never have thought of 'incalculable' in a thousand years."

"Somerset Maugham says that one ought never to use long words when short ones would do," Robin interposed.

"Then we'd better ask him to stay," said Lucy. "He'd be happy as the day is long in this house."

"So should I," said Robin gallantly, rising to his feet. "I'm sorry to say we've got to leave it this very minute. It's twenty past eleven, and I've got to get up at crack of dawn. There's a banana boat due tomorrow. I'm also sorry that my wife got drunk and broke your cocktail shaker."

"I'll buy you another first thing in the morning," I said to Bimbo.

"I saw one in Rodrigues' yesterday. It's very large indeed and made like a bell and you ring it instead of shaking it."

"I shall never speak to you again if you do," said Lucy. "As I said before in my cups a glass jug's the thing."

"I'll buy you a glass jug then."

"That would be silly because we already have four."

We walked through the house and got into the car. Robin switched on the ignition, let down the side window, and waved to Bimbo and Lucy on the verandah steps. "I really am sorry about Dickie," he shouted magnanimously. "I'll give Simon hell in the morning."

"Okay, okay—no hard feelings."

They both waved back and we drove away into the moonlight.

FIVE

I suppose before I go on any further I really ought to explain a little about Samolo itself and its history, in fact I should probably have done all that at the beginning and got it over, and indeed I would have except that I'm not very good at even reading about the relative sizes of populations, imports and exports, longitudes and latitudes, etc., let alone writing about them. However, what must be must be, and it's no use expecting people to be interested in a whole lot of other people getting into a frizz about a royal visit in a faraway British Colonial Possession if they haven't a clue as to where that particular B.C.P. is and how it became a B.C.P. in the first place and what it's like when you get there.

There is of course a local guidebook which was published in the early twenties for the benefit of visiting Kaiyeenis (the Samolan word for strangers) and I could, I suppose, save myself a great deal of trouble by quoting from it, for its information is fairly accurate and its moral tone impeccable, but it is excruciatingly dull and so aridly *un*evocative that I shall resist the temptation and press on on my own. However, like most books of its sort, it has moments of unconscious humour, and these I shall certainly quote if occasion arises, if only to prove how moral bias and excessive gentility can batter the most indisputable historical events out of shape until they are completely unrecognizable.

Samolo is the largest of an archipelago of thirty-four islands, seven of which are uninhabited and a few privately owned. The whole group was discovered by Captain Evangelus Cobb in the year 1786. They are of volcanic origin and situated in the southwestern Pacific. Latitude 18 degrees north and longitude, if you are still interested, 175 degrees south.

The first missionaries arrived in 1821, a whole boatload of them. They were on their way to spread the Light in Fiji and the Tonga Islands but their ship, *The Good Samaritan,* got into a violent storm and was wrecked on the reef just off Bakhua Point.

Quite a lot of them were drowned, but those who survived decided that they had had enough of sea travel and could get on with the job here just as well as in Fiji, and so here they stayed and multiplied exceedingly.

The Samolans received them politely and with the utmost kindness, and the reigning King Kefumalani and his Queen Merolia gave them grants of land and listened civilly and without comment while they explained about Christianity being absolutely the only sure way of saving their souls from eternal damnation.

Actually they were lucky in their timing because had they arrived only a few years before they would have been faced with King Kopapapus, who was another cup of tea entirely and lacked the spirit of old southern hospitality to an alarming degree. He was apparently one of those old-world tyrants of the Heliogabalus type, full of wickedness and strange perversions and given to throwing his discarded favourites, both male and female, into the crater of Fuminnaiyo, which is now an extinct volcano but was then very active indeed and erupted exuberantly about five times a year.

The only active volcano we have now is FumFumBolo on the island of Noonaeo where the Frobishers, who, alas, are coming to stay next week, have a vast cocoa plantation. I say "alas" because although they are kindly, cheerful people and entertain us lavishly whenever we fly over to Noonaeo for a weekend, the noise they make singly and together is nerve-racking.

To me FumFumBolo is a romantic mountain because it is tied up with so many of the fascinating old Samolan legends. From the highest point of our land, above the banana plantations and just where we adjoin the Stirling property, you can, in very clear weather, see the blue conical outline of it with a little wisp of smoke climbing up into the sky and making a grey cloud.

There are several ancient songs about it, and one of these which was translated into English in the early part of the nineteenth century is worth quoting. The first part of it describes Bolo, the Samolan water god who, when he was dying, suddenly observed that his old enemy FumFum, the goddess of fire, was in tears. With a last gallant gesture he puts out the flames around her and takes her to his heart—

> Then a mountain rose from the sea
> And its summit was wreathed in flame
> And that is the fabulous history
> Of how the volcano came . . .

Then there's another charming bit that comes later:

> When FumFumBolo lights the sky
> No monkeys chatter, no parrots fly,
> No flying fishes skim the bay
> And every sea bird hides away.
> The salamander leaves the sand
> Even the turtles understand
> When God is angry
> They move inland.

Fuminnayio, our own volcano, is as extinct as the dodo. He is locally known as "Old Tikki," and there hasn't been a peep out of him for over a century. He is the highest peak of the Lailanu Mountains and dominates the whole island. In latter years the Tourist Board have decided to cash in on him and so they organize expeditions to the summit which are most exhausting and uncomfortable and entail staying the night in an insect-ridden guesthouse, rising before dawn, and clambering up a frightening trail on muleback for four hours. Robin insisted on me doing this when I first came out here and although it was certainly impressive when we got to the top, the descent was torture on account of my saddle slipping and my mule continually lying down, usually on the uttermost edge of a precipice. Robin said that this was entirely my own fault for being frightened and yellow-livered and allowing my fears to communicate themselves to the mule. Mules, he said, although the most sure-footed animals in the world, were naturally high-strung and could be upset and made nervous by the least thing which, as I pointed out with some heat, was sheer nonsense because anyone sitting on my mule for five minutes could tell that it hadn't the trace of a nerve in its whole beastly little body and was merely stubborn, lazy, and exclusively concentrated on getting me off its back and into the nearest ravine as soon as possible.

Anyhow the Lailanu range stretches from Paiana Head in the east to Cobb's Hill in the south, and this southern coast is where all the best beaches are and where, of late years, all the tourists are too and the newest hotels and what the residents describe as "The Riffraff."

The guidebook says:—

The South Shore, where beaches of the finest white coral sand abound, together with limpid lagoons of azure blue, secluded coves, palm-fringed inlets and exotic verdure, epitomizes for the weary traveller all the tropic charms with which writers of adventure stories have tantalized us since time immemorial."

This turgid little paragraph sums it up all right, but it was written a long time ago before the triumphant march of progress had vulgarized the exotic verdure and palm-fringed inlets with indirect lighting, crammed the secluded coves with scarlet, blistering bodies, bottles of sun-tan oil, bathing cabanas, snack bars, speedboats, and even two night clubs. The whole area, from the eastern end of Narouchi Beach to beyond Cobb's Cove, was comparatively uninhabited excepting for five or six private beach houses owned by the wealthier members of the plantocracy whose plantations lay back in the hills. But now it has no less than nine American-style hotels, three motels, and a rash of erratically designed beach bungalows which are rented for astronomical prices for the winter season.

However the South Shore, whether we like what's happened to it or not, has now become a force to be reckoned with. Its tourist facilities attract an increasing number of visitors each year, and although we of the older stratum of society, smug and superior in our houses on the foothills behind Pendarla, may sniff disdainfully and pull aside our skirts, we have to admit that the government's determined "tourist trade policy" has brought the island undreamed of prosperity and set our hitherto rather insecure economy on a firm basis.

It has also, inevitably, done considerable damage to the Samolan character in that particular district. The Samolan people are guileless, engaging, and friendly, and in spite of the missionaries' frantic attempts to imbue them with a respectable sense of sin, they have remained to this day cheerfully amoral.

This inherent amorality, harmless in itself and utterly devoid of any vicious implications is now, naturally enough, I suppose, becoming corrupted and commercialized. Before the advent of heterogeneous wealthy pleasure seekers from the Brave New World it would never have occurred to the average Samolan that his or her physical attributes were saleable. To Samolans, sexual indulgence is as natural, enjoyable, and unimportant as eating mangoes. The missionaries, as I said before, did their utmost to convince them to the contrary but without the slightest success, but where Christian argument failed, the Almighty Dollar ironically succeeded, and nowadays, on the South Shore at least, there is hardly a lissom chambermaid or a muscular beach boy who is not gaily prepared to make the supreme sacrifice for suitable remuneration and the glory of the Tourist Board.

Without doubt all this is to be deplored, and I thoroughly disapprove of it myself but, as usual, for the wrong reasons. The sexual aspects of the situation do not shock me nearly so much as Robin says they should, but what does fill me with dismay is that lighthearted, uninhibited, and hitherto fundamentally innocent young creatures who once accepted the pleasures their bodies afforded them without question, without prurience, and without even the need of restraint, are now becoming wary and calculating and are acquiring, probably without being aware of it, distorted values even more insidiously destructive than those originally proffered to their ancestors by the missionaries.

SIX

On the morning following our dinner with Bimbo and Lucy the skies opened and the rain fell as though some demented celestial fiend was emptying it out of a gigantic bucket. Robin and I had our breakfast on our verandah as we usually do, but although it is strongly roofed and has a wide overhang we had to move the table to the very back of it and turn up all the mats.

Nanny appeared with the children, who were in an exuberant mood and clad in raincoats. Nanny was also wearing a raincoat with an attached "pixie-hood" which hung down at the back and looked like a jellyfish; her expression was morose and her eyes dead with resignation.

"This rain!" she said gloomily, making a little clucking noise with her tongue which caused Robin to wince and rattle the pages of *The Reaper*. "Just fancy! And at this time of the year too, and without a word of warning from the wireless. I'm sure I don't know what I shall do if that windscreen wiper goes wrong again."

"It oughtn't to," I said. "Cummings fixed it only last week."

"He didn't fix the door though, it still won't shut properly and if you slam it it sticks and you can't open it again."

"That," said Robin, "is entirely the fault of the British working-man," and I knew from his tone that he was going to be tiresome. "In the dear old days English cars led the world; American millionaires fell over themselves to buy Bentleys and Rolls-Royces and Talbots and Armstrong-Siddeleys and——"

"Not Austins," I interrupted. "No American millionaire ever fell over anything to buy an Austin."

"It's the five-day week," Robin went on. "The five-day week is robbing us of our prestige abroad and our integrity at home. Can

53

you imagine what the first Queen Elizabeth would have said to the five-day week?"

" 'Od's fish,' I expect, and 'I am Harry's daughter.' " I said. "She used to say that very frequently."

Robin lowered *The Reaper* and glared at Nanny. "We have sold our birthright," he said accusingly, "and betrayed our inheritance. We have also, thanks to fainthearted politicians and enfeebled trades unions, lost our national genius for improvisation."

"You certainly need a lot of that to get out of an Austin when the door sticks."

"It's the windscreen wiper that's really worrying me," said Nanny. "If it goes wrong again in this downpour I really don't know what I shall do. The last time it happened was when I was bringing the children back from the Scout rally and there we were stuck on the worst part of the Paiana Road: the rain was so thick I couldn't see my hand before my face."

"Why should you have wished to?"

"It's all very fine to make jokes, Mr. Craigie," Nanny said with spirit, "but to drive about these dreadful roads in the pouring rain with the traffic going in all directions and the wiper not working is terribly dangerous, it really is. I shouldn't mind so much for myself but it's the children. After all I am responsible for them, aren't I?"

"Absolutely," said Robin cheerfully. "If so much as a hair is hurt on their evil little heads I shall hold you answerable in a court of law."

"I haven't got an evil head, Daddy," said Simon.

"You most certainly have," said Robin. "Which is conclusively proved by your having that bump on it."

"I haven't got a bump on mine," interposed Cokey. "Neither has Janet."

"Go along, Nanny," I said. "Try the windscreen wiper before you start and if it doesn't work I'll take the children in the wagon."

"I hope it doesn't then," cried Simon. "I want to go in the wagon with Mummy."

"Be quiet, Simon, and say good-bye nicely," said Nanny firmly.

Simon laughed loudly and began to caper about the verandah crying "Good-bye nicely" at the top of his lungs. Then Janet and Cokey started jumping up and down crying "Good-bye nicely" too and the general turmoil continued until Nanny managed to grab all three of them and take them away.

Robin returned with a grunt to *The Reaper* while I poured myself out another cup of coffee with my ears strained anxiously to catch the sound of the car starting. After a few moments it did, and I watched it battling its way slowly along the drive with the raindrops bouncing off its roof like glass beads.

"You really mustn't make fun of Nanny in front of the children, Robin; it undermines her authority over them and puts her at a disadvantage."

"Nanny was born at a disadvantage," said Robin without looking up. "What little personality she has, which is negligible, invites mockery."

"Maybe it does, but it's unfair of you to let them see that you're laughing at her. We pay her to look after them and keep them in order, and on the whole she does her job very well."

"All right, all right, but I still think they'd be better off with a nice jolly Samolan girl who wouldn't mince about in a plastic mackintosh and fill their minds with stale platitudes."

"Nice jolly Samolan girl would let them do exactly what they liked from morning till night and have no control over them whatsoever. Nanny, with all her mincing, *is* reasonably firm with them and they respect her."

"Respect is not enough," said Robin. "They should adore her, all children should adore their nannies and run to them with their tiny troubles and climb into their laps and be lulled to sleep. If any of our children climbed into the lap of this angular nonentity they'd be lacerated."

"Your conception of a Nanny's duties is romantic rather than practical," I replied with some asperity. "In any event I see no point in our children being continually lulled to sleep, and any time they feel a sudden urge to pour out their tiny troubles they are perfectly free to climb into my own lap or even yours, although as a regular routine I should be inclined to discourage it."

"Which only proves what I have long suspected." Robin rose and stretched. "That you are sadly lacking in the more tender maternal instincts." He handed me *The Reaper*, kissed me lightly on the forehead, and went into the house.

I glanced at *The Reaper's* front page, noting, without particular emotion, that the Peace Conference in Geneva had come to an impasse; that the Prime Minister had stated in the House of Commons that although the situation in the Middle East had deteriorated rapidly during the last few days there were still grounds for hope that an amicable settlement might be achieved; that the Foreign Office had issued a statement dissociating itself entirely from the dubious activities of one of its ex-attachés in Copenhagen; that the Archbishop of Canterbury was confined to bed with a feverish cold; that His Excellency the Governor had opened a new branch of Barclay's Bank in Duke Street, Pendarla; that Mr. Aneurin Bevan had made an explosive speech at Llandudno in which he referred to the Tory government as bloodsuckers; that the President of the United States had said that all that was needed in Indonesia was a firm hand, and that an elderly lady had fallen off her bicycle outside the Royal Samolan Institute and been treated in the Kineua Hospital for slight concussion.

The rain continued to crash down monotonously, and I stared at it absently while Eulalie meandered slowly in and out clearing away the breakfast things.

The one thing that always gives me the most indigestible food for thought is the basic inconsistency of human endeavour. At that very moment, I reflected, there were millions of people all over the globe working away like beavers to find cures for cancer and serums for this and that and lovely drugs to ease pain and make you go off into a dreamy coma without permanently injuring any of your complicated tissues, while at the same time millions of other people were planning the most complex new explosives to blow all the cures for cancer, the serums, and the lovely drugs to smithereens. There was tension in the Middle East, tension in Indonesia, still more tension in South Africa, and another threatened dock strike in England. There were also millions of people prostrating themselves in Buddhist temples, wailing in mosques, kneeling in Protestant churches, and genuflecting in Catholic cathedrals and all patiently praying for spiritual salvation, personal happiness, an assured position in afterlife, victory in war, and damnation to their enemies of the moment who, probably only a few years ago, were their gallant allies. And then there were the children who in recent, more hopeful years, were reading *The Green Fairy Book*, *The Red Fairy Book*, Hans Andersen, Grimm,

Dean Farrar, E. Nesbit, *The Wide Wide World,* and the works of
Mrs. Molesworth and were now entirely occupied with space fiction and voyages in cylindrical, pressurized air vehicles to the faraway stars where they encounter curiously shaped characters in
crash helmets who have warlike intentions and an immense capacity for organized irrigation.

Those children's brains with all their little cells expanding and
contracting and multiplying themselves as we are told cells are
supposed to do, how could they possibly escape being distorted and
addled by so much mechanized and arid romanticism? What in
the name of Heaven or Hell or God or the Devil or Krishna,
Buddha, Mahomet or the Holy Trinity were they going to dream
up when they were matured and straining at the leash and ready
to get cracking?

Having discarded, or never even acknowledged, all the prettier
dreams, the fairies, pixies, gnomes, enchanted woods and mushroom rings; having, throughout their impressionable, formative
years, been glutted with the new jagged fantasies instead of the
old sentimental ones, into what ungainly shapes are they going
to twist the glowing world? It is, it is indeed, a sobering thought,
a more than sobering thought, a thought depressing and shocking
enough to bring you down with a wallop, to dent your pleasure
domes and demolish your foolish ivory towers leaving you ex-
posed to bleak weather and the wild winds. And yet I suppose
this thought is older than the oldest hills and has struck at the
hearts of middle-aged mothers since the first syllable of recorded
time. To be a mother is from first to last a constant agitation whichever way you look at it. Young, old, or middle-aged, poor Mum is
in trouble from the word go. Leaving aside for a moment the well
advertised compensations—the pattering feet, the loving chubby
arms round the neck, the prides and the glories—there is always
the other side of the medal, the desolate side, where reasoning
and unreasoning fears grow and flourish like weeds. Fears of acci-
dents and high temperatures and sudden death, fears also of other
loves stealing away the young heart and setting it up in opposition to familiar allegiances, and this fear of course is a terrible one
because it exists, as a rule, only in the subconscious where it gnaws
at the vitals and blows itself up with horrid spleen into a serio-
comic monster, a permanent music-hall joke, a mother-in-law.

I know now as I knew then, sitting staring at the rain slamming down on the coco palms, that a day will inexorably come when I shall be a mother-in-law and be forced to try so hard, so very hard, to be tactful and sympathetic and to bite back salutary advice, and try even harder to pretend to myself and to everyone else that the wedding was *charming* and the bride a darling and *so sensible* and that I couldn't be happier or more *relieved* that Simon had chosen to fall in love with someone so eminently suitable in every way. And all the time, behind and below my expert dissembling, my deep deep heart will be sick with jealous loathing and I shall be longing to fly at the "sensible darling," tear her veil off, and slap her silly simpering face.

Depressed by my reflections and the drumming of the rain, I wandered aimlessly down to the back verandah which was a shambles with all the furniture crammed against the back wall. In the far corner there was a leak in the roof, and Tahali had placed an enamel slop pail underneath it to catch the drops which fell every few seconds with a sharp "ping."

Robin went off in the Jeep taking Jock and thereby frustrating the heart-to-heart talk I had intended to have with him about the garden. I had my usual quarter of an hour in the kitchen with Clementine, who was in one of her "defeated" moods and received every suggestion I made with an expression of abstracted resignation: feeling unequal to the effort of jollying her into a more cheerful frame of mind, I issued a few halfhearted orders and left her leaning against the sink and rolling her eyes mournfully as though she had retreated to the last bastion of her moral defences and knew beyond a shadow of doubt that all hope was dead.

At about eleven o'clock the rain stopped abruptly, the clouds rolled back over the foothills to the high mountains, and the sun burst out making the Pareanda leaves glitter like green sequins. Tahali and Eulalie appeared and replaced the verandah furniture, the enamel slop pail was whisked away, and Westinghouse caught a land crab before I could stop him. Westinghouse is exquisite, disdainful, and a full-blooded murderer and although I am grateful to him for keeping the rat situation under control, whenever I find him crunching up other poor unhappy creatures I want to flay the life out of him. I know that it is Nature's Way and

The Law of the Jungle and all that and that he is only obeying his instincts and that he is not a Thinking Reed and therefore not to be blamed like Torquemada and Caligula and a whole lot of other human beings who should have known better. I also know that it is useless to whack him or bash at him with a newspaper because I am up against Forces That Are beyond My Control and that my sudden and, to him, inexplicable rages will only confuse him and, in the long run, quite possibly discourage him from killing the rats. This of course is Robin's argument, and although I see the logic of it I know in my heart that nothing would ever discourage Westinghouse from murder. He is a born killer and glories in it. On this occasion I flew at him with *The Reaper* as usual and as usual he evaded me and, with the land crab dangling and twitching from his mouth, disappeared down the steps into the garden.

I had settled myself comfortably and was on the point of beginning a long chatty letter to Mother when I heard the sound of a car arriving. My heart sank like a stone because I loathe and despise morning callers, but it rose again when Tahali ushered Bunny Colville onto the verandah. Bunny Colville is one of those men whom you couldn't *not* be pleased to see in almost any circumstances. He is tall and dark and going a bit grey at the sides, his manners are charming, and he radiates vitality. He is gay, idle, dissolute and has an appalling reputation for unscrupulous dalliance. He also has "private means," and when he finally emerged from his cloak-and-dagger activities in the war he inherited from some remote uncle a sugar plantation at the southern end of Paiana Bay.

When he first came out here ten years ago he knew nothing whatever about growing anything and had never clapped eyes on a sugar cane in his life. In the interim he has learnt enough to pay an efficient overseer and that is all. He built an airily uncomfortable beach house on the edge of his plantation, and to this he comes every year for two or three months and spends all his time doing underwater fishing with an Aqua Lung and a spear gun and green rubber flippers on his feet. He has had a succession of different loves to stay with him, sometimes chaperoned, sometimes not. If these paramours are interested in barracuda, lettuce coral, blowfish, and other wonders of the deep, so much the better for them. If they are not, and prefer more social delights, they are out of luck and incidentally so are we because Bunny, with gay insouciance, foists them off on us and returns lightheartedly to the reef. We have had a fairly mixed bag up to date. A film starlet with enormous bosoms and a tiny, determined mother; a poetess with wide-set mad eyes and an urchin crop; a tough sun-battered lady journalist from California who dived better than Bunny did, swam like a fish, and was a great success until she contracted septicaemia from a coral scratch and had to be carted across the island in the middle of the night and deposited in the Pendarla Hospital where she remained in a critical condition for several weeks. Then there was poor Carola James, who had just been divorced and flew out to Bunny under the delusion that he would marry her and cherish her for the rest of her life. Actually he cherished her for two and a half weeks exactly, after which she returned somewhat bitterly and covered with mosquito bites to her sister's house in Ovington Square.

In between these ill-starred romances he had managed to have a few local flings which, apart from causing a certain amount of gossip, were without significance and, as far as we were concerned, far less trouble than the importations.

Of late, however, his habitual nonchalance had suffered a sharp jolt in the shape of Eloise Fowey, whom he had encountered quite by hazard in the Grandstand at Doncaster and fallen for hook, line, and sinker. Eloise Fox-Barron, before she married poor Droopy and became the Duchess of Fowey, had served briefly with Sandra and me in the M.T.C. She had recently been the most publicized debutante of the year, was staggeringly lovely and absolutely idiotic. But idiotic or not we were forced to admit that her effect on any man she met was immediate and devastating. She had no brain, no ability, no capacity for concentration, and only a very small trace of schoolgirl humour, but what she had in superabundance was every single chemical ingredient that combines to make one hundred per cent effortless sex appeal. Sandra and I tried over and over again to rationalize this phenomenon to ourselves and to each other but without any success. We could understand easily why men should be infatuated by her looks, for there was no denying that her looks were flawless, but what we couldn't understand was that they could cheerfully endure her company for more than a few hours. Not that she wasn't perfectly amiable and well disposed, but she really was such a cracking fool that we couldn't believe that any reasonably intelligent man, however demented he might be by physical desire, could possibly wish even to say "good morning" to her after the desire had once been gratified. But the disconcerting truth was that they did. They wanted to marry her, to live with her, to lay their lives at her feet. For them an imagined future with her at their sides offered no fears: on the contrary it glowed with anticipatory bliss, and when in May 1946 she finally announced her engagement to Desmond Fowey, known rather unkindly as "Droopy," hearts of oak creaked and groaned and disintegrated from White's Club to John O'Groats.

For Bunny, dear Bunny, the unscrupulous, egocentric, perennial bachelor, to be lured by such obvious bait was really cruelly ironic, if true, and rumour had it that there was no longer any doubt. He was mad about her and she was mad about him and the whole of London was aware of it with the exception of the unfortunate Droopy.

Bunny hoisted himself onto the verandah rail and sat with his elegant legs dangling. He was wearing blue linen slacks, red *espadrilles,* and an eye-searing sports shirt, multicoloured with a pattern of pineapples, palm trees, and hula dancers in grass skirts.

"That," I said, "is one of the most hideous shirts I have ever seen."

"Yes, isn't it?" he replied cheerfully. "I bought it at the airport in Honolulu because the air hostess had just emptied a cup of coffee over me."

"Why don't you give it away?"

"I've tried to, but nobody will have it. Even my garden boy turned it down."

"Send it to the 'Princess' for her next sale of work. She could arrange a whole stall round it."

"If I do that she'll write and thank me and ask me to tea, and if I go to tea the admiral will tell me about his encounter with Lord Jellicoe in the First World War and if the admiral tells me once more about his encounter with Lord Jellicoe in the First World War I shall cut my throat."

"Would you like a drink?"

"It's on its way," said Bunny. "I asked Tahali to make me a strong horse's neck. I ordered one for you too."

"That was very thoughtful of you, but I don't like drinking in the middle of the morning. It makes me feel beastly for the rest of the day."

"Nonsense," said Bunny. "A horse's neck is what the middle of the morning's for. It will fortify you and mellow you and I want you to be both fortified and mellowed because I have something very important to tell you."

"Don't tell me . . ." I settled myself comfortably in our old "planter's chair" and put my feet up on the footrest. "Just let me guess."

"It's a dead secret," said Bunny. "And you really must swear not to breathe it to a living soul, at any rate not yet."

"Pending the official announcement, I suppose?"

"Official announcement!" Bunny looked startled, at which moment Tahali appeared with the horses' necks on a tray which he placed on the table.

"They look very dark, Tahali. Did you put in any ginger ale at all?"

Tahali grinned. "The commander say he wish for drink of great strength," he said. "So I put mostly brandy and a little lime. But there is ginger ale here with opener all ready, and I make peanut butter sandwich if Mistress would desire it."

"No thank you, Tahali," I said. "Mistress does not desire a peanut butter sandwich now or at any other time, and you know it perfectly well."

"The master enjoy peanut butter sandwiches immensely," said Tahali. "And so also does Miss Nanny. I make them for her every time she take children for picnic." He looked reproachfully at me, bowed, and withdrew.

"You've hurt his feelings," said Bunny. "You're slowly undermining that boy's initiative. Soon he'll be nothing but a cringing slave."

"Don't be silly and get on with the secret."

"What did you mean about an official announcement?"

"Nothing," I said, handing him his drink. "It just slipped out. Tell me the great secret and I promise to react suitably. I'm really getting very good at it."

"Getting very good at what?"

"Dissembling," I replied. "Robin called me a dissembler and a liar and a fawning sycophant only last night on our way to the Chalmerses'. And all because I did exactly what I'm doing now."

"And what the hell's that?" Bunny looked bewildered.

"Pretending not to know something that I do know so as not to deflate you and spoil your fun."

"This is a very curious conversation," said Bunny, taking a swig at his drink. "Don't you think we'd better unwind and go back to the beginning?"

"By all means. You said you had something important to tell me."

"Correct."

"You then told me not to breathe it to a living soul, at any rate, not yet."

"Correct."

"And then I said, 'Pending the official announcement, I suppose,' and then Tahali appeared with the drinks."

"You mean you *know* what I'm going to tell you?"

"I'm afraid so, dear," I said gently. "So do quite a lot of other people."

"They couldn't possibly." Bunny was obviously disturbed. "I only knew it myself this morning."

"This is a small island, Bunny dear," I said. "A very tiny jewel in the Imperial Crown. No secret can remain a secret for more than a few hours here."

"Who told you?"

"Sandra originally. She also swore me to secrecy."

"Sandra!" Bunny slapped his knee forcibly. "That explains it. You were in the M.T.C. together, weren't you?"

"Certainly we were. We formed fours and wheeled right and stamped about Lowndes Square for ages, and I fell down one day when we were marching past Derry and Toms."

"When did she tell you?"

"Yesterday afternoon. She was in quite a state about it."

"You mean she was upset?"

"Not exactly upset, but filled with forebodings."

"Oh God!" Bunny groaned.

"She said that it would probably end by her being carried off in a strait jacket."

"I fail to see why she should concern herself so much. After all it isn't really any business of hers. She'll only have to see her once or twice at most as a sort of official politesse."

"She'll have her in Government House for three days and nights."

"What nonsense. She doesn't necessarily have to stay at Government House at all. And that, dear Grizel, is what I came to see you about. You see she can't possibly stay with me, can she?"

"Have you gone raving mad?"

Bunny put down his glass on the rail beside him, screwed up his eyes, and, leaning forward, stared anxiously into my face. "Who," he enquired, "do you imagine that we're talking about?"

"The Queen, of course. I seem to have been talking about nobody else for the last twenty-four hours."

"The Queen! Oh Lord!" Bunny started to laugh.

"Do you mean to say you didn't know the Queen and Prince Philip were coming to the island? That that wasn't the dire secret you were havering about?"

"Of course it wasn't. I was talking about Eloise."

"You mean she's coming too?"

"She isn't coming *too*, she's just coming. She's arriving tomorrow fortnight."

"Oh, Bunny, you really are incorrigible." I got up and fetched the cigarette box from the table. "Who is she coming with?"

"Nobody," said Bunny. "That's just it. She's flying out alone."

"Even Eloise couldn't be as idiotic as that."

"What's so idiotic about it?" said Bunny defensively. "You know the situation perfectly well. She can't bear being separated from me any more than I can bear being separated from her."

"Not only is she an English duchess," I said irritably, "but she is a highly overpublicized one, in addition to which she is monotonously alluring and wreaks havoc wherever she goes. Can you imagine the effect on this island if she arrives out here unchaperoned and lives in sin with you in your awful little beach house?"

"It's much less awful since you saw it last," Bunny said pacifically. "I've had the big room repainted and all the furniture recovered."

"That's beside the point and you know it."

"Of course I know it, Grizel. That's the reason I came to see you suddenly this morning. You're an old and dear friend and one of the few people in the world I can really trust. I know as well as you do that we shall have to be terribly discreet. I also know as well as you do that she can't possibly stay *openly* with me in my awful little beach house or anywhere else. But she has got to stay openly somewhere, hasn't she?"

"She hasn't *got* to come at all. It's absolute madness."

Bunny left the rail and began wandering about the verandah looking hangdog, I lit a cigarette and prepared myself for what I knew was coming next. Bunny flung himself onto the swing seat, which gave a loud screech of protest.

"You don't like Eloise really, do you?"

"I don't exactly not like her, but we just haven't very much in common."

"She thinks the world of you, honestly she does. She's always saying how wonderful you were in the M.T.C. and how kind you were to her too."

"Then she must have a very lovely nature," I said, "combined with a most unreliable memory."

"She said you helped her and encouraged her and stood between her and trouble scores of times."

"I also strained every nerve to get her transferred to another unit because she irritated me to madness. Now look here, Bunny——" I sat up purposefully and looked him firmly in the eye. "Stop dithering about and come to the point and don't waste any more time trying to convince me that Eloise thinks the world of me and looks upon me as a sort of guardian angel, because it just isn't true. Eloise doesn't give me a thought from one year's end to the other, we don't even send each other Christmas cards, and the only reason that I may have temporarily reappeared in her mind again is because she knows that I am a friend of yours, that I live here on this island, and that I might turn out to be useful to her."

"My God!" said Bunny morosely. "What bitches women are about each other. It's quite terrifying, it really is."

"Don't let it upset you unduly. It's the result of centuries of oppression in a man-made world."

"If you'd been born a decade or so earlier you would have been one of those harpies who tied themselves to railings and bit innocent policemen to the bone." Bunny looked at me accusingly.

"Very likely," I replied. "And Eloise wouldn't. Please don't imagine that I am blind to the obvious distinction you are drawing in your mind between us."

"I'm not drawing any distinctions in my mind. I am only still hoping against hope that you'll be sympathetic and kind and help me in this bloody difficult situation."

"May I point out that this bloody difficult situation is entirely your own silly fault?"

"Maybe it is," said Bunny. "But that doesn't make it any the less bloody. I can't help falling in love, can I?"

"You could if you put your mind to it. Why don't you concentrate on deep-sea fishing?"

"Now you're being flippant, and it's beastly of you when you know what a state I'm in."

"You've concentrated on fishing before with triumphal results. Why don't you do it again and get on with loving Eloise when you're back in England? She'll wait, she's a fairly lackadaisical character. You can take her home some lettuce coral and a few conch shells. Why in heaven's name let her come out here and complicate things and make a rip-snorting scandal?"

"There's no need for there to be any scandal at all if you'll only be a real chum and co-operate, instead of moralizing at me like a Victorian deaconess."

"Supposing I were a real chum as you call it and co-operated like mad? What would this co-operative chummery let me in for?"

Bunny gave a sudden smile in which wistful appeal and calculated charm were admirably blended. "The snows are melting," he said, "and blossom by blossom the spring begins."

"Prettily said, dear, but it doesn't answer my question."

"The moment has come——" He paused, wiped away the smile, and assumed a contrite expression which was so palpably false that I had to bite my lip to prevent myself from laughing. "The time has come for me to confess, abjectly and without evasion, what I intended to tell you at the very beginning before we got into all that cross-talk about the Queen."

"What have you done?" I said grimly.

"I wrote to Eloise two weeks ago and told her to tell Droopy and give out to all her friends that she was flying out here to stay with you!"

"Bunny!"

"I followed this up by sending her a cable in your name inviting her, most affectionately, to spend two months with you. The cable ended 'With love, your old friend, Grizelda,'" he added.

I looked at him in frozen horror. "How dare you do such a thing —without even asking me? I'll never forgive you."

"I intended to ask you, honestly I did, and then I thought better of it."

"Oh!" My voice quivered with rage. "So you thought better of it, did you?"

"If you had said no at that stage," he said reasonably, "the whole plan would have been balled up and I should have been in the soup."

"I say no now and you *are* in the soup."

"Grizel!"

"It's the most unwarrantable piece of impertinence I've ever heard of. You ought to be ashamed of yourself."

"I am," said Bunny. "I'm bitterly ashamed. You have only to look at me."

"I don't have to look at you and I don't have to speak to you either, ever again. Please go away."

"I haven't finished my horse's neck."

"Damn your horse's neck, and you needn't imagine that you can get away with this by being facetious and whimsical. I'm really angry."

"I know," said Bunny sadly. "I thought you would be."

I got up, went to the verandah rail, and stood there with my back turned to him, staring at the far hills and trying to control my temper. At this moment Tahali came out of the house with a cablegram on a salver. I took it, slit it open irritably, and read it in silence. "Dear Grizelda terribly excited arriving twenty fifth BOAC Flight 429 is there anything I can bring you love Eloise."

"Thank you, Tahali," I said in a flat voice. "There is no answer."

Tahali grinned and withdrew, and I handed the cablegram to Bunny and returned to my chair.

"What are you going to do?" he said after a long pause.

"I'm not going to do anything. You, on the other hand, are going

67

to do a great deal, and the first thing you are going to do is to get into your car, drive to the post office, and send Eloise a cable saying that all plans have been unavoidably changed. You can then return to your house, pack your fishing equipment, take the first plane to England, and explain to her exactly why."

"Grizel, please—please be reasonable."

"Reasonable!" I could hear my voice rising. "You quite unscrupulously forge my name, place me in a hideously embarrassing position, and then expect me to be reasonable. Did you seriously imagine for a moment, however demented you may be by this asinine infatuation, that I would dream of having Eloise Fowey to stay with me for two whole months? Why, I'd rather lie down and let a truck run over my head than have her in the house for two days."

"But you won't have to. That's the whole point."

"What do you mean?"

Bunny got up from the swing seat and stood looking down at me pleadingly. "She won't really be staying with you at all, she'll be staying with me. All I wanted you to do was to supply a sort of 'cover' from the social point of view. She knows that perfectly well, she won't get into your hair for a moment, I swear she won't."

"Do you really believe that you and the Duchess of Fowey can live in a beach house on this small island without anybody finding out about it?"

"My house is isolated, miles away from the South Shore. Nobody ever comes near my bit of the coast, and there aren't even any local neighbours nearer than Bana-lua. If you met her at the airport, gave one lunch party for her, and invited her to a meal or two every now and then, nobody would be any the wiser."

"Do you want to marry her?"

"Yes. If Droopy could be persuaded to divorce her."

"Oh, Bunny!"

"I tell you I'm in love with her, really in love, and she is too. I know I've bashed about a good bit hitherto, but this is the real thing. We'd get married tomorrow if we only could. I know you don't care for her much but she is a darling when you really get to know her, and you never have really got to know her, have you? I know that you and Sandra both thought she was a dithering ass in the M.T.C., but after all she was very very young at the time and anyhow that sort of thing isn't her dish . . ."

"In wartime lots of people had to do jobs that weren't their dish," I said sternly. "Neither Sandra nor I was exactly born to the parade ground."

"You and Sandra both happen to be well organized and efficient human beings. Eloise is completely different. She's never been efficient in her life."

"I think getting her hooks into one of the most eligible dukes in England might be described as fairly efficient."

Bunny turned away. "You really hate her, don't you!"

"I do not hate her," I replied hotly. "I don't know her well enough to hate her. If you love her and she loves you that's your affair and hers, but it certainly isn't mine and, fond as I have always been of you, I do think you have gone much too far in trying to involve me in a situation that is bound to end in trouble. You visit Samolo for a few months every year, but you might remember that I live here. If this idiotic business blows itself up into a full-size scandal, which it almost inevitably will, you and she can go away and trail your tattered reputations through the divorce courts while I am left with the debris."

"You mean you definitely won't agree to help?"

"How can I, Bunny? Do be fair."

"All right then—we won't say any more about it." He gave a wry smile. "I really didn't think you'd feel quite so strongly about it. I'll have to think up something else."

"Why on earth can't she come out with some girl friend or other and stay at a hotel?"

"I thought of that in the first place, but to stay in a hotel on this island would be insanity if you had anything you wanted to conceal. Also I don't believe she has any friend whom she could trust and who would be available to make the trip."

"Is she so sure that she can trust me?"

"Everybody trusts you, darling. It's just one of those things." He shrugged his shoulders. "That of course is the basis of my whole evil plan. If Eloise came here as your guest all problems would be solved automatically and nobody would suspect a thing. After all my house is only seven miles away in case any emergency should arise."

"Seven miles of very bad road."

Bunny must have sensed that I was weakening because, with a tender smile, he took both my hands in his and proceeded to swing them backwards and forwards rhythmically as though he were playing a game.

"You're quite sure that I shall give in, aren't you? Quite certain of getting your own way?"

"Not absolutely *dead* certain," he smiled disarmingly, "but sort of hopeful."

"Has it never occurred to you that this devastating 'carry-all-before-it,' 'knock-'em-down' charm of yours might one day fail?"

"Of course. But it hasn't so far, has it?" He shot me a quizzical look. "Or has it?"

"No, it hasn't exactly failed, but I warn you not to overwork it, with me at any rate. I'm beginning to notice cracks in it, signs of wear and tear." I turned away from him again.

"That was quite unkind. And what's more I believe you really meant it."

"Yes," I said. "I think I did."

He came up behind me and placed his arm lightly round my shoulders. "Perhaps I didn't realize quite how much I was asking," he said gently. "If you truly feel that you can't help me over all this, I promise you faithfully I shall understand. This isn't calculated persuasiveness, I swear it isn't. I admit I'm an unscrupulous self-centred bastard and that I'd go to almost any lengths to get my own way, but in this case 'almost' is the operative word. I wouldn't sacrifice one jot of your real affection for me even for Eloise, and that's saying a good deal because I love her very much."

"Oh, Bunny!"

"I know you don't approve, and think I'm an ass and she's an ass, but there it is. There's no accounting for the whys and wherefores of people suddenly falling in love with each other. It just happens, and you're caught, and reason flies out of the window. In this instance of course the joke's on me. I'm on a bad wicket and I know it, and, to do her justice, Eloise knows it too. She's quite willing to make a complete break and come to me openly and take the consequences."

"What's holding her back?"

"I am really. I can't bear the idea of her sacrificing her position and her reputation and enduring all the squalid publicity of a divorce and then finding out, when it's too late, that it wasn't worth it. We've discussed it from every angle and decided to go on as we are for at least a year before busting the works wide open."

"Among all the angles you discussed it from, was the wretched duke's point of view touched on at all? After all he is her husband."

"That note of sarcasm in your voice was quite unnecessary. Of course we discussed Droopy's point of view. That's one of the things that's worrying her most."

"Yes, I expect it is."

"You can believe it or not, as you like, but she is very fond of him. Naturally she isn't in love with him now, any more than he's in love with her, that all died down years ago, but they're excellent friends."

"Does he suspect that you and she are, to put it romantically, lovers?"

"Of course not. Droopy would never suspect anyone of anything. He lives in a world of his own."

"A fairly insecure one, I should say."

"He isn't remotely interested in anything outside his estates and his race horses. He pays no attention to Eloise whatsoever except when he takes it into his head to give a vast house party for Goodwood or something, then he expects her to be on tap every minute of the day and night and run it for him."

"Run it for him? Oh, Bunny!" I burst out laughing. "Eloise couldn't run a sewing bee."

"That's where you're wrong. She's a wonderful hostess. You haven't seen her for ages, you only remember her as a silly inexperienced young girl."

"I certainly do, distinctly."

"Well, she isn't now," Bunny said sulkily. "You'll see for yourself."

"Yes," I sighed wearily. "I suppose I shall."

"You mean you will help, you will do what I ask?"

"I can't say yes or no definitely until I have discussed it with Robin."

"Yes, of course, I see that."

"I don't think he has ever envisaged me in the role of a conniving Restoration 'madam.' It might be rather startling for him."

"I'll be eternally grateful—I swear I will."

"Never mind about that for the moment, just listen to me seriously. Before I agree, or ask Robin to agree, I must tell you that I heartily disapprove of the whole business. As I said before I neither like nor dislike Eloise, she means nothing to me either way and I doubt that she ever could. But I do happen to be very fond of you, and it's for that reason and that reason alone that I am even considering involving myself. If I *can* persuade Robin and I *do* take on this highly unenviable responsibility for your sake, you must promise to abide by the rules I lay down."

"Obviously I'll do anything you say."

"In the first place she'll have to stay in this house a minimum of three nights a week. On the others you can have her to yourself and fetch her and return her with the utmost discretion. In the second place whether she likes it or not, she will have to do her bit socially and open sales of work and bazaars if requested and never, in any circumstances, be seen alone with you in public. In the third place she will have to stay at Government House for a couple of nights. I'll fix it with Sandra, I'm lunching there today anyhow. She'll probably have a fit! And last but by no means least, my dear, you have got to promise to behave yourselves and not let me down and make me look an abject fool which God knows I am."

Bunny flung his arms round me and gave me a resounding kiss. "You are a dear darling great big wonderful doll!" he cried exultantly, "and I'll never get over your sweetness to me until the day I die."

"As you seem to be getting into the habit of sending Eloise cables from me," I said, "you had better send her another one telling her to bring out the *Oxford Book of Quotations* and some Earl Grey tea from Jackson's in Piccadilly."

"Okay, pal!" He flashed me a quick, dazzling smile. "I'll do it now this minute." He blew me a kiss, disappeared swiftly into the house, and a moment later I heard the noise of his car starting.

SEVEN

There were only four of us lunching at Government House; H.E., Sandra, Chris Mortlock (the A.D.C.), and me, so we had it on the verandah looking out over the garden. It was tolerably cool and had a greenish, translucent under-the-sea quality because the shades were let down almost to the ground and we could only get glimpses through the sides of the garden blazing in the sunlight. The food, as usual, was adequate but uninspired and Sandra, much to my surprise, suddenly became aware of it.

"This won't do," she said firmly. "This really won't do at all. This *is* Government House and not a down-at-heel private hotel in the Cromwell Road."

"What's the matter, dear?" H.E. looked up vaguely from his plate of macaroni cheese.

"Everything," said Sandra. "She'll have to go."

"Who will have to go where?"

"The cook of course." Sandra rang a little silver bell. "There must be some cold ham or tongue or something. This is inedible."

"It tastes all right to me," said H.E. mildly.

"Only because your mind's on other things. If you really were thinking seriously for one minute about what you were eating you'd have thrown your plate straight over your shoulder at the first mouthful—like Ludwig of Bavaria," she added.

"As a matter of fact I rather like macaroni cheese." H.E. smiled reminiscently. "It takes me back to my prep school, and if Ludwig of Bavaria was given to throwing platefuls of it over his shoulder he must have been even dottier than I thought."

At this moment Paiano, the G.H. butler, came onto the verandah.

"Bring some cold ham or tongue and salad as quickly as you can, Paiano," said Sandra, "and tell Thelma to come and see me in my sitting room the moment after lunch."

Paiano bowed and withdrew. Sandra sighed and took a piece of toast out of a silver rack in front of her and waved it at Chris.

"She can't even make toast," she said. "Feel that, it's like coconut matting."

Chris laughed and obligingly pinched the piece of toast. "It is a bit soggy, I must say."

Sandra sighed again. "What is so awful is that I know perfectly well that it's all my fault. I have no 'flair' for food. 'Flair' is something you're born with, like Marjorie Davenant. Nobody's even had a poached egg in her house that wasn't absolutely ambrosial and nobody's ever had a poached egg in this house that wasn't either too runny or too hard and anyhow tepid."

"When the Blaises were here the food was even worse," I interjected.

"That," said H.E., "could have been more happily phrased."

"Grizel's quite right to be truthful. The whole trouble with people like us in tremendously high positions for which we are quite unfitted is that we are surrounded most of the time with sycophants who never come out boldly into the open and tell us the truth."

"Cuckoo never does anything else."

"Cuckoo doesn't count, she is unique. She prides herself on saying what she thinks, but it hasn't yet dawned on her that she is entirely incapable of thought. Thelma must go."

"How long has she been here?"

Sandra turned helplessly to Chris. "How long *has* she been here?"

"Six months. She came last October when the other one went away to have the baby."

"*She* doesn't look as if she were going to have a baby, does she? That would ease the situation enormously."

"You're weakening already," said H.E.

"I hate being beastly to people and screwing up my courage to deliver them body blows and watching their faces fall and their eyes fill with tears. I'm no good at it and never have been."

"I'll talk to her," said Chris.

74

"Oh do, Chris dear, and be really firm. I've deluged her with cookbooks including that *Perfect Hostess* one and *Gourmet* and I never stop cutting out recipes from American magazines for appetizing little luncheon snacks, and all we get is this everlasting macaroni cheese." She turned to me. "Do you think she should go straight away or be given one more chance?"

"Good cooks are very rare on this island, and I don't suppose she is all that bad really; all she needs is keeping up to the mark."

"Encourage her more," interjected H.E. "Perhaps she lacks confidence. Find out something that she does well and praise her extravagantly for it."

"I've been trying to find out something she does well for six months. Whatever happens we shall have to get someone else for the royal visit. This sort of thing would be too shaming."

"Call up Juanita," I suggested. "She might lend you one of the Kelly's Tavern cooks. After all she's renowned for having the best food of any hotel on the island."

"I can't call up Juanita until it's settled about the royal lunch."

"It is settled," said H.E. decidedly.

"No, darling, it isn't, not really. I know you think you've won, but I've still got quite a lot of irrefutable arguments up my sleeve. You agree with me, don't you, Chris?"

"It's nothing whatever to do with Chris," said H.E. "And it's unfair of you to try to make him commit himself."

"I wish I knew what you were talking about," I said plaintively.

"Juanita telephoned me the first thing this morning and offered to arrange a select and delicious lunch for the Queen and Prince Philip when they do their tour of the island and of course I said yes at once, A, because I love Juanita and Kelly's is far and away the most amusing hotel here; and B, because they will have to lunch somewhere. Then George flew into a passion and said it would be hideously undiplomatic and upset all the other hotels and that we should arrange for old Sir Albert to give them lunch at Bingall's Bay. Now there is one thing that I wouldn't wish on my worst enemy and that is to have lunch with old Sir Albert at Bingall's Bay, or anywhere else for that matter. He's a cracking old bore and the house is pitch-dark and so filled with vast furniture that you feel as if you were stumbling through Maple's."

"Dark or light, furnished or unfurnished," said H.E., "it would still be far more suitable than Kelly's Tavern. I have no intention of allowing the Queen to be stared at by all those American millionaires in beach clothes."

"It would be better than being stared at by old Sir Albert and all his ghastly relations. Anyhow Juanita would give the party in the big private bungalow at the end by the tennis court, and so no millionaires would be able to stare at anyone."

"Juanita is *not* going to give the party in a private bungalow or anywhere else," said H.E. "Juanita is not going to give the party at all. And that is final."

"But I've already said yes."

"And I've already said no."

Further argument was prevented by Paiano coming in with the cold ham and the salad, but there was tension in the air and we all helped ourselves in silence. I caught Chris's eye and he gave an imperceptible shrug. Sandra, with a dangerous edge in her voice, went on talking.

"We must all bend our minds," she said brightly, "to think of different ways of boring our royal visitors to death. First of all they must be welcomed at the dock by the church choir—this incidentally has already been suggested. Then we must make a hard-and-fast rule to invite no one under the age of sixty-two to the state banquet. Alma Peacock, who is already straining at the leash and hasn't been off the telephone since yesterday afternoon, can easily be persuaded to give a gala production of some weighty classic, her little amateur theatre group doesn't know the meaning of the word fear, they've already done *Hamlet*, *Mourning Becomes Electra*, *Young Woodley*, *Blithe Spirit*, and *Antony and Cleopatra* with Alma herself as Cleopatra. I see no reason why on this special occasion they shouldn't attack something really impressive like *The Trojan Women* or *Medea* . . ."

"I should dearly love to see Alma as Medea," said H.E. equably.

"Then," continued Sandra, "we must organize a series of interminable native dances. Ivy Poland will, I know, be only too willing to whip up her pupils into a frenzy of endeavour—then——"

"How you do rattle on," said H.E. "This ham is even worse than the macaroni, it's as hard as iron."

"That's the Deepfreeze," I said helpfully. "Samolans love putting everything they can lay their hands on into the Deepfreeze."

"I think I am going mad," said Sandra.

Later on, when the not very comfortable lunch was over and Sandra had taken me to her sitting room and slammed the door, she kicked off her shoes, as usual, and flung herself onto the sofa.

"What did I tell you?" she said. "It's going to be unadulterated misery from beginning to end. George has been in this stubborn, tiresome mood ever since we first had the news that they were coming. I could willingly throttle him when he digs his feet in and won't see anyone's point of view but his own."

"You're not bad at that yourself."

"All I'm trying to do"—she ignored my interruption—"is to make this royal visit unlike all the other royal visits the poor dears have to go through. I should love to think that years and years hence, when the Queen is a very old lady with a cap like her great-great-grandmother, she will say, looking back wistfully over her long and triumphant reign—'Ah Samolo!'"

"She might say 'Ah Samolo' anyhow, it all depends on the intonation."

"You didn't let me finish. I would like her to say, 'Ah Samolo—that lovely lovely island where we had the happiest time of all . . .'"

"And all because of that delightful Lady Whatever-her-name-was," I said, continuing the fantasy enthusiastically, "and that charming friend of hers who was so helpful, you must remember dear, Mrs. Grizel What-do-you-call-it, with those three entrancing little children who gave us those bouquets so prettily."

"Royal personages however old they are always remember names," said Sandra firmly. "And so there would be none of that Lady What's-her-name or Mrs. What-do-you-call-it, and I can tell you here and now that I intend to cut bouquet presenting down to the minimum and so it's no use your raising Simon and Janet and Cokey's hopes in *that* direction."

"It was only an idea."

"The thing that's really worrying me is Juanita." Sandra got up and began walking about the room. "I love Juanita and I really can't bear to hurt her feelings. George is really being insufferably pompous over the whole thing."

"Juanita can take it," I said. "Juanita is tough."

In this I was perfectly right. Juanita certainly is tough. She is a formidable character with a personality like a battering ram and has a well-deserved reputation for speaking her mind in trenchant and quite unequivocal language. She was born on the island and her forebears were full-blooded pirates from whom she has inherited what Robin calls her "buccaneer" quality. She runs her hotel brilliantly and is impressed by no one unless they happen to be exceptionally talented and even then she has to like them first. She is a wonderful friend and an implacable enemy, and any visitor to the fabulously expensive Kelly's Tavern who has the temerity to complain about anything or raise her ire in any way finds himself packed up and bouncing away in the station wagon before he knows what's hit him. Poor Lady Blaise used to be absolutely terrified of her and shook like an aspen whenever she put her nose round the doors of Government House. Sandra, on the other hand, adored her from the first moment that she clapped eyes on her; she spends a night at the Tavern whenever she can get away and sits for hours on the terrace after dinner while Juanita regales her with hair-raising stories of the bad old days. Robin adores her too because she was sweet to him when he was a young man and used to teach him to spear octopus on the reef by torchlight.

"I haven't quite given up hope." Sandra lit a cigarette and wandered over to the window where she stood looking out over the vivid garden with its jacarandas, poincianas, and tulip trees flaming against the background of misty purple mountains. "You see, it isn't as if Juanita suggested it from any base motive. She neither needs the publicity nor wants it. I know her only idea was to help and of course it will give her enormous pleasure to be able to give the Queen and Prince Philip probably the only edible food they'll get on the island. I shall have to think of a way of getting round George."

"He seems to have set his heart against it fairly definitely."

"Yes." She pondered for a moment. "That's because I lost my head and tackled the whole thing in the wrong way. I shouldn't have said yes in the first place without consulting him. I do see that. Tact has never really been my strong suit where George is concerned. I really must try to mend my ways and that is all there is to it."

"Why not call up Juanita now, this minute, and explain the

whole truth and nothing but the truth and tell her to hold her horses for the time being?"

"I did say yes so very definitely and enthusiastically."

"She'll understand. She's nothing if not sensible, and she's certainly not an umbrage taker."

"I'll ring her up later," said Sandra thoughtfully. "After I've had another, more tactful go at George. Actually he doesn't care for old Sir Albert any more than I do so I am sure that I can squash that little scheme anyhow. In the meantime you'd better grab a pencil and a piece of paper and we'll start separating the sheep from the goats."

"Oh Lord, must I?"

"Of course you must. You promised. Laura would do it automatically if she were here, but she's in Honolulu with that mad old mother of hers and won't be back until the twenty-fifth. We'd better begin with the garden party, that's fairly easy. It's the more exclusive functions that are going to torment us."

"The twenty-fifth!" My heart sank. "Before we begin on the lists I have something to ask you."

Sandra shot me a suspicious look. "What sort of something?"

"It's not so very awful really, only rather peculiar."

"What *are* you talking about?"

"It's Eloise Fowey," I said with a rush. "She's coming to stay with us, on the twenty-fifth."

"Eloise Fowey!" Sandra stared at me in astonishment. "What on earth for?"

"Well—she sort of wants to," I said rather lamely.

"Is she coming alone?"

"Yes—Droopy can't get away. I haven't seen her for years, as you know, but I had a sweet cable from her—and——"

"There's something behind this." Sandra screwed up her eyes and looked at me penetratingly. "I can smell it a mile off."

"I don't see why poor Eloise shouldn't come to stay with me if she wants to and I want her to."

"But you *can't* want her to. She's a crasher and you know it."

"I believe she's improved a lot since the old days—I mean I don't think she's nearly as idiotic as she used to be."

"That wouldn't be difficult. She was virtually half-witted."

"She was certainly beautiful, you must admit that."

"Of course she was," said Sandra quite crossly. "She was so damned beautiful that she disrupted the whole outfit, upset discipline, ruined morals, and never did a stroke of work."

"I know all that but she was quite nice really. I mean she wasn't in any way a beast."

"She was a fool. I'd rather have a beast any day than a fool and so would you. I can't think what's happened to you, you must be out of your mind. She'll have Robin falling flat on his face at her feet the moment she steps into the house. Have you thought of that?"

"Of course I have," I replied testily. "But he won't. He's far too sensible. Robin would never fall for such obvious bait."

"I shouldn't bank on that if I were you. After all getting the gentlemen is all she knows anything about. Male sensibleness has a curious way of disintegrating when faced by that particular form of predatoriness. Look at Bunny Colville! He's apparently mad about her—— Bunny Colville! Oh!" She stopped short. "I begin to see."

"I don't know what you're talking about," I said hurriedly.

"Oh yes you do. You know perfectly well. You've let Bunny get round you, isn't that it?"

"Yes, I suppose I have in a way, but I put up a gallant fight. He really put it so that I couldn't possibly refuse."

"What does Robin say?"

I hung my head. "He doesn't know yet."

"Really, Grizel!" Sandra went off into peals of laughter. "You really are the most awful pushover in the world. You should be ashamed of yourself."

"I am," I said humbly. "But being ashamed of myself isn't going to help. I've given my word that I'd stand by Bunny and help him all I could. That's what I want to ask you about really. I said I'd try to persuade you to have her here for a few days."

"Oh, Grizel! How could you when you know how much I've got on my mind?"

"Only for a couple of days, three at the outside. After all she is an English duchess, you'd have to do something about her anyhow. Entertaining prominent visitors to the island is what Government House is for, isn't it? You've often said yourself that it's like a badly run railway hotel."

"Not all that badly run."

"It was your phrase, not mine; I'm only quoting."

Sandra stubbed out her cigarette irritably. "All I can say is it's damned inconsiderate, as though I didn't have enough to harass me without having to watch Eloise languishing about under everybody's feet and pouting at the A.D.C.s."

"There's only one A.D.C., and I'm sure Chris won't mind being pouted at, and anyhow you've got ample excuse not to have to see much of her, except at meals."

"Meals!" Sandra moaned and threw herself down on the sofa again. "Meals in this house are torture enough as it is, and the sight of Eloise disdainfully spooning up a tepid cabinet pudding will humiliate me more than I'm humiliated already."

"Nonsense," I said firmly. "You're not in the least humiliated, you're just in a thoroughly gritty mood about everything. You don't happen to be interested in food and what wines go with which, it's something that was left out of you when you were born, like being colour-blind or not being able to play the piano. It's not *your* fault. And anyhow it doesn't matter nearly so much as you think it does. Nobody expects the cooking in Government Houses to be good any more than they expect the cooking on British railways to be good. It's just part of our tradition. You're working up a sort of complex about it."

"Thank you, dear," said Sandra. "You are very comforting."

"Good. Now then . . ."

"Now then what?"

"Will you rise like a glowing phoenix from the ashes of your scratchiness and have Eloise to stay for three or four days?"

"You said three at the outside just now."

"Well, three at the outside then?"

"I suppose I shall have to, but only under the strongest protest, and I must also add that I disapprove thoroughly of the whole shady business."

"Very well," I said meekly.

"And," Sandra went on, "if you've been weak enough to let Bunny get round you that's your affair, but I warn you here and now that if you find yourself involved in a highly unsavoury little scandal, which you very probably will, I shall wash my hands of you entirely and disown you."

"All right," I said. "Fair's fair. I'm most grateful to you and you're a darling."

"You can let me know later when the tiresome ass wants to come, but you must give me at least a week's warning."

"I promise."

"Now then"—said Sandra in businesslike tones—"we'd better get on with the lists. We'll start by eliminating the worst horrors. You read out the names and I'll make the notes."

She balanced a writing block on her knee, we both lit cigarettes and set to work. As Sandra had foreseen, the garden-party list was fairly easy because all we had to do was to put a little cross meaning "yes" against practically every name. It had to be a free-for-all anyhow, and in such a vast crowd even the unsuitables would have few opportunities to make beasts of themselves. What was not so easy, however, was the list of people to be presented. This had to be written out on a separate piece of paper and discussed and analyzed with scrupulous care. Happily there were very few people on the island who were absolutely beyond the pale, but there were certainly a few borderline cases. When we had worked and written in and scratched out and argued for at least two hours the list was added up to one hundred and forty-three people.

"It's no good," said Sandra. "My head's going round like a humming top and I just can't think any more. For God's sake let's have some tea and relax for a minute." She got up and rang the bell. "Here we have one hundred and forty-three living breathing human egos, each one of which is completely convinced that it is his right to be presented to Her Majesty the Queen. And on the other hand we have a very definite directive that in no circumstances whatever must there be more than fifty. This, if my arithmetic is correct, which it seldom is, leaves ninety-three eminent inhabitants of Samolo to be hurt, embittered, and mortified for the rest of their natural lives. It also means angry letters to *The Reaper*, angry letters to George and me, and a seething cauldron of social discontent, the steam from which will asphyxiate us whenever we visit a hospital or open a bazaar or preside at a committee meeting."

"I like the bit about the seething cauldron of social discontent and the steam."

"It's all very fine to laugh, but it's true and you know it. What *are* we to do?"

"When we've had a nice cup of tea we'll go through it again and cut some more, ruthlessly and without regard to the consequences. That's the only way. If people want to get hurt and treasure up bitterness, they'd better get on with it. Anyone with any sense will know that they can't *all* be presented. If I were you I should harden your heart and rise above the whole thing."

"Put yourself in poor Maisie Coffrington's place for instance. If you were her and had lived here all your life and suddenly found you were not on the presentation list, what would you do?"

"What Maisie Coffrington usually does, drink myself to a standstill."

"Well, not Maisie Coffrington then, think of somebody else . . . what about Daphne Gilpin? She comes from one of the oldest families in Samolo. What would you do if you were Daphne Gilpin and found yourself unpresented?"

"This is silly," I said, "and you're merely working yourself into a state. In the first place *if* I were Daphne Gilpin I would not live with Lydia French at Fisherman's Hole. I would not throw bottles at her even if I did, and I would not wear grubby corduroy trousers at the races. But as I am not Daphne Gilpin the whole discussion becomes academic and irrelevant."

"Do you think it's really true about them throwing bottles at each other?"

"Perfectly true. It's happened several times. I've heard it on the best possible authority."

"How curious it all is." Sandra shook her head thoughtfully. "I suppose they wouldn't do it unless they really enjoyed it."

"Whether they enjoy it or not it seems to me sufficient reason for them to be crossed off the presentation list."

At this moment Paiano came in with the tea on a little movable table which looked like a tray but had legs that shot down.

"That little table comes from Peter Jones," said Sandra, "and I couldn't endure life for a split second without it. It's exactly the right size for everything, and it has a baize top when the tray isn't there so you can play patience on it. I have one in my bedroom, there's one in the library, and I've sent for some more. Would you like one when they come?"

"Very much indeed."

"Then you shall have one, and believe me you'll never be away from it and you'll be grateful to me until your dying breath. Paiano, please remember that if and when the new tables arrive one must be sent immediately to Mrs. Craigie."

"Very good, my lady." Paiano smiled, ravishingly exposing a great many gleaming white teeth, and went out.

"Paiano's wife has just had another baby," Sandra said, pouring out the tea. "I can't imagine how he finds the time."

"Samolans always find the time, that's what makes the place so invigorating."

"I think you must mean that the other way round," said Sandra, handing me a cup. "The cake's all right because I had some yesterday, but if you take my advice you'll avoid those sandwiches like the plague. They look to me as if they had peanut butter in them." She took one, bit into it, and put it down with a grimace of disgust. "I was quite right," she said. "They have."

We had just finished tea and were about to grapple with the lists again when H.E. came in with a letter in his hand.

"You'd better deal with this, darling," he said handing it to Sandra. "It's from Maisie Coffrington explaining that she met the Queen several times when she was a little girl and is so looking forward to seeing her again. I suppose she'd better be put on the presentation list."

"We've just scratched her off."

"Then scratch her on again," said H.E. amiably, and went out closing the door gently behind him.

I left Government House at about six o'clock in the middle of a first class Vista-Vision, Samolan sunset. The avenue of poincianas leading to the side entrance, which I always used rather than the main gate because it saved me about a quarter of a mile, was ablaze with scarlet, and the sky behind the silhouetted mountains changed from pale yellow to pink, from pink to mauve and from mauve to deep blue as though it were being controlled by an over-enthusiastic chief electrician from some celestial switchboard.

There is little or no twilight in Samolo, none of that lovely drawn-out gentleness of English summer evenings with rooks cawing in the high elms and sheep bleating and the light slowly slowly changing and fading into dusk. Here, it is vivid and dramatic and over in a flash; the sun gets nearer and nearer to the rim of the horizon and then takes a sudden, last-minute dive into the sea and disappears: for a few minutes the sky glows with every imaginable colour and then night has come and the stars are out and you have to switch on your headlights.

I drove home slowly because I wanted to give myself time to think out the best way of breaking the news to Robin of Eloise's imminent arrival. There is a good deal of healthy, old-fashioned Scottish rectitude in Robin's character, and bits of it pop out when you least expect it. Not that I least expected it over the Eloise business; on the contrary, I was fully prepared for a stormy scene ending with him stating flatly that he would have nothing to do with it at all. There was no possible doubt about it. Sandra had been perfectly right when she had said I was a pushover. I should never have allowed Bunny to persuade me. I felt furious with myself for being so weak, and by the time I had arrived at the house I was determined that if Robin showed the slightest signs of disapproval I would call up Bunny immediately and tell him that he would have to find someone else to cover up for him.

When I had put the car in the garage and let myself in I was greeted by delighted shrieks from upstairs which told me only too clearly that Robin had come home early, was helping to bathe the children and overexciting them thoroughly so that they wouldn't calm down and go to sleep for hours.

When I went into the nursery Nanny was sitting, rigid with disapproval, looking out of the window. Her pursed lips and expression of bridling resignation explained wordlessly but unmistakably that she had done her best and could do no more. She rose when I came in and twisted her face into a wintry smile.

"Mr. Craigie is in the bathroom with the children," she said in a flat voice. "They are playing submarines."

"What fun!" I replied brightly. "But I think we had better stop them now, don't you?"

"They should have been in bed half an hour ago." Nanny maintained her martyred smile. "I did suggest to Mr. Craigie that he come up later when they were settled down, but I fear I was overruled."

At this moment the bathroom door flew open and Simon, Janet, and Cokey rushed into the room stark naked, pursued by Robin with a large wet sponge. Janet and Cokey ran screaming like engine whistles into the passage and Simon dived under the bed.

"Do put that sponge back in the bathroom, dear, it's dripping all over the floor."

Robin gave me a tremendous wink and, unperceived by Nanny, made a gesture as though he were going to throw the sponge at her. Simon, peering out from under the bed, gave a shriek of delight.

"Go and get the twins, Nanny," I said. "I'll deal with Simon."

"Good evening, dear," said Robin. "We've been having a little romp."

"So I see." I took the sponge from him and went into the bathroom with it. It was a difficult task to get Simon out from under the bed, and when we finally succeeded he was covered in dust and had to be bathed again. Nanny retrieved Janet and Cokey from the landing and forced them into their nightgowns. Taken all in all it was about half an hour before order was restored. It was when I was bending down to kiss Simon good night that he delivered his bombshell.

"Do duchesses wear crowns?"

I stared at him in amazement. "What on earth made you ask that?"

"Like kings and queens and princes and princesses?"

"Why do you want to know? What put the idea into your head?"

"Because of the one that's coming to stay with us!" Simon hoisted himself up onto the pillow. "Janet says they wear them all the time and I say they don't."

"Who told you a duchess was coming to stay with us?"

"Daddy did," replied Simon. "When we were getting ready for our bath. He said she was a real *bona fide*, dyed-in-the-wool, streamlined job and we should have to bow down and put our foreheads on the ground every time we said 'good morning' to her."

"Daddy was talking nonsense," I said with my brain whirling.

"Do you mean it isn't true? That she isn't coming after all?"

"No, darling," I said, "she is coming all right, but you won't have to bow down and put your foreheads on the ground. Daddy was joking."

"What are we to call her?"

"Aunt Eloise," I said firmly. "And as often as possible."

"But she's not a real aunt, is she?"

"No, but I'm sure she would love people to think she was."

"She is a real duchess though?"

"Yes, darling." I bent down and kissed him. "For the time being anyhow."

"Do you mean she might stop being a duchess suddenly?"

"We must all do our best to prevent that happening." I laughed rather wildly. "Now snuggle down and try to go to sleep like a good boy."

"I'm sorry about putting our foreheads on the ground being only a joke. We were going to start practising tomorrow morning."

"Never mind. Kiss me good night and go to sleep."

Simon twined his arms round my neck and hugged me. "I'm an enormous bear," he said, "and I'm going to hug you until you burst into a million pieces."

"That's a charming thought and I appreciate it more than I can say, but I should appreciate it still more if you would, instead of being an enormous bear, be an amiable well-behaved little boy and get under that sheet and relax." I forced his wriggling little body down onto the bed and drew the sheet up over him. "I have to go and have my bath and change my dress."

I found Robin on the lower verandah blandly contemplating the stars and sipping a gin and tonic. I mixed one for myself and sat down on the swing seat which, as usual, gave a shriek of protest.

"That damned thing needs oiling," he said. "It has needed oiling for several months."

"I know it has. I've been meaning to do something about it but I keep forgetting."

"To mean to do something about something and not do it is slipshod and indecisive," said Robin reprovingly. "You should be firm, marshal your wandering faculties, and buy an oil can. You should also curb your rapidly growing passion for intrigue."

"I don't know what you're talking about."

"You've been sly and underhand again."

"Don't be silly, I haven't been anything of the sort."

"Oh yes you have. First of all there was all that unnecessary secrecy and dissembling about the royal visit, and now there's this shameful conspiracy about Bunny and his duchess. I don't know what is happening to your character, it's deteriorating with every breath you take. I expect it's Sandra's influence—she's one of those scatterbrained, fluttery creatures without any moral fibres."

"Nonsense," I replied. "Sandra's fairly creaking with moral fibres and she's about as fluttery as a cash register when she really puts her mind to anything. Also you love her as much as I do and it's no use pretending you don't."

"Is she in on this lark too?"

"What lark?"

"Bunny and his duchess of course. Did she put you up to it?"

"Of course she didn't—on the contrary she fought like a steer when I asked her to have Eloise to stay for a few days."

"Why did you ask her?"

"Because I promised Bunny I would this morning. He suddenly appeared out of the blue and went on coaxing and persuading until I gave in, and what's more I've been regretting it ever since. If you disapprove you only have to say so and I'll telephone him now and say the whole thing's off."

Robin gulped down the remainder of his drink and went over to the table to mix himself another.

"That's roughly the treatment he gave me. He grabbed me in the bar of the Royal Samolan where I was having a peaceful drink with Siggy, insisted on my lunching with him, and poured out the whole sordid story. He said you'd been a doll and were a wonderful friend and that he felt guilty about having asked you to help him without consulting me first. He's obviously in a bad way, isn't he?"

"I presume you gave in too, just as I did?"

Robin came back to his chair. "What else could I do? The poor chap was in a terrible state."

"The poor chap's a monster."

"Of course he is." Robin laughed, "We all know that. He's always been a monster where women are concerned, but this time I think it really is serious, he's been hooked."

"That's his lookout," I said crossly. "I've been thinking it over very carefully, and I have come to the conclusion, strongly influenced by the scatterbrained Sandra, that we really oughtn't to have anything to do with it. Apart from personal inconvenience and social complications it might very easily involve us in all sorts

88

of trouble. Do let's telephone him and get out of it before it's too late."

"We can't." Robin sipped his drink meditatively. "We've both said 'yes.' It would be mean to go back on our word, besides"—he looked at me with a gleam in his eye—"I'm rather looking forward to entertaining this glamorous, coronetted siren. It'll ginger up the colony no end."

"The colony will be gingered up quite enough with the royal visit."

"Is she as fascinating and alluring and beautiful as Bunny thinks she is?"

"All that and more," I said briskly. "She's an absolute dream, in addition to which her intelligence is quite staggering. You'll be astounded by her incisive knowledge of books and pictures and international affairs."

"You're being sly and underhand again," said Robin. "It's quite obvious that you loathe the sight of her."

"Actually the sight of her is the only part of her I find tolerable. However, be that as it may, for Bunny's sake and auld lang syne we are going to be landed with her. You can rely on me to behave with impeccable manners and lavish every attention on her providing that you and I have a clear understanding before she so much as sets foot in the house."

"Clear understanding?" Robin looked at me guilelessly.

"Yes. And the clear understanding is that you swear to behave properly."

"I don't know what you mean."

"You know perfectly well what I mean. I want no veiled glances, no roguish innuendoes, and no long intimate rides round the plantation. In fact I do not intend to have any repetition of the Rose Cavendish episode."

"The Rose Cavendish episode, as you call it, was entirely built up in your own silly mind and, if I remember rightly, you gave me your solemn promise never to mention it again."

"Well, I have mentioned it again, so there, and what's more I shall go on mentioning it incessantly if I catch for one fleeting second that sheepish, lecherous look in your eye."

"Sheepish and lecherous don't seem to go together."

"Never mind about that. You will promise, won't you?"

"What happens if I fall madly, passionately in love with her?"

"Just see to it that you don't."

"How can I possibly guarantee that? Here I am, a healthy male in the prime of life married to a jealous, possessive wife a whole year and a half older than I am. How can I, faced suddenly with a beautiful, seductive woman of high degree, promise to control the hot blood coursing through my veins, swear, in advance, to crush down ruthlessly my natural, primeval urges?"

"It's no use trying to be funny. I'm serious."

"In which case," said Robin, "you're not only sly, underhand, secretive, jealous, and thoroughly disorganized, but you're a fathead in the bargain."

EIGHT

There are two schools of thought about cocktail parties; one says that they are absolute hell and one of the curses of modern civilization, and the other claims that they are a boon and a blessing to men and enable people to get together socially with the minimum of trouble. Personally I am inclined to hover between the two points of view. They can be absolute hell and make your head ache and your feet ache and involve you in a whole lot of time-wasting small talk as well as filling you up with highly spiced and indigestible "appetizers" so that when you finally get home to dinner you have no appetite at all and wish only to be lying in a cool, white bed in a clinic and sipping beef tea. On the other hand they are far far less wearing than dinner parties or luncheon parties, and you can at least make a getaway when it becomes too unbearable.

However, whether we like it or whether we don't there is no doubt that in small colonial communities the cocktail party as an institution has irrevocably come to stay.

In Samolo there are usually three or four a week and frequently more and the same groups of people foregather, wearing more or less the same clothes and discussing more or less the same things. The same drinks and the same canapés are served with only slight variations when some energetic hostess has discovered some new recipe in an American magazine.

We give one on an average of about once in every two months and they're no worse really than anybody else's; everyone appears to enjoy them and they all say how lovely it's been and when they've all gone Robin and I wander about among the debris nibbling the leftovers and finish up by having scrambled eggs on a bridge table on the back verandah.

On the evening following our momentous decision about Bunny and Eloise we went, dutifully but rather gloomily, to Mrs. Innes-Glendower's. The news of the royal visit had been announced in that morning's *Reaper*, and so we knew what we were in for. One of Mrs. Innes-Glendower's most tedious characteristics is her infinite capacity for reminiscence. She is not a bad old girl really, but she certainly does live in the past, so much so that Robin says that he can't imagine why she thinks it worth while to come down to breakfast. The past in which she lives so enthusiastically is heavy with grandeur. She is the widow of a general who, at some period of his doggedly mediocre career, had been attached, in a minor capacity, to the royal household. These clouds of brief glory have been trailed by Mrs. Innes-Glendower ever since. She remembers, only too vividly and at the drop of a hat, countless quaint and charming little royal anecdotes, most of which are devoid of any point except the important one that she herself was present at the time. All of us in Samolo have heard them so often that we know them by heart, and when any new blood appears on the island such as Pug and Connie Bright or poor Elmer James and Bruce Wheeler, our hearts sink and we have to sit mute and helpless while the flood washes over us and them.

Royal snobbery, in moderation, is rather a good thing, I think, and I am all in favour of it. The crown is a symbol and as such is, or should be, of tremendous importance. We are used to the tradition of royalty and have been brought up to believe in it and respect it and love it. I, being thoroughly British and sentimental to the core, would hate to live in a country in which there was no regal pageantry and no chance of suddenly seeing the Queen drive by. This I know can be described as reactionary emotionalism which perhaps it is, but reactionary or not I feel it very strongly, and when the gutter press alludes to our royal personages by their Christian names and smears their private affairs with its grubby little clichés, I feel deeply angry and somehow ashamed. I want the symbol to go on shining, to go on being out of reach, and I am thankful to say that in our country and its colonies and dominions, it still does, in spite of all efforts to belittle it. All this, however, does not mean that I am entirely in sympathy with Mrs. Innes-Glendower. She carries her adoration of royalty so much too far that she sometimes makes me want to spring onto the nearest table and sing *The Red Flag* if only to shut her up.

Upon arrival we parked the car at the end of a long line of other cars and walked up the drive to the house. The house is fairly hideous, but the garden is lovely and the low row of casuarina trees sang to us in the breeze as we passed. Beyond their humming noise, and far far away, we could hear the surf pounding on the Narouchi reef.

Mrs. Innes-Glendower greeted us at the top of the verandah steps. We could hear from the timbre of her voice that she was in a state of high excitement.

"Isn't the news splendid?" she said as she led us through the oppressively furnished drawing room and out onto the patio at the back where the party was assembled. "Naturally I had heard the rumours, nobody has been talking about anything else for days, but I never really quite believed it until I saw the official announcement in *The Reaper* this morning. Apart from everything else it will be so good for the island. For me personally of course it is particularly thrilling, having known the Queen since she was a little girl. And what a remarkable little girl she was too! So charming to everyone and yet so—how shall I put it?—so genuinely royal. I remember on one occasion when she was quite tiny, I think it was at one of the garden parties, some dreadful woman rushed up to her and wrung her hand like a pump handle without curtseying or anything . . . my dear—she absolutely froze her!"

"How?" enquired Robin.

"She just stood there," Mrs. Innes-Glendower lowered her voice dramatically, "and looked right through her. It was quite extraordinary, the woman literally *slunk* away. I remember the Queen Mother, she was the Duchess of York then of course, caught my eye and we nearly laughed outright, we honestly did! It was a trivial incident but somehow *significant*. One felt that the child, even at that tender age, was aware of her heritage, was already preparing herself to face her destiny—do you know what I mean?"

Robin opened his mouth to reply, but I knew by the glint in his eye that he was going to say something flippant and so I jumped in before he had a chance.

"Of course I know what you mean," I said, "and I couldn't agree more. I never had the honour of knowing her personally as you have but I have always noticed, even in photographs and newsreels, that she had unassailable dignity, a certain *je ne sais quoi*," I added weakly.

"That's exactly it," cried Mrs. Innes-Glendower with enthusiasm. Robin shot me a quizzical look which I ignored, and we were swept out onto the patio.

Mrs. Innes-Glendower's parties, although not particularly exciting, were always well done and the setting was enchanting. Beyond the patio, which was prettily lit and filled with about fifty people all chattering at the tops of their voices, the garden stretched away into the darkness. A vast banyan tree in the middle of the lawn had coloured lights on some of its lower branches while on the right of it, in a circle of flaring native torches, a group of young Samolan musicians in vivid sarongs were singing discreetly and plaintively. All the old Samolan songs have a plaintive quality because they are mostly concerned with unrequited love and farewells and gentle, archaic sadnesses. There are a few more cheerful ones in swifter rhythms but even these, harmonically, have a dying fall. The hotel dance bands on the South Shore disdain, as a rule, the ancient music and go in for modern jazz with, to my mind, excessive zeal. This, naturally enough, I suppose, is a case of demand creating supply. Most tourists are quite content to hear the "real thing" once or twice, but their transient hearts yearn for more familiar strains, with the result that they get all the latest American musical comedy tunes played fairly erratically and very very loudly.

Mrs. Innes-Glendower, fortunately, had had the good taste and sense to realize that music at a cocktail party should provide a gentle background rather than a noisy performance, and the old melodies, thrummed on the ukuleles and sung quietly by muted male voices, floated out over the dark garden and mingled agreeably with the trilling of the tree frogs.

Mrs. Innes-Glendower left us and went to greet the admiral and the "Princess," who had clanked up the hill convulsively in their Morris Minor and were now, judging by the noise, trying to park it. We drifted over to the bar, asked for gin and tonics, and joined Buddha and Dusty Grindling and Maisie Coffrington, who was already showing signs of wear and tear. Buddha and Dusty are great friends of ours: his real name is Terence but he is known as Buddha because, whenever there is an argument going on and he has had a few drinks, he affirms defiantly that he considers Christianity a total failure whereas Buddhism still remains pure and unsullied and radiates religious tolerance and every other kind of tolerance. We are all quite used to this and nobody pays attention any more. He is a dear man, small and bright-eyed and highly intelligent. Dusty, his wife (baptized Hermione), is tall and impressive-looking with wide grey eyes and a talent for appearing to be cool and collected and impeccably groomed in all weathers and all circumstances. I knew by Buddha's stance that he was in one of his *épater le bourgeois* moods. Dusty was sipping her drink calmly and looking over his head at the mountains.

"I am glad you've come," he said, kissing me absently, "because you, unlike many others that I could name, occasionally understand what I am talking about. The obtuseness of most of my friends on certain subjects of vital importance to us all, is to me a grave and quite fabulous mystery."

"What's up?" asked Robin. "What are you ranting about now?"

Buddha fixed him with a bright brown eye. "I am not ranting yet," he said, "but if I have to listen to any more of the hysterical nonsense about the royal visit that I have been listening to all day, I most certainly will rant. Not only will I rant in a manner that would put the late Sir Henry Irving to shame, but I will shout and roar and bang my head against the nearest wall."

"If you started by doing that," interposed Dusty gently, "you'd knock yourself out and we should be spared all the rest."

"My wife is trying to undermine me as usual. She has been trying to undermine me for seventeen agonizing years. She is much bigger than I am, otherwise she would never have been able to drag me to the altar in the first place."

"It wasn't an altar, dear," said Dusty. "It was the Caxton Hall Westminster."

"I have been told a hundred times if I have been told once," went on Buddha, ignoring her, "that the imminent visit of Her Majesty the Queen and His Royal Highness the Duke of Edinburgh will be GOOD for the island!"

"Of course it will," said Robin. "Every ass knows that."

95

"Exactly. Every ass knows that and, if you will forgive the direct implication, every ass says that, but what every ass hasn't taken into consideration is that the statement is nothing but a sentimental, wishful-thinking fallacy. In actual fact the exact contrary will prove to be the case. You mark my words."

"Rubbish," said Robin equably. "You're on the wrong wicket old boy, as usual."

"This 'Playing Fields of Eton' phraseology sickens me, but I will let it pass for the moment and continue to elaborate my theme——"

"Maisie wants another drinkie." Maisie Coffrington slipped her arm affectionately through Buddha's. "Maisie wants another little drinkie very badly."

"Maisie may *want* another little drinkie very badly," said Buddha, detaching himself from her grasp, "but if Maisie *has* another little drinkie she is liable to fall flat on her little facie. Where was I?"

"Nowhere in particular," said Dusty.

Buddha shot her a withering look and continued: "Before I go any further I wish to make it quite clear that when I say the royal visit, far from being good for the island, will be very bad for the island, it is in no way intended as a reflection on the royal visitors themselves."

"Damned generous of you," said Robin.

"They are handsome and charming and gracious and will do the job as efficiently and intelligently as they do all their other jobs, but—and it is a very big but indeed—the very fact of their coming here will cause incalculable social, moral, economic, industrial and political confusion . . ."

"Why should it?"

"In the first place it will work social snobbery up to an even higher pitch than it is already. Ordinary citizens who hitherto have been reasonably contented with their lot will suddenly, egged on by their wives, swathe themselves in delusions of grandeur, become power-conscious, overambitious, and start jockeying for position and conspiring to get special presentations and honours, and if that isn't morally reprehensible I should like to know what is. Secondly, the hotels and shops will double and treble their prices, which are astronomical enough as it is, thereby upsetting the economic status quo which God knows is wobbly enough already. Thirdly, the native handicraft industries will go completely haywire and, instead of concentrating on their conventional mats and palm thatch and bamboo, will deluge us with hideous raffia bags and coasters and screens and whatnots appliquéd with crowns and coats of arms and uneven E.R.s, cunningly wrought in coloured straw and sequins. Politically of course the whole business will have far-reaching and disastrous results. All the Samolan Nationalists who, up to now, have been perfectly happily screaming abuse at the government and scrawling communistic slogans on public buildings will, again egged on by their wives, bend the knee and genuflect and allow themselves to be coaxed and cajoled, thereby completely vitiating their power as a healthy opposition. But over and above all these desperate dilemmas in which the royal visit will place us, there is one worse than all the others put together, one that nobody up to date seems to have envisaged . . ."

"Tell us," said Robin. "Don't keep us in suspense. I'm already on the verge of tears."

"The press!" Buddha paused dramatically. "The press of the world will converge upon this wretched little Pacific paradise and leave it looking like Hampstead Heath on the morning after Bank Holiday. They will impart an air of scruffiness to the loveliest day. They will huddle in cliché-sodden groups in all the bars of all the best hotels. There will be pallid, narrow-headed oafs from Fleet Street and pseudointellectual political correspondents with corduroy trousers and enlarged Adam's apples; vivacious sob sisters who will describe our royalties in the same terms as they would describe Hollywood movie stars: social columnists from America; smart, well-dressed women with friendly manners and hearts of stone and from England, an impecunious lordling or two, and one or two anaemic fashion writers in badly cut print frocks. The whole dreary unappetizing lot of them will come tumbling out of aeroplanes at our feet and, what is more, we shall have to be nice to them, we shall even, if asked to do so by high authority, be compelled to ask them to our houses, because the fallacy of the Power of the Press is still rampant in this decaying and foolish world."

"I have a great friend who is a journalist," I said. "She's a darling."

"Then she must be a very bad journalist," snapped Buddha. "No good journalist could go on being a darling even if she had started as one."

At this moment Michael Tremlett came up and looked anxiously at Maisie, who was teetering slightly and trying to focus her eyes on the lights in the banyan tree. Michael is a nice enough boy. Robin says he is "wet" and I suppose he is, in a way, but he is devoted to poor Maisie and looks after her loyally; he also has a definite talent for interior decoration.

"Time to go, dear," he said, a trifle sibilantly. "We said we'd be at Jane's at seven thirty and it's that now."

"I don't want to go to Jane's," said Maisie. "I can't abide her."

"You love her," said Michael with gentle firmness. "You know you do. Everybody loves dear old Jane."

"I do not love dear old Jane," Maisie's voice rose belligerently. "Dear old Jane's a bore, and what's more she gets even drunker than I do."

Michael laughed shrilly. "You're wonderful, Maisie, you really are!"

"The last time I dined there," continued Maisie reminiscently, "she sat in a fruit salad."

"Perhaps she'll do it again if we hurry." Michael gripped her firmly by the arm. "Come along."

We watched him lead her away, piloting her with practised skill through groups of people and up the two wide marble steps into the house.

"That boy certainly earns his keep," said Buddha, "but I suppose he wouldn't do it unless he enjoyed it. There is a strange seedy magnificence in the sight of young English manhood devoting all its deathless energy to looking after a drunken neurotic old enough to be his mother."

"Perhaps he is genuinely fond of her," I suggested. "She's a lonely creature and I suspect that he is too. Also, apart from her drinking, which I admit is tiresome, she has many excellent qualities."

"The nobility of your nature, my dear Grizel, puts me to shame," said Buddha. "You always have a kind word for everyone, which is admirable in itself but death to general conversation. You are out of place in this jagged century; you should be living your life in a small Victorian village and concentrating on minor good works."

"You misjudge me," I replied sharply, "and if you start attacking me with your *Literary Digest* phrases I shall be only too delighted to prove to you that I have most emphatically *not* got a kindly word for everyone, so there."

"Go it, old girl," said Robin.

Buddha sighed. "That 'so there' lowered the tone of your whole sentence," he said sadly.

At this moment Mrs. Innes-Glendower bustled up with Hali Alani. Hali Alani is the most decorative of our island "lions." He is strikingly handsome, about thirty-two, and the Prime Minister of the People's Imperial Party, which is now in power. He is considered by most of the elders of the community to be a bit of a lightweight, and it is more or less taken for granted that all important decisions and policies are controlled from behind the scenes by his father, Punalo Alani, who is old and wise, was educated in England, and looks like a little withered nut. In spite of Hali's outward light-weightness, which is a great asset socially, he is far from being a fool, added to which he has considerable personal charm. H.E. is a bit suspicious of him but Sandra dotes on him, in fact almost everyone in the colony dotes on him excepting naturally the supporters of the S.S.N.P., the Samolan Socialist National Party, which is very left-wing indeed and works up agitations and strikes and small discontents whenever it can. Fortunately, however, the Samolans are a mild and temperamentally cheerful people: they are uninterested in politics and sensible enough to realize that they are perfectly happy under the aegis of the British. If there were a great deal of poverty and industrial disorders the S.S.N.P. might have more chance of working them up to an embittered realization of their wrongs, and the disingenuous slogan "Samolo for the Samolans" might have more effect. As it is, however, they are not conscious of having any particular wrongs, and the idea of Samolo being for anyone else but Samolans has never occurred to them. This acquiescent attitude of course runs directly counter to modern "progressive" political thought which is based on the assumption that British imperialism was, at its best, evil, capitalistic, and money-grubbing and is now done for anyway. The Samolans really don't know anything about

British imperialism. The island was handed over to the British in the eighteen-fifties by King Kefumalani I, who considered—wisely, as it turned out—that they could administer and control it more efficiently than he could. No blood was shed; no native populations were ground down under any iron heels; in fact nobody was ground down in any way apart from a few pirates who had to be exterminated for the common weal. The present agitation, by the Labour Party at home, the Russians in Moscow, the Americans in Washington, and the S.S.N.P. here, for Samolo to break free from the British yoke and achieve dominion status, has very few supporters in the whole Samolan archipelago. In the first place, such a drastic change would obviously entail a lot of responsibility, and the Samolan people are fundamentally irresponsible and know it. In the second place, they consider themselves to be fairly treated, and even if there are occasional causes for dissatisfaction they instinctively prefer the devil they know to the more incalculable devils they might encounter if they suddenly found themselves out on their own without their old British Nanny to run to.

H.E., who comes from a brilliant socialist family, was frankly bewildered by this Samolan *laissez faire* when he first came out here, but he has since become used to it and, I believe, secretly rather likes it. At any rate Hali Alani and his father Punalo are cheerfully determined reactionaries and, speaking personally, I hope and pray that they will remain in power for a long time to come.

"Hali," said Mrs. Innes-Glendower exuberantly, "lunched at Government House today and he is full of the most exciting information."

"What about?" enquired Buddha, and I knew from his tone that we were in for trouble.

"The royal visit of course." She turned to Hali. "Tell them about your idea for the old FumFumBolo prayer dance in the moonlight. It really would be perfectly lovely and I'm sure quite unlike anything they have ever seen before."

"I suspect that by now the Queen and the Duke of Edinburgh have seen so many unique traditional native dances that they might both quite conceivably faint dead away at the very thought of having to endure one more."

Hali smiled disarmingly. "I see that dear Buddha boy is this evening in a dark mood," he said. "He will make stony ground for any idea I have for entertaining Her Majesty."

"Dear Buddha boy is against the whole enterprise from the start," said Robin. "He's been roaring away like one of those men at the Marble Arch on Sunday afternoons."

"I have never been to London which is for me most pitiful," said Hali. "Why is there this roaring at the Marble Arch?"

"It is to prove to visiting foreigners that we are a free country," said Buddha. "We go to almost any lengths in England to prove fallacies to foreigners."

"I fear that I am all in the sea," said Hali.

"Dear Hali," I said, slipping my arm through his, "don't worry about being all in the sea. Your intuitions are quick, in the sea or out of it, and you are quite right about Buddha being in a dark mood. He has been insufferable for the last half an hour but he doesn't really mean to be, it's just that his ego, being larger than most people's, always drives him to take the opposite view from anyone else's . . ."

"Now look here, Pollyanna Borgia . . ." began Buddha, but I silenced him.

"Shut up for a minute, dear. I am just trying to explain your tiresome and overcomplicated character to Hali because, as you well know, I always have a kindly word for everyone." I turned back to Hali. "He is just as excited as we all are about the royal visit, but for some reason best known to himself he wants to prove that he is a cut above such sentimental snobberies. This is just his 'line,' and we must all accept it and laugh at him as we always do."

"Come away, love," said Dusty, taking Buddha by the arm. "Grizel has worsted you and you must learn to take your medicine like a man . . ."

All would have been well if at that particular moment poor Mrs. Innes-Glendower hadn't flung herself enthusiastically into the breach.

"I can't understand anybody not being absolutely thrilled about the royal visit," she cried. "It's the most wonderful thing that's ever happened to the island and, apart from all the pleasure it will give, it will do so much *good!*"

This was too much for Buddha, who broke away from Dusty's restraining grip and rounded on Mrs. Innes-Glendower.

"Think more carefully, woman," he said menacingly, "before you make such utterly fatuous statements. You, suckled and nurtured by middle-class respectability, you, whose spiritual home is Cheltenham, have not and could never have the faintest conception of the perilous issues involved in this misguided and quite unprovoked royal descent upon our hitherto tranquil little community. Our peaceful harmless existence will be shattered into a million pieces, our moral fibres will be weakened and sodden by ghastly, meretricious patriotic hysteria, eminent citizens of hitherto unblemished integrity will cringe and grovel, and finally, when our royal guests depart and the flag waving is over and the hysteria subsided, nobody will be speaking to anyone else."

"In that case," said Mrs. Innes-Glendower with praiseworthy dignity, "I should like to start now by not speaking to you. Please take your husband away, Dusty. He has obviously had too much to drink, and I do not care to be spoken to in that tone in my own house." With this she turned and left us.

"Now you've done it," said Robin.

"The woman's a relic! And she has a mind like an Edwardian hair-tidy and——"

"Relic or not," said Dusty, "we've just been thrown out of the house, so we had better go with a good grace; come on, you can send her some flowers and a note of apology in the morning."

"Apologize! What have I to apologize for?" Poor Buddha's voice was defiant, but underneath I could detect the beginnings of remorse.

"For a great many things," said Dusty patiently, "but principally to your hostess for telling her that she was suckled in middle-class respectability and that Cheltenham was her spiritual home."

"What is this Cheltenham?" enquired Hali.

"It is a very pleasant little town in England," I replied, "filled with retired colonels and admirals and ex-ambassadors and their wives. They play golf and bridge and go for drives and live on the memories of their past grandeurs."

"And what, if you will forgive one more question for the betterment of my English idiom, is an Edwardian hair-tidy?"

"That's a bit more difficult to explain," said Robin. "It's really a sordid little cornucopia into which Edwardian ladies stuffed bits of their hair that had come out in the comb, and a cornucopia"—he went on hurriedly to forestall Hali's next question—"is that trumpet-shaped thing that Ceres, the goddess of plenty, used to throw all the fruit and vegetables out of."

"Thank you," said Hali. "You have made it all most clarified."

"Come home, Buddha." There was a note of strong authority in Dusty's usually lazy voice. "Come home at once." She gripped him firmly by the arm and led him away. Mrs. Innes-Glendower, who was talking to the Turlings on the other side of the patio, turned and watched them go.

"This may very possibly develop into one of those island feuds," said Robin. "Which will end in making everything very uncomfortable for everybody. We'd better stick around until we get an opportunity to pour a little oil."

"I will then leave you," said Hali. "For I am dining with my papa and he gets hopping irritable if I am late. I cannot tell you how sorry it makes me to have been present at such a wicked little drama of society. Buddha boy is most naughty when he insists on mounting his boxes of soap, but he is a very sweet and lovable fellow taken by and long."

Hali bowed, smiled engagingly, and went off to say good-bye to Mrs. Innes-Glendower. Robin and I sauntered out onto the lawn and sat on a seat underneath the banyan tree. I felt suddenly oppressed, as I so often do at cocktail parties, with a vague sense of futility. There they all were, the people we lived our lives with, the men in their white jackets and the women in their flimsy coloured frocks, some of them were close friends whom we genuinely cared for, others were casuals whom we liked well enough, and some were acquaintances whom we met from time to time and had no particular contact with, but we knew them all. We knew their names and their faces and where they lived and what their business was, and of course they knew us too, just so much and no more, and month after month, year after year, we all met and remet each other on occasions like this and drank gin or rum together and talked and talked about this and that and meanwhile Time was scurrying by and before we knew where we were all our various children would be grown up and married and divorced and we should be grandparents, or not as the case might be, and then we should be old and crotchety and begin to die off. Now of course we had a mutual interest, an excitement that bound us all together, the royal visit. But when that was over and we sank back again into our beautiful but stagnant pond, everything would go on again just exactly as it had gone on before, and it seemed suddenly unbearable. All the little sillinesses and social trivialities; Buddha and Mrs. Innes-Glendower wouldn't speak for a few weeks and then it would all be made up and forgiven and forgotten, then someone else would have a row with someone else and *they* wouldn't speak for a few weeks and people would take sides and discuss it and wallow in it until that too was made up and forgiven and forgotten.

Robin, who was smoking peacefully and staring up into the branches of the tree, must have felt my depression oozing out of me because he patted my hand affectionately.

"The thoughts of youth are long long thoughts."

I sighed. "Mine were far from being the thoughts of youth. They were the thoughts of rapidly advancing age."

"Cheer up," he said. "You don't look a day over fifty."

"It's the waste that's depressing me," I said. "The wicked waste. I once had a nursemaid when I was very small, and whenever I left any tapioca pudding, which I detested, on the side of my plate, she always said 'Wicked Waste!' and now I feel as if all the tapioca I had ever not eaten had collected itself into a great cloud and was smothering me."

"A truly Tchekhovian thought."

"Do you ever have the feeling that nothing really matters in the least bit, and that every minute of our lives that should be immensely valuable isn't valuable at all and that we're all wandering through the years in a sort of dreary vacuum?"

"Of course, I am a positive martyr to those sorts of reflections. I frequently stop the car in the middle of the road when I am rushing off to see someone and say, 'What's it all for?'"

"Don't laugh at me, I'm serious."

"Oh no you're not," said Robin. "You're just feeling depleted and tired and bored and you want to put your feet up."

"I don't think that even having my feet up would entirely banish this sensation of cosmic futility."

"Them's mighty big words to use at a cocktail party."

"We're not at a cocktail party. We're outside it, at least I am. Not only do I feel that I'm outside the cocktail party but I feel that I'm outside the whole of existence and just looking on rather miserably, like those psychics who leave their bodies in the middle of the night and look back at themselves asleep in bed."

"I don't mix with those sorts of people," said Robin. "As you know, in my position I can't be too careful."

"I love you very much," I said.

"Aha!" Robin rose to his feet. "Now I see it all·clearly. Sex, nothing but sex, let's go home and to hell with smoothing Mrs. Innes-Glendower's ruffled feathers."

"Men are all alike," I murmured, following him across the lawn. "No spiritual quality."

I am frequently saddened when I realize the width of the gulf that separates me from the heroines of those modern psychological novels written by our leading women novelists. These heroines, although that perhaps is not quite the right word for them, have a sensitivity, an awareness, a sort of pleasantly neurotic perception of all the little "nuances" of daily life, in which I am temperamentally lacking. They appear to be able to pin down a moment either of irritation, or ecstasy, or nostalgic sadness with such satisfactory precision. For them, every minute of the day is rich with vital implication. I am sure that this sensory acuteness has its disadvantages, that it makes them more vulnerable to the impact of annoying trivialities, more deeply lacerated by pinpricks, but nonetheless I envy them. Not because I am not perfectly happy as I am, really, but because I feel that it would make me more interesting as a companion to Robin.

It would be so lovely to be able to analyze, swiftly and with immediate accuracy, the motives behind people's behaviour; the predominant emotional atmosphere in a room full of people. It would also be lovely, in some of those quiet moments when we are alone together, to be able to dally with abstractions and apply delicately witty literary allusions to the events of the day. I have tried this once or twice when we have been sitting on the back verandah after dinner and looking up at the stars, but it has never been a real success. On one occasion when I had just finished an infinitely subtle book by Rosamond Lehmann and was feeling my intellectual oats, I embarked on what I hoped would turn out to be a profound and stimulating discussion of our own personal relationship: I placed it deftly on a series of different emotional planes: physical, spiritual, domestic, etc., etc. It was an exquisite evening and the fireflies were flitting back and forth across the lawn while far away in a distant village there was some sort of a party going on and the sound of the drums, muffled by distance, was wafted to us in gentle gusts by the quiet breeze, and I was really doing quite nicely and warming to my work when Robin suddenly sneezed and said he wondered if he was going to have a cold. When I had flown upstairs and routed-about in the bathroom for some Phensic, found it, and administered it to him in a nice strong whisky and soda, I sat down again and tried to recapture the mood but it was shattered irrevocably and I couldn't get my thoughts to clamber back onto the right level of light, wistful introspection. I made one abortive effort and said something about human happiness being dependent on one's capacity for being able to make adjustments to changing circumstances and the physical mutations of growing older, and, above all, Time. Time, I said, although reputed to be the Great Healer, was frequently nothing of the sort. Time, assisted by dull routine and daily familiarities, was responsible for more hitherto happy relationships breaking up than it was given credit for, and if only more people had the sense to realize this they would take more trouble to break the routine and minimize the familiarities and always be on the *qui vive* to be different in some way and prepare little surprises for one another. I was once more beginning to gather impetus when Robin gulped down the last of his whisky and said that, speaking of Time, he had a little surprise for me which was that it was ten to eleven and that he for one was going to bed.

I had failed, as usual, by choosing the wrong moment, whereas they never failed—Miss Lehmann, Mrs. Woolf, or Miss Bowen—attractive, brilliantly cerebral creatures, to know the moment, to recognize it clearly for what it was and to analyze it down to its tiniest subtlety. I am bound to admit, however, in fairness to myself, that I do think they occasionally fail in other ways in which I actually don't. In the first place they are, as a general rule, pretty wretched, whereas I am resilient and cheerful as a cricket for many hours of every day. In the second place I do feel that perhaps they torture themselves unnecessarily by sensing psychological implications in quite casual words or gestures: words and gestures in fact that actually mean no less and no more than they appear to mean. If they were in my place, for instance, Robin's bleak lack of interest in my conversation and his abrupt dismissal of it would have plunged them immediately into a morass of melancholy introspection. They would have probed behind his words to find hidden, subconscious discontents with life in general and with themselves in particular. Their poor hearts would have drooped and died with the quite unconfirmed suspicion that the fabric of their married happiness was wearing thin; that their words and thoughts no longer communicated themselves as once they had when passion's flame was burning more brightly; that this sudden, callous jamming of their wave lengths indicated the beginning of the end; was a sign that the lyric spring and summer of love was over and that dank autumn was at hand and that there was nothing to look forward to but dead leaves and ashes and the protracted drudgeries and makeshifts of disenchanted proximity.

What wouldn't have entered their minds perhaps, but which most certainly entered mine, was the possibility that Robin really was going to have a cold, in which case he would inevitably be feeling irritable and uncomfortable and would be in no mood to listen to high-flown philosophical dissertations from me or anyone else.

On the night that we drove home together from Mrs. Innes-Glendower's cocktail party there were no overtones to plague us and no unspoken psychological intuitions to make us wary of each other and spoil the tranquil pleasure of the drive. Mrs. Innes-Glendower's house is high up on the foothills behind Narouchi Beach, and the road down from it, although twisty, is full of charm. First of all it winds through banana plantations which belong to the Stirling family, who have one of the oldest and most picturesque houses on the island. We could see the lights glimmering in the windows as we passed. Then there is a straight bit where the road narrows and runs through an ironwood grove and over a little white bridge. The trees are thick on each side and although you can smell the sea and hear it, you can't see it at all until suddenly the road swerves sharply to the left and it lies there in front of you with rows of coco palms making spidery shadows on the sand. The reef here is about three quarters of a mile from the shore and the rollers eternally pounding on it make a long line of foam which gleams phosphorescently in the moonlight.

Robin drove across the road and onto a small bluff covered with wiry grass and sea grape and shut off the headlights and the engine. I, always a slave to tradition, fumbled in my bag and lit a cigarette for each of us. He took his automatically in silence and we sat quite still for a few minutes without saying a word, and the very fact of our sitting there together staring mutely at the line of surf and the stars and the gently moving feather dustery coco palms which occasionally made a little noise like the sound of hand-clapping far away, made me aware that, acute psychological perception or no acute psychological perception, I was very fortunate and very happy.

NINE

The two weeks between Mrs. Innes-Glendower's cocktail party and the arrival of Eloise Fowey were overcrowded and increasingly hectic. In the first place Sandra telephoned me and bullied me into agreeing to be on the entertainment committee for the royal visit. This meant attending meetings with Ivy Poland, Alma Peacock, and the rest of the local Little Theatre group, all of whom are filled with enthusiasm and grandiose ideas but unfortunately lack the professional experience and technique to carry them out. In addition to this I had to endure several heart-to-heart talks with Bunny Colville, who was churning himself into a frenzy about the imminent arrival of Eloise, and on top of it all the Frobishers arrived from Noonaeo for a ten days' stay.

Now the Frobishers are a sweet couple and I am devoted to them. They are goodhearted and cheerful and have entertained us several times with the utmost hospitality on their vast cocoa plantation, but alas, the noise they make singly and together is nerve-racking. There are five of them all told. Bob, Molly, and three children, two boys and a girl, who are round about the same age as mine, and they all have peculiarly penetrating voices. Molly, in addition, has a laugh which can be heard from one end of the house to the other. It is more a bray than a laugh really, and every time she does it one looks instinctively at the sky to see if it is going to rain. The children shriek on a higher, more sustained note than any other children I have ever met, and of course my children catch it from them and the result is pandemonium. Bob, who is tall and handsome and never stopped winning cups for his athletic prowess when he was young, has a mania for telling funny stories. One after the other they surge out of him, and whenever he pauses for breath Molly is ready with a full-throated bray to prompt him. Certain people have a natural gift for anecdote, a special talent for picking unexpected words to surprise you into a sudden chuckle regardless of whether the story is intrinsically funny or not, but poor Bob is not one of these. He presses on with dogged zeal to the inevitable pay-off, disdaining irrelevant adornments until he arrives at the hideous moment when you know beyond a shadow of doubt that you are expected to give a merry peal of spontaneous laughter. Actually Robin is better at this than I am and generally manages to be on cue when the time comes whereas I become numb after a while; my mind begins to wander, and I am frequently caught with a vacant stare and no clue whatever as to what has been said.

It is pathetic to watch people you like and respect being urged by their own egos to hold the floor at all costs, to strut in temporary limelight, to show off, and all in order to bolster themselves up with the illusion that they have been the life and soul of the party. I could imagine the poor darling Frobishers bouncing into bed together after one of their usual anecdotal orgies and Bob saying, with a note of whistling-in-the-dark, hopeful complacency; "Well, I think the evening went off very well, don't you?" and Molly, with every female instinct rallying to reassure him, murmuring, "Thanks to you, dear, entirely thanks to you, but I do wish you had told them the one about the two parrots!"

I remember once asking Robin when we were staying with the Frobishers, and we ourselves had bounded into bed worn out after many hours of sustained cheeriness, why he didn't take Bob aside, man to man, and explain to him tactfully that we really didn't like listening to funny stories nearly so much as we pretended to and that a much better time would be had by all if we could just gossip away about general topics and discuss the weather and the crops? But he said he really hadn't the courage; that poor Bob would be mortally hurt and that there was nothing for us to do but grin and bear it. I replied wearily that I was perfectly prepared to *bear* anything within reason but it was having to *grin* so much that was getting me down, whereupon Robin delivered a few ennobling platitudes about tolerance and taking people as one found them, and went to sleep.

Anyhow they were on us, children, funny stories, and all; and the house, as usual, resounded to their din. There were, also as usual, inevitable fights and squabbles and dramas among the children. Timmy and Mickey Frobisher, being a few months and a year older than Simon respectively, were rather inclined to lord it over him and order him about, which frequently led to disaster. Sylvia, the girl, and Janet and Cokey got along all right, but there was no genuine basis of affection between them.

The ten days' visit passed noisily but more or less uneventfully except for one occasion when Bunny invited us all over for a picnic lunch on his beach, and even that wouldn't have been particularly eventful but for one incident which, although we were unaware of it at the time, was later to have alarming repercussions. The children, all yelling at the top of their lungs, were crowded into a small rubber boat and rowed, by Bunny, out to the reef. Bob, Molly, Robin, and I were on the beach lazily packing up the remains of the lunch which had been sent down from the house in a large hamper. Suddenly we heard a burst of yelling even louder than usual, and looked up to see that the boat had collapsed. This didn't worry us unduly because all the children can swim like porpoises; Bob and Robin, however, ran into the sea and swam out to help Bunny to get the boat right side up again. Molly and I watched, without much maternal agitation, the commotion going on. By the time the men had righted the boat Timmy Frobisher and Simon arrived on the beach, rather out of breath because it was quite a long swim for two little boys. They plumped themselves down on the sand and asked for bananas and so I routed about in the hamper and produced some, then it was that Simon said casually, "Mickey's hurt himself."

Molly jumped to her feet. "Hurt himself—how?"

"It was nothing much," said Timmy. "When the boat upset he fell on a sharp bit of coral and cut his leg."

"Badly? Did he cut it badly?"

"Not really," said Simon indifferently. "But he made an awful fuss."

"So would you," said Timmy hotly, "if you had nearly cut your foot off."

Molly gave a scream. "Cut his foot off!" She ran quickly down the beach and, plunging into the water, swam frantically towards the approaching boat.

I shook Timmy. "Is it really bad or are you making it up?"
"It bled a lot—all the water was pink."

"It always is," said Simon, munching his banana, "when you
bleed in it."

I left them both and walked down to the sea's edge and out into
the shallows. Molly had reached the boat and was helping Robin
and Bob to push it. In it were the other children and Bunny holding Mickey on his knee. Mickey, needless to say, was screaming
like a banshee. When the boat got into the shallow water Bunny
handed Mickey to Molly, who carried him ashore. The other children, rather subdued, scrambled out of the boat and stood round
while we examined Mickey's wound. It was a nasty cut just below
the knee and was still bleeding. Bunny ran up to the house for
some disinfectant and a bandage, meanwhile Molly tried, unavail-
ingly, to soothe Mickey's sobs. When Bunny returned we dabbed
the cut with Milton and bandaged it, and eventually Bob and
Molly carried Mickey up to the car and went off to find Dr. Bowman, who lives only a few miles away. When they had gone and
the immediate drama was over the children stopped being subdued and all started screaming again so Bunny and I left Robin to
cope with them and strolled along to the far end of the beach.

"Lucky it was this side of the reef and not the other," said
Bunny. "That child bled like a pig. If it had happened a little
farther out we would have had all the sharks in the neighbour-
hood snapping around."

"Don't," I said with a shudder. Sharks and barracuda are my
special nightmare, and although I have accustomed myself over
the years to the children flinging themselves in and out of the
water whenever they feel like it, my mind is never completely at
ease. I know that most of the beaches on the South Shore are well
protected by reefs and that there have never been any recorded
fatalities except for one foolish woman who dived from a boat
one moonlight night in the middle of Pendarla Harbour after a
gay drinking party at the Royal Samolan and had both her legs
bitten off.

In these seas it is not wise to bathe at night even in the lagoons
unless they happen to be shallow and entirely encircled by reef.
And even then, leaving aside the possibility of big fish, there are
other menaces such as sleeping sting rays or purple jellyfish which

float about on the surface of the water trailing long, poisonous tentacles which wrap themselves round you and disfigure you with painful weals for weeks afterwards. Bunny of course, with his passion for spear fishing, suffers from no fears, but then Bunny does not happen to be the anxious mother of three young children.

When we had got to the end of the beach we sat on the edge of a little wooden landing stage and dangled our feet in the clear, blue-green water.

"Before you go," said Bunny, "I want your advice on some new covers I've bought for the big room."

"What colour are they?"

"Sort of reddish."

"Oh, Bunny! Red is rather a hot colour for this climate."

"Wait until you see them," he said earnestly. "They really are very pretty and much lighter and more cheerful than the old ones."

"That, dear, wouldn't be difficult. What have you done about the spare bedroom?"

"That's a leading question," he replied, "and the answer is nothing."

"Well, you ought to be ashamed of yourself. The bed is like a board, the table by the side of it wobbles, and the shutter flaps back and forth all night because the bolt's broken. I know because I've slept there, or rather tried to sleep there. Eloise will have a fit when she sees it, after all she has been used to considerable luxury."

"I had not counted on Eloise using the spare bedroom overmuch," said Bunny.

"That is no affair of mine." I looked at him austerely. "And what is more it is the one aspect of the whole business that I resolutely refuse to discuss."

"Well, you brought it up, all this talk about bedrooms."

"Whether Eloise uses it or not that bedroom should be entirely redone," I said firmly. "It isn't fair to your friends. Just because you happen to be allergic to all forms of physical comfort and are perfectly happy dossing down on straw mattresses and eating things out of tins, it doesn't necessarily follow that other people feel the same way. And while we're on the subject of general house renovation," I went on, "have you done anything about the rats?"

"Rats? What rats?" asked Bunny innocently.

"Listen, my dear," I said gently. "You forget that I had the house for a whole month last summer. There is nothing about it that I don't know. And one of the principal things I *do* know is that a cosy little family of rats inhabit that dank room between the kitchen and the dining room. I know this, not from hearsay or idle gossip, I know it because I have seen the beastly things time and time again with my own eyes. I have also heard them scampering about among that dusty collection of shells in the middle of the night."

"You exaggerate," said Bunny. "There may be one or two harmless little field mice."

"What I saw were not field mice, they were rats."

"You're not to go filling up Eloise with all these lurid inventions. Promise me you won't."

"I've promised quite enough already."

"You've been a dreamboat, and so has Robin, I'll never forget it as long as I live." He offered me a cigarette from rather a crumpled package. "And if you want to be just a little teeny bit more noble, you'll let Robin and the others go home when they bring the boy back from the doctor's, and stay behind with me and I'll mix you a sublime martini and we'll go over the house together from stem to stern and I'll do anything you say."

"I can't stay long. We're taking Molly and Bob to dine with Juanita at the Tavern."

"No more than half an hour. I'll whisk you home in a flash."

"Not over that road, you won't." I sighed. "Poor Eloise."

"Why do you say that?"

"I was thinking how many times she will be dragged back and forth over those appalling bumps."

"Do you think she'll hate it here?"

"I haven't the faintest idea. As I have already explained I really don't know her very well and I haven't clapped eyes on her for years."

Bunny flipped a shell into the sea and watched it skim over the ripples.

"I suppose you and Robin think I'm a bloody fool about all this."

"I don't know what Robin thinks, but I most certainly do. I think you're both behaving like idiots, but we've been into all this before, haven't we? And it's really no use going on about it. She's arriving next Monday and that's that."

"You still think it wiser for me not to come to the airport?"

"Really, Bunny, you're carrying on like a besotted schoolboy."

"That sounds highly unattractive."

"It is highly unattractive. For heaven's sake pull yourself together. There is no question of your coming to the airport, and you know it perfectly well. You will come to us for dinner as arranged and see Eloise for the first time then and not a moment before."

"And when may she come here?" he asked meekly.

"That will be decided when we have discussed it with her. In the meantime I suggest that you get rid of those rats."

"Field mice," said Bunny. "You will do what I ask about going over the house with me, won't you?"

"I can't stay more than half an hour."

We walked back along the beach and found the children in a state of wild excitement because Robin had found a fair-sized blowfish. There the poor thing lay on the sand, blowing itself out and subsiding again while Cokey and Janet prodded it with a bit of stick. Sylvia stood farther off looking scared, and Timmy and Simon were capering about emitting war whoops.

"Either kill it," I said to Robin, "or put it back into the sea. I can't bear to see it going on like that."

"It's not a feeling thing," he replied. "All that gasping and blowing is entirely muscular."

"Muscular or not it's obviously perfectly wretched," I said. "For heaven's sake do something about it."

"If we took it home Mummy could keep it in a tank," suggested Simon.

"We haven't got a tank and you're not going to take it home." I turned to Robin. "Please, darling, do as I ask, the children have had their fun, do put it out of its misery."

Robin waded into the sea, deposited the blowfish, and brought back Timmy and Simon. Bunny shouldered the picnic hamper, the three girls collected the towels, and we climbed up the steps to the house.

In fairness to Bunny I must admit that although the place leaves a lot to be desired architecturally, it is ideal for the particular kind of life he likes to live when he's out here. First and foremost there is the beach, a perfect crescent of coral sand, completely private and enclosed by small headlands at each end. The house is built on a bluff about fifty feet above sea level and is surrounded on three sides by a grove of wild almond trees and casuarinas. The wild almonds grow out flat like umbrellas, and the more you lop them off the more they spread so that there is always plenty of shade.

Bunny had certainly gone to great trouble to make our day by the sea a success. When we climbed up the flight of concrete steps and we grownups had had showers to wash off the salt and the sand, we came out of the house to find a tea table set under the trees. Cynthia, his housekeeper, a coffee-coloured, ramshackle woman of about forty whose hair was always coming down, had obviously been goaded into prodigies of endeavour. There were two large iced cakes and stacks of thick tomato and cucumber sandwiches; there was even a covered dish of hot buttered toast, but this was a failure because the toast was tepid and had, I suspect, been made in the morning. However when we had collected the children from different parts of the garden they fell on the repast like a swarm of locusts and wolfed at least three quarters of it.

Bob and Molly arrived back with Mickey, still inclined to whimper, but professionally bandaged, and he was made much of by all of us because he had apparently been very brave and submitted to Dr. Bowman's cauterizing his wound with manly heroism. None of us was completely convinced by this because Mickey had shown no conspicuous signs of heroism during or since the accident, but we accepted the story at its face value and stuffed him with chocolate cake.

I explained to Robin that I had agreed to stay back for half an hour with Bunny to advise him about the house, upon which he gazed innocently at the far horizon and proceeded to hum "Just a Love Nest Cosy and Warm" under his breath until I stopped him with a sharp kick on the shin.

Eventually they all piled into our station wagon. The Frobisher children shrieked of course because it was not in their nature to get into a car or out of a car without shrieking, but the noise was muted by the amount of food they had eaten and they drove off down the rutted drive in a cloud of dust.

"You really have been very sweet, Bunny," I said as we went into the house. "To have taken so much trouble and given us such a lovely day. I do hope you weren't bored stiff."

"Not a bit. As a matter of fact I'm quite fond of children really."

"To be fond of children is one thing," I said, "but to be fond of the Frobisher children shows that you have a capacity for saintly compassion which I had honestly never suspected."

"They certainly are noisy little buggers, but after all look at their parents. Any child brought up in the constant proximity of Bob's jocularity and Molly's neighing would be forced to yell its head off in sheer self-defence."

"It's probably good training for them. The world is getting noisier and noisier every day. You can't even order your groceries in Mrs. Ching Loo's now without being deafened by that screeching radio."

"That's entirely calculated," said Bunny. "Mrs. Ching Loo is a very shrewd gal. The more shindy that's going on, the more distracted you get, and you order masses of stuff that you don't really need in a sort of demented trance. It's the same technique as revivalist meetings really, the impact of increasing noise on vulnerable nervous systems. If you are submitted to enough concentrated din you're bound in time either to see the light or buy twenty tins of Campbell's mushroom soup instead of two."

We went into the house and Bunny sat me in a chair with a copy of *Life* magazine while he mixed a martini. Cynthia wandered in with a yellow plastic pail of ice and wandered out again. I suddenly laughed.

"What's up?" enquired Bunny over his shoulder.

"I was just wondering what Eloise will think of Cynthia," I said. "She's probably become used to serried ranks of footmen by now. Cynthia's amiable nonchalance might be a bit of a shock."

"Cynthia's a treasure," said Bunny. "I admit her appearance is against her and her cooking is lethal, but she looks after me like a mother and runs the house beautifully."

"Bunny," I said firmly. "Cynthia may be a treasure and look after you like a mother, but she most emphatically does not run the house beautifully. In fact she doesn't run the house at all. I presume Eloise is not bringing a maid with her?"

"Of course she isn't."

"Has it struck you that she might require some washing and ironing done occasionally? Cynthia couldn't even press a pocket handkerchief."

"Eloise is perfectly prepared to rough it." He handed me a glass and poured the martini into it. "I warned her that life here was on the primitive side. What on earth would she want things washed and ironed for? She'll be in a bathing dress most of the time."

"She might, just every now and then, like to get into something fresh when she takes off her bathing dress."

"What do you suggest?"

"I suggest that you get someone else in, even if only by the day, as a sort of lady's maid."

"Anything you say," said Bunny meekly. "I think it's all damned nonsense and that you're underrating Eloise if you think she's only a pampered doll, but I agreed to do anything you say and I'll keep my promise. How can I get a maid?"

"I'll try for you. I'll ask Clementine. She has a sister I think who might do."

"You're a darling . . ."

"Never mind about that. Let's go over the house."

We went over the house. The spare-room bed was still as hard as iron, the table beside it still wobbled, and the shutter was in the same state as it was when I had had the house six months before. Bunny's bedroom was a bit better, but it was austere to the point of asceticism, in addition to which the walls were lined with valuable but repellent coloured engravings of reptile and insect life. There were coiled snakes, evil looking tarantulas, and a terrifying picture of a black scorpion fighting to the death with a spider.

"These," I said, "must all be put away in a cupboard immediately."

"They're fascinating, and they're quite beautiful too in a sort of way."

"I can tell you here and now that their particular beauty will

118

not be appreciated by Eloise any more than it is by me. They're perfectly repulsive. Promise me that you'll take them down."

"Anything you say, lady. But I must have something on the walls. The place will look like a hospital."

"Better that than a reptile house. I'll find some flower pieces or something."

We went over the house meticulously, and I made as many helpful suggestions as I could, aware while I was making them that actually, on account of my own proven inadequacy as a housewife, I was the last person in the world to whom Bunny should have turned for such advice. I could imagine only too clearly Robin's gleeful mockery had he been present to hear me laying down the law with such bland authority. Behind my outward display of domestic bossiness and assumed matronly superiority over poor Bunny, my conscience taunted me with the broken rings in Robin's shower, the insecure lamp on the back verandah, the eternal creaking of the swing seat and numberless other humiliating imperfections in my own house. It was painfully obvious to me that almost any other married woman on the island was better equipped to give Bunny the help he needed. Lucy Chalmers for instance would have known in a split second what to do about the arrangement of the furniture in the big living room, whereas all I could do was to stare at it glumly and, with a slavish desire to please, admire the new slip covers which were quite hideous. However, I could at least comfort myself with the reflection that compared with this bleak, overmasculine barrack, my own establishment, with all its defects, was a palace of sybaritic luxury.

It is a curious fact that men of Bunny's type who make a life's work of fascinating, or being fascinated by, women of all sorts and kinds, have so little sense of those trivial graces of life which to most women of taste have become essential. In this modern age, with all its evil potentialities and its alleged decadence, there are certainly more minor material advantages available to the female sex than ever there were before, among which, to name only two, are cleaning tissues and soft toilet paper. In both of Bunny's bathrooms I need hardly say there were neither. There was of course toilet paper; hard, sullen rolls of it, of a quality and texture that could be useful only for filing the nails. The face towels were harsh and ungiving and the bath towels so meagre in size and material

119

that no one, male or female, could hope to dry themselves with them in less than a quarter of an hour. Then there was the question of soap. Good soap, even in the farthest-flung colonies of the British Commonwealth, is quite easy to get. Why then should Bunny, the fascinating, the darling, the great lover, provide for his loves vast, unyielding hunks of what looked like Cheddar cheese? When I questioned him patiently about this he merely giggled and shrugged his shoulders and said that he personally didn't approve of high-scented soaps for two reasons: A, that they destroyed the body's natural odours and B, that they made him sneeze. And when I replied that I would rather endure hay fever and croup than the body's natural odours, he said that I was a pernickety old goose and that overcivilization was the greatest curse of the age.

We had what was left of the martini and went outside for a moment to look at the reflection of the sunset. Bunny's house faces due east, and although he has the pleasure of seeing the sun pop up out of the sea while he is having his breakfast he cannot see it set because the Lailanu Mountains are in the way. The reflection however is often lovelier than the actual setting. We stood in silence for a little, watching the sea swiftly change from deep blue to lavender and then to quiet grey. There was a line of small dark clouds on the horizon looking like clipped poodles' heads against the darkening apple-green sky. Bunny pointed to it with an imperial gesture.

"Who would worry about scented soap and toilet paper when they can look at that?" he demanded.

"I would," I replied, "if I happened to be in urgent need of either."

"Women are extraordinary cattle. They're always moaning and bellyaching about romance and beauty and when it's suddenly spread out before them like a glowing oriental tapestry all they can think about is toilet paper."

"That is unjust, rhetorical, and entirely irrelevant," I said with some asperity. "In the first place I am not given to moaning and bellyaching about romance and beauty, and in the second place I was not thinking about toilet paper. You brought that up. And in the third place it is hardly becoming for you, in your present highly equivocal situation, to refer to women as cattle."

"It was only a figure of speech," said Bunny. "And as a matter of fact I am devoted to cattle."

"If that were really true, and you had merely invited a placid, cud-chewing heifer to visit you, we should all have been saved a great deal of inconvenience."

"*Touché,*" said Bunny, and, slipping his arm affectionately through mine, he led me to the car.

TEN

On the morning that the Frobishers were due to leave I awoke earlier than usual and stared, sleepily and happily, at the ceiling on which the sun, shining through the shutters, made a symmetrical pattern like staves of music. I was conscious of an inward lightness, a lifting of the spirit. For a few days at any rate, before Eloise came, we should have the house to ourselves. It is not that I dislike having people to stay; on the contrary I enjoy it very much, anyhow to begin with. I love the arrival, the showing of the house and garden, the exchange of mutual gossip, and the cosy, enthusiastic feeling of friendliness. This particular pleasure, however, seldom lasts more than a day or two. The newness of having strangers in the house, the fun of making plans to entertain them, begins to wear off and a faint but unmistakable tedium sets in and small irritations and resentments rear their nasty little heads. The guests, whoever they may be, become somehow pervasive and there seems to be no getting away from them. There they are, spread about the sitting room or the verandah when you want to talk to the cook about the meals or the gardener about the vegetables. There they are, cheerful and loquacious and ready to be amused, just at the moment when you want to sit quietly at your desk and plough through the grocer's book and make out a list of things for Nanny to get in the town. Then, dear God, there are the shopping expeditions, the enforced standing about in the Arts and Crafts shop while they argue about raffia table mats, coloured native scarves, ash trays, and other suitable, packable novelties to take back as presents to their loved ones. These expeditions are the worst trial of all, really, because you invariably start off with high hopes and a certain complacent pride at being able to take them to exactly the right shop where they can find exactly what they want and then, as the high hopes and the pride begin to wilt, you begin to curse your own stupidity in not letting them take the car and do their shopping on their own: you stand about helplessly fingering things on the counter and wishing, with growing exasperation, that they'd get on with it, hurry up, buy whatever it is they want, and come away.

I had endured all this, inevitably, with the Frobishers, with the added exacerbation that they had insisted on taking the children as well. One particular morning was vividly etched on my mind as the nadir of the Frobishers' visit. It was a rising crescendo of horror from the time we drove away from the house in the car until the last gruesome incident when, laden with parcels, hot and exhausted, we sat down to have ices on the new terrace of Rodrigues' store and Sylvia attempted to fondle Blanche Worthing's terrier which was tied to the leg of an adjacent table. If I had seen what was happening in time I could have averted the catastrophe because both of Blanche's terriers are well known to be highly neurotic and suffer from all kinds of peculiar canine complexes. Unfortunately Bob had just embarked on one of his stories and I was staring at him dully like a rabbit at a python. There was a sudden snarl and a piercing shriek and, from then on, pandemonium. In point of fact the actual bite was so tiny and superficial that you could hardly see it, but the Frobishers en masse made such a hullabaloo that you'd think that the child's hand had been severed at the wrist. We got up and pushed our way, parcels and all, through the gathering crowds and drove to the hospital where Bob, Molly, and the howling Sylvia were taken charge of by dear old Dr. Aluna and I was left with Mickey and Timmy in the outpatients' waiting room. The doctor apparently said that as it was little more than a graze a tetanus injection would be unnecessary, so he disinfected it, bound it up, and that was that. Poor Blanche of course kept on telephoning to know if the child was all right and sent round a vast box of chocolates which mollified the Frobishers, who were grumbling threateningly about lawsuits and people who owned savage dogs being a menace to the community.

Now at last, at long last, they were going, flying back home to their large, rambling plantation house on Noonaeo where they could all bellow to their heart's content.

Robin was snoring in the next bed; a gentle rhythmical, non-aggressive little snore. I peered across at him in the half-light. He was lying on his back with one knee humped up under the sheet and his pyjama jacket was open—I noticed with dismay that there were two buttons missing. We had both decided, years before, that sleeping in the same bed, although it admittedly had its points, was unhygienic and uncomfortable. It's all right of course in the beginning when the "being in love" part of marriage is still a-growing and a-blowing, when the promise of physical ecstasy is ever-present and a small unpremeditated movement or gesture can ignite a sudden spark which grows into a swift fire burning the world away and leaving you dazed and enchanted in the most intimate of all quietnesses. But later, when habit and familiarity dull the magic a little and values and balances are adjusted, during those dangerous years when you are forced to realize that love is no longer quite what it was and not yet, not yet quite as it should be, then is the moment to separate a little, to give your heart time to accept and understand the inevitable adjustments. Physical passion is surely the slyest and wickedest joke played by nature on the human race, for after all it is only the human race that ever falls for it. Or rather, it is only the human race with its passion for complicating everything, that has clothed it with so much significance, so much illusion and ecstasy and heartbreak. The other worlds around us—the animal world, the insect world, the bird world, and the fish world—are void of the intricate, contrived delusions with which we stubbornly endow our basic urges. No bull moose has died for love. No amorous tabby has gone into a decline because the blue Persian next door has found satisfaction elsewhere, and although we are all aware of the apocryphal hypothesis of the monkey and the typewriter, no anthropoid, however gifted, has yet managed to write a love sonnet. It is only we humans who insist on entangling the spiritual with the physical, and although this insistence has unquestionably inspired prodigies of literature and music and art in general ever since we started to scratch away with those flints on the walls of our primeval caves, it has also played merry hell with our nervous systems.

How fortunate it was, I reflected, leaning on one elbow and contemplating the sleeping form of my husband and the father of my children, how very very fortunate that neither of us was temperamentally unstable or tortured by insatiable sex appetites or given to desperate, unbecoming desires. I naturally knew this to be true of myself, but I also knew, beyond doubt and eager wishful thinking, that it was true of Robin too. Whether or not it would always be so there was no knowing; at some predestined moment in some wretched future year his body might turn from me to someone else, but that his heart could leave me I would not and could not believe. As though my still ardent but somewhat complacent love for him had suddenly pierced his dream, he put an end to his snoring with a violent grunt and woke up. He turned, in order to snuggle down into the pillow, and caught me looking at him.

"What are you doing?" he said in a voice still furry with sleep.

"Nothing particular, just looking at you."

"Well, don't, because there's no future in it and I am very busy at the moment and it distracts me."

"What are you busy at?"

"I was in the middle of releasing little Mickey Frobisher from the belly of a shark and you interrupted me."

"I didn't make a sound."

"You were staring at me and your vibrations woke me up. Do stare at the ceiling or your mother's photograph or something and let me go back and finish the job."

"You'd better leave Mickey in the shark. It's time to wake up, anyhow."

"Eulalie hasn't swum in with the tea yet."

"She'll swim in in a minute." I got out of bed. "It's a lovely morning and I'm going to open the shutters." I made a movement towards the window, but he grabbed my leg, pulled me down onto his bed, and delivered a smacking, highly unromantic kiss on the side of my neck.

"Do you know what I would do if I were the hero of an American novel?" he said, continuing to hold me in a vicelike grip. "I'd give a hoarse, strangled cry and cup both your blue-veined, pointed breasts in my muscular hands."

"In that case I'm glad you're not," I replied, trying unsuccessfully to wriggle free from his grip. "In the first place they're not nearly as pointed as they once were, and in the second place I would rather Eulalie didn't come in and find us scrambling about like Japanese wrestlers. Do let me go."

"No self-respecting American he-man would dream of letting a new day begin without a bit of breast-cupping." Robin tightened his grip and I struggled harder, at which moment of course Eulalie did come in with the tray. Robin giggled and let go of me and I hurried, with as much dignity as I could muster, back into my own bed.

Eulalie, with studied indifference, arranged the tray on the bedside table, moved across to the windows, and opened the shutters, flooding the room with strong sunlight. Then, with an oblique look at Robin, she wandered slowly out, closing the door, rather pointedly, I thought, behind her. "A minute later," said Robin, "and she'd have had the thrill of her life."

"There I think you underrate her," I said. "It would take more than the spectacle of a middle-aged couple romping on a bed to thrill Eulalie."

"Middle-aged yourself," said Robin, yawning, and, after scrabbling about with his feet to find his bedroom slippers, he went into the bathroom and started his usual morning assault on his teeth. I poured out the tea absent-mindedly, wondering why it is that men always make so much more noise over their ablutions than women do.

Communal breakfast on the verandah with the Frobishers, our children, their children, and Nanny was as appalling as ever. The Frobishers yelled, the children squabbled, the dogs barked, Nanny made her clucking noises of overt disapproval, but I remained serene and unmoved by the prevailing tumult because my whole being was glowing with the blissful, heart-warming reflection that it was the last time. In less than an hour my children would be on the way to school and in less than two hours the Frobishers would be zooming home high above the shiny sea.

As I had to attend the meeting of the Samolan Amateur Dramatic Society at eleven o'clock, Robin, with saintly grace, had agreed to drive the Frobishers to the airport. The actual moment of departure was unduly prolonged because Timmy suddenly complained of violent pains in his stomach and Molly whisked him off to the lavatory while we all stood about in the drive and made conversation. Eventually, after I had had ample time to torture myself with visions of them missing the plane which only goes twice weekly, they reappeared. Last good-byes were screamed all over again, Bob roared a few final jocular witticisms, and at long long last away they went. I walked slowly through to the back verandah where I stretched myself in a long chair, lit a cigarette, and allowed the blessed, peaceful emptiness of the house to wrap itself round me. Westinghouse appeared from the garden and sat down in a patch of sunlight and washed himself. There was complete silence, except for the hand-clapping sound of the coco palms and, far away in the distance, the occasional muffled hooting of a car on the Narouchi Road. The pale green bamboos on the other side of the ravine moved their feathery fronds languidly in the morning breeze as though they too were waving a relieved farewell to the Frobishers.

The meeting of the S.A.D.S. took place in the back room of the Art Institute. I arrived a few minutes late, having had the usual difficulty of finding somewhere to park the car. Everybody was standing about gossiping, and a long table was impressively set out with pads and pencils and individual ash trays. I greeted Buddha and Dusty and Cuckoo Honey, who was wearing a tiny hat with a knob on the top, like the lid of a jar of preserved ginger. Alma Peacock, impressive in a flowing print with an eye-searing pattern of white pineapples on a pink background, took the chair and we all arranged ourselves round the table. Alma is an admirable character in many respects. She is kindly, resolute, enthusiastic, and industrious. Under her ebullient leadership the S.A.D.S., which she started from scratch many years ago, has certainly achieved some creditable if occasionally overambitious productions. There is, however, something about her personality, a certain incongruous schoolgirlishness, which always makes me want to laugh whenever I look at her. On the other hand Ivy Poland, who runs a dancing school in Queen Street and has achieved local fame with her "Ivy Poland Dancers" without whose ardent modern posturing no annual pantomime is complete, retains no endearing aura of long-ago School Theatrics. She is professional to the core, sharp as a needle, and is reputed, when unduly irritated, to fly into ungovernable rages. Her mouth droops a trifle at the corners, and it is not difficult to envisage her whacking the shins of the I. P. Dancers with a cane when their jetés and coupés are clumsily executed. It is difficult however, looking at her now, a small grey woman in her middle forties, to imagine her in her far-off heyday as a ballroom dancer floating glamorously into the Palm Court of the Grand Hotel, Folkestone, on the arm of some agile and suitably betailed male partner, and more difficult still to picture her in even earlier years flitting through the enchanted forest of "Where the Rainbow Ends" as a will-o'-the-wisp. Nevertheless that, we are led to believe, is her authentic background and it would ill become any of us in our distant colonial isolation to question it. It is scarcely necessary to add that there exists between her and Alma a state of decently veiled hostility which only on very rare occasions has been permitted to blaze into open warfare. The rest of the committee, apart from Buddha, Dusty, Cuckoo, and myself, consists of Peter Glades and Esmond Templar, who landed hand in hand on the island in 1949 and set up an antiques shop, Michael Tremlett, Brinsley Martin, and Keela Alioa. Brinsley Martin is our main character actor and is chiefly remarkable for his prowess at elaborate make-up. He has seldom appeared in any production, wigged, padded, lined, and crepe-haired, without a spontaneous round of applause at his first entrance. On one or two occasions, however, his passion for visual characterization has led to disaster as on the famous night when he was playing the inquisitor to Letty Togstone's St. Joan and his entire nose fell with a soft thud into her outstretched hands. Michael Tremlett, although lacking any outstanding histrionic ability, is an efficient stage manager; Peter Glades and Esmond Templar are enthusiastic but occasionally petulant artistic supervisors, and Keela Alioa, our star turn as an actor, is on the committee in an honorary capacity as representative of Samolan interests. He is in his mid-twenties and extremely handsome, and his performance of Hamlet in modern dress was the talk of the island. It was an all-Samolan production, and as their idea of modern dress consisted mostly of brilliantly coloured sarongs the visual effect was quite enchanting.

When we were all seated and the buzz of conversation and the scraping of chairs had died down, Alma whacked the table with a little hammer and embarked on a lengthy speech which glowed with royalist enthusiasm and was peppered with splendid phrases such as "Allegiance to the Crown" and "Our Imperial Visitors" and "Showing the Flag," etc. When she had finished and sat down amid a few grunts of assent and muttered "hear hears" everyone began talking at once until she had to whack the table again for silence.

There is something about well-intentioned, amateur committee meetings that induces in me a feeling of claustrophobia, I feel trapped and hopeless and quite incapable of constructive thought or concentration, and this one was no exception to the rule. It droned on for two solid hours, during which time I drew hideous faces on the piece of paper in front of me and tried to wrench my mind away from Eloise and Bunny and whether or not the Frobishers had got off all right. Hot sunlight filtered through the slats of the venetian blind, and outside in the street the noise of gears changing and dogs barking and klaxons hooting made it difficult at moments to catch what anyone was saying, and everyone, as usual, was saying a great deal. It was finally decided after many impracticable suggestions had been put forward and discarded that an ordinary theatrical production in the local Playhouse would be inadequate and that what was needed was something on a much larger scale. At this point Cuckoo Honey sprang to her feet and delivered a stirring eulogy of a military tattoo she had seen in Darjeeling when she was a little girl—— "It really was magnificent," she said, her nose growing quite pink with remembered emotion. "The cavalry came charging through a gap in the hills and all the people who had been besieged in a fort for weeks cheered and cried and then the fort went up in flames and everyone sang 'Abide with Me.'"

"A curious moment to choose," said Buddha in a loud whisper, but Cuckoo ignored this and went on. "What I really mean is," she said, "that it made a tremendous impression on the natives, and I do honestly think that we should try to do something on those lines. After all we *are* a British colony and we have got the Royal Shropshires."

"We have also got several gaps in the hills," said Dusty, "but I still don't think a military tattoo is quite the answer."

"Speaking as the only 'native' present," said Keela with gentle acidity, "I cannot feel that my brother Samolans at this present time would be so easily impressed by sudden chargings and flames and a great display of British militancy. It would puzzle them, and when Samolans are puzzled they laugh."

"It was only an idea." Cuckoo sat down rather crossly.

"What about a lovely medieval pageant?" suggested Esmond Templar. "With the Knights of the Round Table and everybody in armour and wimples and that sort of thing."

"I should think that would puzzle the Samolans into hysterics," said Dusty.

Alma rose to her feet authoritatively. "Our main object," she said sternly, "is not only to entertain the inhabitants of our island but to give pleasure to our royal visitors."

"Hear hear," murmured Peter Glades and giggled. Alma shot him a disapproving look and continued, "I have, as you know, given this matter a lot of thought and I am aware that we have very little time at our disposal, but I am convinced that what we really should do is to present Her Majesty with something that she could see nowhere else, something indigenous to our island and entirely Samolan. Ivy is in complete agreement with me over this . . ." She smiled at Ivy Poland, who nodded austerely. "We discussed it yesterday after the Bleekers' cocktail party, and as the idea was originally hers I now take pleasure in asking her to explain it to the committee." Alma sat down and there was a slight pause while Ivy blew her nose delicately and rose to her feet.

"The idea is this," she said modestly. "An historical water pageant." She paused, unfortunately long enough to allow Buddha to mutter "Good God!" and then went on. "We thought of telling the story of the island beginning with the legend of FumFumBolo in which my girls could do a ballet as water sprites. Then the landing of Captain Cobb and the missionaries and so on right up to the present day. We also"—she smiled encouragingly at Cuckoo —"thought of enlisting the aid of the Royal Shropshires, in fact I have already telephoned Colonel Shelton warning him that we might call on him to help us. They are a fine body of men and would do splendidly for pirates in the earlier scenes . . ."

"Where on earth do you propose to do all this?" interrupted Buddha.

"Cobb's Cove," replied Ivy triumphantly. "It would make an ideal setting. We have it all planned in our minds. We could have grandstands built round the semicircular beach and the two headlands would provide wonderful wings for entrances and exits. The Samolan Electrical Company and the Royal Shropshires between them could organize the floodlighting. We also propose to ask

Kerry Stirling to write the libretto, probably in blank verse, and persuade dear Inky Blumenthal to compose a score based on traditional Samolan folk music—you all know how brilliant he is at that sort of thing—and we thought, as a grand finale, that the church choir, which we've got to use anyway, could come sailing in on a barge singing, while the Royal Shropshires, having changed back into their uniforms, would march down that path from behind the Turlings' bungalow and assemble on the beach and do a sort of trooping of the colours!" She paused, smiling expectantly, and then rather abruptly sat down. There was silence for a moment or two, which was broken by Esmond Templar clapping his hands and crying enthusiastically that it was a marvellous idea.

"It's not 'trooping *of* the *colours*,'" said Buddha. "It's 'trooping the colour.'"

"I remember being taken to see it for the first time when I was a tiny little girl," said Cuckoo. "Daddy had six months' leave and we stayed at the Hyde Park Hotel and I cried my eyes out!"

"The Hyde Park Hotel can be depressing," murmured Dusty.

"Come, come," cried Alma firmly, "to our muttons!"

From then on everyone began talking at once and the noise was deafening.

An hour or so later when I was sitting on the back verandah, sipping a gin and tonic and feeling as if I had been run over, Robin appeared looking cheerful.

"God's in his heaven," he said, "the Frobishers are in mid-air, and all's right with the world." He clapped his hands and yelled for Tahali. "How was the meeting?"

"Noisy, but on the whole fairly successful, I suppose. It has been decided to treat the Queen and Prince Philip to a water pageant."

"Very suitable for the rainy season. Where's it going to take place?"

"Cobb's Cove."

"Better and better, the mosquitoes in Cobb's Cove at that time of the year are well known to be larger and more virulent than anywhere else on the island. You'd better arrange for everyone to wear heavy veils and have quinine served in the entr'actes. Also"— he went on, warming to his subject—"there is almost certain to be a sou'wester blowing, in which case the sea will be very rough indeed."

"Nonsense. The sea is never rough in Cobb's Cove, it's almost completely sheltered."

"It all depends from which direction the wind's blowing. I've bathed there when the waves were mountainous."

At this moment Tahali appeared and Robin ordered a pink gin.

Just as we were finishing lunch Sandra rang up. "What's all this nonsense about a water pageant?" she asked rather crossly.

"It's nothing to do with me. I just sat there. Alma and Ivy cooked the idea up between them."

"It's sheer madness. How are they going to do it and who's going to play what?"

"None of that has been definitely decided yet, it was only a preliminary discussion. All I know is that the church choir is coming round the headland in a barge and the Royal Shropshires are going to be pirates and troop the colour on the beach."

"They can't troop the skull and crossbones in front of the Queen; it would be *lèse-majesté*."

"They're only going to be pirates in the first part, then they're going to change back into their uniforms."

"Where?"

"Behind the Turlings' bungalow, I believe."

Sandra snorted. "The whole thing's idiotic," she said. "You must think of something else."

"I've already explained that it's nothing to do with me. I just sat there."

"You should have jumped on the idea at the outset. What's the use of serving on a committee and never uttering? You have no moral courage, that's what's wrong with you."

"As a matter of fact," I said with spirit, "I think it might be quite charming if it's done well."

"Then you must be dotty. What about parking space? I suppose nobody gave that a thought!"

"No, I don't think they did, as I said just now it was only a preliminary discussion."

"There isn't room to leave a tricycle on that bit of road behind Cobb's Cove."

"There's room for a thousand tricycles and several motor busses on that vast playing field just beyond the Chesley Hutchinsons', and it's hardly ever used for anything."

"All right, all right, have it your own way." There was a resigned note in Sandra's voice. "You'd better come to lunch the day after tomorrow and tell me what else you've planned."

"I haven't planned anything. You'd better ask Alma and Ivy to lunch, they're the real culprits."

"I'd rather die," said Sandra. "You come anyway." Then she rang off.

ELEVEN

The few days between the Frobishers' departure and Eloise's arrival passed all too swiftly. Nothing particular happened. I lunched at Government House as commanded and found that Sandra had rather come round to the idea of the water pageant. "At least it will be different," she said, "and of course it might be very funny indeed. I can't wait to see the church choir come rolling round the headland in a barge and singing their lungs out, it will be so much better than having them standing in serried ranks and bellowing into one's face like they do in the Town Hall. And the dear Royal Shropshires will adore being pirates and clambering about with cutlasses in their mouths, they have so little fun as a rule, stuck up there in those gloomy barracks month in month out. Of course the weather problem is a bit of a worry, but I think with any luck it will be all right; even in the rainy season it only pours seriously for a few hours every morning. The only thing we have to dread is a real rousing sou'wester. That of course would wreck the whole enterprise."

"It certainly would," I agreed.

"We usually have at least a day's warning anyhow," she went on cheerfully, "but I do really think there should be some sort of undercover alternative got ready in case the worst happens."

"Easier said than done."

"It's no good being defeatist. That's the committee's problem, and as you're serving on the committee you really must see that they have something prepared."

"How can I?"

"Just put your foot down."

"What alternative do you suggest that I suggest?"

"Really, darling." Sandra looked at me reproachfully. "I don't know what's been happening to you lately, you seem to have lost every scrap of initiative."

"I am only serving on the damned committee at your special request. I have absolutely no authority to put my foot down. Also I have other things on my mind, such as a husband and a family and a house to run and the Bunny-Eloise situation to cope with."

"That's your own stupid fault for letting him get round you in the first place. When's the silly beast arriving?"

"Tomorrow, at ten forty-five. B.O.A.C. Flight 429. I suppose you wouldn't like to come and meet her with me—just for old times' sake?"

"Certainly not. I disapprove strongly of the whole sordid business. I consider I'm doing quite enough by agreeing to have her here for three days. By the way, when do you want me to have her?"

"Sometime within the next two weeks."

"It's no good being vague and slapdash about it, you must let me know exactly. The house may be chockablock. I know we've got two Burmese ministers and their wives on the third and fourth and a woman from the British Council who's been doing a lecture tour in Japan."

"What does she lecture about?"

"I'm not sure, something to do with the Victorian novelists, I think, and their influence on modern literature."

"Do you think that will really interest the Japanese?"

"Of course. Everything interests the Japanese, they're keen as mustard on British culture and progressive Western ideas."

"I wouldn't call a lecture on the Victorian novelists exactly progressive."

"You never know. Imagine a group of those hissing geisha girls crouched over a really good translation of *The Mill on the Floss*. It might alter their whole view of life!"

"Will the sixth or seventh be all right for Eloise?"

"Yes, I suppose so." Sandra heaved a deep sigh. "But not a split second more than three days—swear it!"

"All right. I swear it."

TWELVE

The airport is about half an hour's drive from Pendarla and is a hive of cheerful inefficiency. Also no effort has been spared to make it the most hideously uncomfortable place to wait about in. The "Passengers' Lounge" is furnished with forbidding, uncushioned wooden chairs with sharply sloping seats on which you are unable to sit forward without sliding back and which cut you cruelly under the knees when you have slid back. There are several glass-enclosed pens opening off this, marked strictly private, and in these you can see the friends you have come to meet standing about forlornly for hours clutching their hand baggage and mouthing at you. You are not allowed to speak to them, nor they to you, until they have passed through Immigration and Customs. Some people get out of hand during this period and make frantic signs and grimaces, but I long ago decided that this was waste of energy so now I just blow a welcoming kiss or two and sit down again and read a book.

Eloise's plane was first of all announced as being on schedule, then, a few minutes after, as being three quarters of an hour late. After about twenty minutes had elapsed a further husky announcement stated that it would arrive at twelve twenty-five. This meant that there wasn't a hope of getting Eloise back to the house before two o'clock, so I shut myself into a hot telephone booth which smelt of Irish stew and called Robin. "You and Nanny had better have lunch on your own because the plane's already an hour and a half late."

"That's one of the silliest reasons for me to have lunch alone with Nanny that I have ever heard," he said. "I shall lunch at the club."

"All right, but try to be back by two o'clock to greet Eloise."

"If I lunch at the club I shall be too drunk to greet anyone."

"Then have something on a tray in the garden."

"That would be too marked. I don't want to hurt Nanny's feelings; she loves having her feelings hurt."

"Then have lunch at the club and drink only soda water."

"That's quite out of the question. You know how popular I am, I can't set foot in the place without everyone plying me with alcohol."

"Don't be tiresome, darling. It's hot as hell in this telephone booth and I'm suffocating. Just tell Clementine and Tahali to stand by with something for us whenever we get there."

"Eloise should have come by sea. If she had come by sea she might have fallen madly in love with someone on the ship and we should all have been saved a great deal of inconvenience. The whole trouble with air travel is that there's no time for that sort of thing."

"I'm going to ring off now darling because the sweat's running off my nose into my bag."

"All right—all right."

I wandered back into the Passengers' Lounge and stared irritably at the display of quaint souvenirs provided by the Royal Samolan Gifte Shoppe. There were the usual dancing dolls in grass skirts, daintily painted shells, table mats made of banana mesh, and a lot of raffia hats with Samolo worked on them in coloured wool. A Pan-American plane was preparing to take off and the noise was ear-splitting, so I went out into the blazing sunlight and crossed the parking lot to the Luana Inn, where you can have a drink in comparative peace. I found myself a table in a corner and ordered a gin fizz. Daphne Gilpin and Lydia French were at the bar throwing dice and knocking back Kala-Kala cocktails. They were both dressed in slacks and shirts and Lydia was wearing very dark glasses which probably concealed a black eye, because Daphne is known to be violent when in her cups. They are our local Lesbians and personally I am quite fond of them. There was a certain amount of gossip when they first set up house together at Fisherman's Hole, but that died down after a year or so and now they are quite accepted, by the sophisticated for what they are and by the innocent as amiable eccentrics. They dress more or less identically, but their temperaments are completely divergent.

Daphne is Samolan-born, dark and clear-cut and immensely capable. She served for a while with Sandra and me in the M.T.C. and could dismantle a lorry engine and put it together again more swiftly and efficiently than the most hairy-chested garage mechanic. Lydia is fair and pretty and a bit of a ditherer. It is her taste that has made their house as attractive as it is . . . Daphne would have been perfectly content with some leather armchairs and a couple of camp beds. Daphne it is who drives the car and the speedboat and disappears under the sea for hours in an Aqua Lung while Lydia arranges flowers, mixes exquisite salad dressings, and occasionally does delicate *gouache* paintings of native girls weaving mats and lying in hammocks. Daphne also holds the purse strings, which I think is the basic reason for many of their notorious rows. They give a cocktail party about twice a year, and these are always good fun if you are wise enough not to stay to the end and become involved in any dramas. Sandra has them to Government House every so often but insists on skirts.

Daphne saw me and waved and they clambered off their bar stools and came over to my table. "What are you doing here?"

"Waiting for the B.O.A.C. plane."

"So are we," said Daphne. "Lydia has a friend on it, Ursula Gannet."

"She's just as much your friend as mine," protested Lydia gently.

"Be that as it may, we shall have her in our hair for a month. What are you drinking?"

"A gin fizz—it will be here in a minute."

"Do you mind if we join you or would you rather be left alone?"

"Of course I don't mind, I'd love it."

Daphne clapped her hands authoritatively and called to the bar boy to bring their cocktails over to my table. "Who are you meeting?"

"Eloise Fowey." I felt suddenly self-conscious and hoped I didn't show it.

"Good God!" Daphne looked surprised. "What on earth is she coming out here for?"

"To stay with me," I replied a little stiffly. "She hasn't been feeling very well lately," I added rather fatuously, "and she thought a little tropical holiday would be a good idea."

"She's wonderful-looking," said Lydia. "I saw a picture of her in the *Tatler* only a few weeks ago."

"I haven't clapped eyes on her since the old M.T.C. days," said Daphne. "She was wonderful-looking then but a bit of a bloody fool, I always thought."

"She's changed a great deal lately."

"When did you see her last?"

"Two years ago when Robin and I were in London. We lunched and dined together a few times, and—and Robin took her to the Festival Ballet," I added wildly.

"I shouldn't have thought that would have been her cup of tea at all."

"'*Sylphides*' got her down a bit, all those white girls rushing in and out, but she enjoyed the more lively ones very much."

"Bring her over to the house sometime," said Daphne heartily. "I'd like to see her again after all these years."

At this moment the bar boy arrived with the drinks and to my relief the subject of Eloise was dropped. I'm not against telling a few whacking lies every now and then when it is socially necessary, but I find it rather a strain and am inclined to get carried away and go much too far. I already regretted having said what I did about the Festival Ballet because I should have to remember to brief Eloise when she arrived and Robin as well. I foresaw that the next few weeks were going to be tortuous in the extreme and that I should be incessantly hopping back and forth between truth and falsehood and probably get myself so inextricably tangled up that I should become a nervous wreck. After we had sat there for about three quarters of an hour, gossiping idly about nothing in particular, there was a sudden harsh crackling noise from the loudspeaker over the bar and an asthmatic voice informed us that B.O.A.C. Flight 429 would be arriving in ten minutes. There was the usual argument as to who should pay for the drinks which was finally settled by Daphne aggressively clapping her hands for the bar boy and signing a chit for the lot. By this time they had had two more Kala-Kala cocktails each and I had had three gin fizzes and I was feeling benign and cheerful and ready for anything. As we walked across the parking space back to the Passengers' Lounge, Daphne said: "I hear the S.A.D.S. are going to do a water pageant for the royal visit."

"Yes," I said. "In Cobb's Cove. It ought to be lovely, don't you think?"

"All depends on the weather," said Daphne laconically. "Have you got an undercover alternative in case of a sou'wester?"

"Not yet, but we're going to concentrate on that like mad at the next meeting."

"Good," said Daphne. "If I can be of any help call on me. If the weather *is* all right you can have the use of my Chris-Craft with pleasure."

"That would be wonderful. It isn't big enough to carry the whole church choir, but it might come whizzing in with the soloists."

"Church choir!" Daphne grunted. "I might have known it. Old Alma ought to have her head examined."

"It isn't really her fault. We've got to use them because Sandra squashed the idea of them greeting the royal party on the dock and there were hard feelings."

"That bloody choir should be abolished. It's always off-key and depresses everybody."

"They did 'Hiawatha' quite nicely at Christmas," said Lydia.

"You only say that because Lua Kaieena sang in it. You've always been crackers about Lua Kaieena."

"I'm not crackers about her in the least," said Lydia with spirit. "I just happen to think she sings well."

"You sat there gaping at her like a teen-age bobby-soxer."

"I did *not!*" cried Lydia, her voice becoming rather shrill. "And I wish to God you'd shut up about it."

"Let's go out on the tarmac and watch the plane land," I interposed hurriedly. "It's due any minute now."

To my relief Daphne gave a curt nod of agreement and strode off towards the swing doors.

"She ought never to drink in the morning," Lydia hissed in my ear. "It always makes her belligerent."

We followed Daphne out onto the tarmac and stood glumly in a row staring at the empty sky. Presently, after Daphne had started to light a cigarette and been reprimanded by one of the airport officials, a white pencil appeared out of the clouds above the deep blue mountains. We watched it in silence as it descended lower and lower until it disappeared behind the airport buildings. A few minutes later we heard the roar of its engines and it came into view again with the sun glittering on its propellers. It landed gracefully at the far side of the airfield and then turned and taxied slowly towards us.

"That's that," said Daphne. "Let's go and have another drink."

"We must just wait and see them all get off," said Lydia. "There'll be lots of time for another drink while they're going through Customs."

"Have it your own way," replied Daphne disagreeably, and again we waited in silence.

At long last, when the steps had been pushed into place and the pilot and two other officers had left the plane, the passengers began to disembark. The first two were spry young men in Palm Beach suits and carrying brief cases. Then there was a slight hold-up because a very old lady in a wheel chair had to be manoeuvred through the door and carried by two stewards down the steps. Then came the other passengers clutching overnight bags and magazines and weighed down with overcoats. In the bright light their faces looked grey.

"There she is," cried Lydia and waved her hand excitedly. A slim woman in a beige coat and skirt and a white hat waved back and joined the group at the foot of the steps which was being held in check by a B.O.A.C. stewardess. So far no one who had disembarked bore the faintest resemblance to Eloise, and I began to feel irritated. If she had missed the plane, which she was more than capable of doing, it would mean that I should have to go through all this again three days hence. Just as I was about to give up all hope, she appeared framed in the doorway with an armful of flowers and a steward immediately behind her carrying two little pigskin bags, one obviously a jewel case, and a fawn-coloured coat. She came slowly down the steps and was greeted at the foot of them by the photographer from *The Reaper*. She posed obligingly while he flashed his camera and then moved off with the other passengers towards the Immigration room. I waved violently to try to catch her eye, but she didn't see me and disappeared from view.

Daphne, Lydia, and I went back into the lounge. "What about that drink?" said Daphne.

"Not for me," I said firmly. "I'll just wait here."

"You don't really need another drink, darling," said Lydia. "You know you don't."

"That's where you're wrong," said Daphne. "I shall need a great many drinks to be able to bear Ursula booming at me morning, noon, and night for the next month."

"You are being difficult, darling, you really are."

"Come on." Daphne grabbed her firmly by the arm. "This madhouse is driving me round the bend." They moved off, Lydia dragging back a little. "See you later, old girl," said Daphne over her shoulder. "Don't forget to bring Eloise over for a drink, and that the Chris-Craft's yours whenever you want it."

I slid into a vacant wooden chair and lit a cigarette. The agreeable effects of the three gin fizzes had worn off, and I was beginning to feel melancholy and a little sleepy. Presently I got up and stood at the entrance to the Customs shed. Eloise was there, well ahead of everybody else with the steward still in attendance. I managed to catch her eye, and she flashed me a ravishing smile and went back to the business of identifying her luggage. She seemed more poised and assured than she used to be in the old days, and she was more staggeringly beautiful than ever. While I was waiting Mr. Seekala, *The Reaper* reporter, came up to me. He is a nice little man with a slight cast in his right eye which is a worry because you can never be quite sure with which one of them he is looking at you.

"You will please to present me to Her Highness, Mrs. Craigie?" he said.

"Certainly. But she's not a highness, only a grace."

"Is it her name that is being Grace?"

"No. Her name is actually being Eloise. Grace is her title."

"Grace of Fowey?"

"No. Duchess of Fowey. Her Grace, the Duchess of Fowey."

Mr. Seekala looked puzzled. "All the same as Loolia, Duchess of Westminster?"

"No. Not quite all the same, and it's not pronounced Loolia either, but Leelia, and she is called Loelia, Duchess of Westminster, because there was a divorce and the Duke of Westminster married again."

"If this distinguished lady should be named Grace instead of

Eloise and the Duke of Fowey divorced and married again would she then be named Her Grace Grace, Duchess of Fowey?"

"Yes," I said hopelessly. "I suppose she would."

"That is something learned," said Mr. Seekala happily. "The titling of the English high classes is always to me bewildering to catch on to."

"So it is to everyone else. Whenever I'm in trouble over that sort of thing I fly straight to Debrett."

"For me in my humble position," said Mr. Seekala, "air travel is beyond the question."

Fortunately at this moment Eloise appeared still accompanied by the steward and embraced me affectionately. "This is all terribly exciting," she said. "And you are an angel to come and meet me. Is Bunny here?"

"Of course not," I said quickly. "Bunny's at school, but he and Janet and Cokey will all be home at teatime and they're dying to see you." I turned to Mr. Seekala. "The duchess always calls my eldest boy Bunny. It's a sort of pet name. This is Mr. Seekala, Eloise. He represents our local newspaper, *The Reaper*."

Eloise shot me a sharp look and then turned her lambent eyes to Mr. Seekala. "How do you do," she said graciously.

"Welcome to Samolo, Grace," said Mr. Seekala, and bowed. "I sincerely hope that your stop with us will be of long duration and both happy and rewarding."

"Thank you," said Eloise. "I'm sure it will be."

"You will be visiting our spots of interest without doubt. There is much in our island to see and love."

"Of course. I want to see everything."

"It is a sadness for us in Samolo that His Highness your husband was not able to come with you."

"I know," said Eloise. "It's wretched, isn't it? But he just couldn't get away. He's not actually a highness," she added, smiling. "Only a grace."

Mr. Seekala's left eye swivelled wildly. "He too is Grace?"

"I've been trying to explain all that," I interposed swiftly. "But don't let's go on about it any more because there really isn't time. We've got to get your luggage into the car, and I am sure that Mr. Seekala will understand if we leave him now."

Mr. Seekala bowed again. "You have been most kind," he said.

"Perhaps I might be permitted to call at the house one of these fine days for a brief conversation with—with"—he hesitated—"with our distinguished visitor?"

"By all means," I said. "Telephone me in the morning."

Mr. Seekala backed away, and I piloted Eloise through the crowd and out into the car park. The steward loyally followed carrying the two bags and the coat. "This is Joe," said Eloise as we went. "He's been absolutely divine to me ever since we left London airport, and on top of all that he gave me these lovely flowers in Honolulu."

Joe shot her a look of besotted adoration and blushed. "It's been a pleasure," he murmured hoarsely.

"I'm surprised they let you bring them through the Customs," I said. "They're usually terribly strict about bringing in growing things."

"Joe tipped them the wink," said Eloise complacently.

At long last when we had finally crammed most of Eloise's luggage into the boot of the car and put the rest on the back seat and Joe, scarlet with emotion, had waved us away, Eloise settled back, scrutinized her face in her hand mirror, and lit a cigarette. "I'm sorry I dropped that brick about Bunny," she said. "I had no idea that little cross-eyed man was a reporter."

"It doesn't really matter," I said, trying to keep irritation out of my voice. "But we really do have to be careful, you know."

"Of course. Bunny explained everything in his last letter. I can never begin to tell you how grateful I am. If you hadn't been such a wonderful friend and agreed to help us I shouldn't be here at all."

"Well, now that you are here," I said a trifle grimly, "we have all got to concentrate on being as circumspect as possible. The only two people who know the true facts of the situation are Robin and Sandra. She's invited you to stay at Government House for three days next week."

"It's very sweet of her," said Eloise. "Do I have to go?"

"Yes. I'm afraid you must. It would look awfully suspicious if, in your position, you didn't stay at Government House at least for a little. This is a small colony and gossip is rampant if given half a chance."

"I never cared for Sandra much in the old M.T.C. days. She was always ordering me about."

"It was her job to order you about, she was your superior officer."

"She needn't have picked on me quite so much as she did. I remember once when I got back a little late after driving some dreary old general to Uxbridge, she flew at me like a tigress."

"I remember the incident clearly," I said. "You were more than a little bit late. You had taken three hours off to dine with Boy Livingstone at Bray. Don't forget that I was your superior officer too."

Eloise gave a little giggle. "You were much nicer to me than she was anyhow."

"At all events," I said, "Government House it's got to be, for three days at least. And if Sandra asks you to any social stuff you will really have to do it, and in no circumstances must you ever be seen in public alone with Bunny."

"I don't want to be seen in public with him, any more than he wants to be seen in public with me. All we want is to be alone together."

"And that," I said, "must be handled with the greatest discretion."

"You're not going to bully me too much, are you?" said Eloise wistfully. "I mean I know I'm being an awful nuisance to you and all that and I really will try to be as good as gold and do everything you say, but I really am in a dreadful state over the whole situation and I don't know what to do or where to turn. That's what's so horrid about being in love, everything gets mixed up and you can't see straight."

"Are you really in love with Bunny?"

"Of course I am. And what's more it's the first time I ever have been really."

"Come, come, Eloise, you can't expect me to believe that."

"But it's true, I swear it. Of course I've had a few swing-rounds in my time and maybe thought one or two of them were the real thing at the moment, but they never were."

"How do you know that this is?"

"Because it's quite quite different. It's been going on for over a year now, and I really have fought against it tooth and nail. I'm absolutely mad about him, and it's no good pretending I'm not."

"Until you and Bunny and Droopy between you come to some

sort of definite decision you've jolly well got to pretend that you're not."

"I suppose you're livid at having me forced on you like this." Eloise gave a little sniff. "And I honestly don't blame you. I feel awful about it, I really do."

"Well, don't," I said. "Everything will be perfectly all right if we're really careful. I admit I was a bit cross at first when Bunny suggested your coming, but that's all over now, and here you are, and we'll all enjoy ourselves."

We drove along in silence for a few minutes. Eloise lit another cigarette and looked out of the window while I wrestled with my conscience. I felt snappy and irritable and was aware that I had been governessy. It was no good, I reflected, taking it out on Eloise. Robin and I had both accepted the situation and she was to be our guest, ostensibly, for the next few weeks. She was obviously well disposed and willing to behave with as much discretion as possible in the circumstances, but the basic trouble was of course that the circumstances should never have occurred. Bunny shouldn't have been idiotic enough to have asked her to come out in the first place, and in the second place she should have had more sense than to have agreed to come. The immediate future bristled with evasions and deceits and appalling complications, and it only needed one false move to spark off one of those "Scandals in High Places" over which the avid readers of the English gutter press could lick their beastly chops for months. I glanced at Eloise out of the corner of my eye; she was staring vaguely at the passing countryside, but her mouth was drooping a bit and she looked unhappy, and suddenly, despite my innate disapproval of the whole business, I felt genuinely sorry for her. It was not for me to attempt to assess or judge the vagaries of other people's emotions. I was lucky. My own emotional problems were negligible and I hoped to God that they would continue to be so, but then I was not and never had been temperamentally inclined to amorous dalliance, nor, I was forced to admit, had I ever possessed that particular chemical attraction which brought out what is known as "the beast" in men. It must be, I thought, difficult to pursue one's life in an orderly manner if every time one asks for a cigarette or a glass of water the nearest male quivers and breathes heavily through his nose and shows every sign of acute lechery. This palpably had been Eloise's problem ever since she was born. There it was, at this very minute, that envied, indefinable sex appeal, emanating from every pore of her as she sat beside me in the Austin, and I reflected grimly that had I been provided with one hormone too many or one too few, whichever it is that makes our sex impulses unpredictable, I would automatically have made a pounce at her. She, happily unaware of my train of thought, looked at her face in her hand mirror again and sighed.

"I look revolting," she said. "Bunny isn't coming to lunch, is he?"

"No. Dinner. But he's coming early, before the others."

"Will there be many others?"

"Only local chums. Bimbo and Lucy Chalmers and Buddha and Dusty Grindling. They're quite gay and you'll like them."

"I'm sure I shall," she replied without enthusiasm. "But what funny names."

"I've never known why Bimbo is called Bimbo, his real name is Henry, but Buddha's called Buddha because he fancies himself as a staunch anti-Christian. Actually he's kindness itself and never stops helping lame dogs over stiles and giving away things."

"How nice," said Eloise absently. "I once had a walk out with a boy who was anti-Christian. He used to do Black Masses at Oxford, at least he said he did, but I expect he was only showing off."

"I wouldn't know how to do a Black Mass if I wanted to. You have to sacrifice a goat or something, don't you?"

"I believe so." She looked out of the window again. "Are those coconuts?"

"Yes. That's part of the Stirling plantation. It goes on for miles and miles."

"Fancy! I never knew they'd be smooth like that. The only ones I've ever seen are those beige hairy ones at church fetes."

"Those large trees with dark green, patent-leathery-looking leaves are breadfruit."

"Do you eat them?"

"Oh yes, often. You can have them roasted or baked or fried, or made into a purée with butter."

"I expect they put on pounds."

"Yes. I'm afraid they do."

"Is Bunny's house far from yours?"

"About seven miles, but the road's fairly terrible."

"Is it nice?"

"Well, it's beautifully situated," I said guardedly. "But it isn't actually the acme of luxury."

Eloise gave a little giggle. "I didn't expect it to be."

"He's very proud of it, and I must say the beach is perfect. I hope and pray you like underwater fishing?"

"I don't know. I've never tried it."

"You will," I said. "You'll be out on that reef wearing flippers and a mask before you can say Jack Robinson."

"I don't suppose I shall mind," said Eloise thoughtfully. "Except of course that I loathe getting my hair wet. Is there a good hairdresser here?"

"Yes. In the Royal Samolan Hotel. He's quite passable but liable to get carried away with the rinses so remember to keep an eye on him."

"When am I going over there? I mean—what's the form, exactly?"

"Well . . . We've been discussing it from every angle, that is Bunny and Robin and me, and we decided that the wisest course was for you to use our house as a sort of basic headquarters and just nip over to Bunny's for two or three nights a week whenever the coast's clear. Bunny can drive you back and forth, or Robin, or I can take you over if need be. The only thing to remember is that you must be prepared to pop back at once if any crisis occurs, I mean if anyone arrives unexpectedly and asks where you are. We'll hash up some kind of code so that when I telephone you'll know there's danger and stop whatever it is you're doing and come whizzing back immediately."

Eloise laughed. "That could be a bit awkward, couldn't it? . . . I just might be out on the reef," she added demurely.

"You know perfectly well what I mean."

She leant over and patted my knee affectionately. "Yes, dear," she said. "I do know what you mean and I think you and Robin are perfect angels to put yourselves to all this trouble and I shall never forget it until the day I die."

"Never mind about that," I said. "Here we are." I turned the car into the drive.

"This place is heaven," said Eloise. "Sheer heaven!"

Robin came to the door to meet us and Eloise, without effort, subjugated him immediately. She opened her eyes a trifle wider than usual and said, "Although we've never actually met I feel that we are already old friends." Upon which he assumed a rather sheepish expression, wrung her hand enthusiastically, and led her into the house and out onto the back verandah, leaving me and Tahali, who was grinning from ear to ear, to cope with the luggage.

"Very beautiful lady," he said breathlessly as he yanked one of her suitcases out of the boot.

"Yes," I agreed, and added before I could stop myself, "that's the cause of all the trouble, cause of all the crime!"

"Crime?" Tahali stared at me in astonishment.

"It's a quotation from an old English music hall song, 'Mister Cupid'—I don't remember much of it really, but all the choruses end with 'It's all through Mister Cupid ev-er-y time.'"

"It sounds a most jolly song," said Tahali cheerfully. "Is it this Mr. Cupid that makes the crimes?"

"It certainly is. He's the god of love."

"If he is a god he is perhaps in the Holy Christian Bible?"

"Actually no. He was at it long before the Bible was ever thought of. He was a Greek myth."

"What is that?"

"I'll explain another time," I said, and followed Robin and Eloise into the house marvelling at my inherent passion for imparting useless information and my complete inability to do it successfully.

THIRTEEN

At about half past eleven that night Robin and I climbed wearily into our beds. The day, for me at least, had been a considerable strain. Bunny had arrived at six o'clock on the dot, outwardly over-nonchalant but inwardly, it was clear, a prey to turbulent emotion. I chatted to him rather distractedly on the back verandah until Eloise appeared looking radiant after her afternoon snooze and wearing a cornflower-blue Balenciaga dinner dress that made her eyes look like gig lamps.

Their meeting was restrained and well conducted, and I suggested tactfully that Bunny might like to take her to the bamboo grove, which is a small plateau on the other side of the ravine, to watch the sunset. He agreed, with admirably controlled alacrity, and off they went down the steps and across the garden until they vanished from view. They returned about an hour later, a few minutes before the others arrived, looking only a little dishevelled. Eloise retired, with the utmost composure, to tidy, while Robin, Bunny, and I sat about sipping our martinis and making conversation.

We were all three conscious of an embarrassed tension in the air which made every word we said sound forced and banal, as though we were strangers struggling valiantly to find a comfortable piece of common ground on which to establish a basis for communication. Finally I could endure it no longer and said, irritably, "This has got to stop."

Robin raised an eyebrow at me. "What has?"

"This ghastly strain," I said. "It's driving me mad."

"I wasn't aware of any particular strain," said Robin with an air of exasperating aloofness.

"Grizel's right," said Bunny gloomily. "There is a ghastly strain and it's all my fault."

I shot him a grateful look. "Well, anyway, let's break it into a million pieces. The others will be here in a minute and we must present a united front and at least look relaxed. Come on, Bunny, out with it, what's causing it? . . . Apart from the general situation, I mean, something must be."

"I want to break a promise," said Bunny. "And being a man of my word I am ashamed of wanting to. I know it was agreed between us that Eloise shouldn't come to me for a few days at least, until she'd really settled in here, and I promised to be good about waiting and not try to force the issue. But seeing her again has completely bitched my good resolutions. I want you to let me take her to the house tonight, after the others have gone. I promise I'll bring her back at crack of dawn. But honestly I don't think I can face driving home all by myself after all these weeks of anticipation. It's more than human flesh and blood could stand."

"Did you discuss this with Eloise?"

"Yes. She wants to, too, of course, but she won't budge an inch without your consent. She's terrified of you."

"So is everybody else," Robin interposed genially. "All the servants and children and dogs cringe and whimper whenever she comes near them."

"Shut up, darling. This is no moment for flippancy."

"I didn't mean that sort of terrified," Bunny went on. "It's just that she doesn't want to upset you."

"Upsetting me is not the point," I said tartly. "It's upsetting the whole applecart that counts."

"I don't see why the applecart should be any more upset if she comes to me tonight than if she came to me three nights hence, particularly if I swear to whisk her back before the servants are up."

I looked at Robin helplessly. He was staring at the ceiling and blowing smoke rings. I knew from his attitude that he was thoroughly enjoying himself and prepared to give me no moral support whatever. Bunny was gazing at me appealingly, like a spaniel waiting for a stick to be thrown for him. I noticed that his eyes looked unusually bright and that he was slightly flushed. There can be no two opinions about it, I reflected, the Ol' Debil Sex can certainly wreak havoc in the human heart when it really sets its mind to it.

"This is the thin edge of the wedge," I said resignedly. "But have it your own way."

Bunny beamed with delight. "You're a saint," he said, "a great-hearted, true-blue saint, and I shall never forget your kindness until the grave closes over me."

"I can recall very few members of the saintly hierarchy who would shamelessly connive at fornication and adultery," I said sharply.

"How delicately you put things, dear," murmured Robin.

"Be that as it may," I continued, "you had better leave, fairly ostentatiously, before the others go. You can park your car—with the lights out, naturally—in that little lane behind the banana shed, you can see the drive quite easily from there, and you can come back when you see Robin put out the light over the front door."

"Apart from your other saintly qualities," said Robin, "you seem to have a positive genius for conspiracy and low intrigue."

"You are a broken reed," I said bitterly. "Your character is unstable and feckless and I am ashamed of you."

At this moment there was the sound of a car arriving. Robin rose. "I'll go," he said. "You stay and do a little more disreputable plotting."

The dinner party went off entirely successfully. Nobody got into any arguments; the food was adequate except for the chocolate soufflé, which had sunk in the middle and looked like a deserted crater. Eloise, although not exactly talkative, was obviously in excellent spirits and contrived, without apparent effort, to captivate everyone, even Lucy and Dusty, who are usually inclined to be suspicious of outstandingly glamorous members of their own sex. We all sat on the back verandah after dinner and discussed island personalities, the royal visit, what was on in the London theatres, and spear fishing. In due course Bunny rose dutifully, glanced at his watch, and said he must be pushing off because he had to get up *very* early in the morning. He gave me an unabashed wink as he said this but fortunately nobody saw it except Robin, who choked. When he had gone Bimbo and Lucy and Dusty and Buddha vied with each other in inviting Eloise to lunches and dinners and picnics. Buddha even suggested an expedition to the top of "Old Tikki" but I squashed that. Eloise, sewing away without undue diligence at a piece of petit point, agreed smilingly to everything and, when they had finally gone, said they were all perfectly angelic and that she would like a drink of water. Robin put out all the lights and locked up the house, and we waited in the dark until Bunny came up the verandah steps. We then all said "good night" to each other in conspiratorial whispers, and Bunny and Eloise went quietly across the lawn together in the moonlight holding hands.

When Robin and I finally were in bed and smoking our last cigarette, he gave a sudden chuckle and said, "There's nothing half so sweet in life as Love's Young Dream."

"Be that as it may," I replied, "there are moments when it can be damned inconvenient."

"You must get out of the habit of saying 'be that as it may' so often," he said reprovingly. "It makes you sound like a family lawyer. You'll be saying 'heretofore' and 'inasmuch as' before you're much older."

"I feel very old indeed at this particular moment."

"Cheer up, love." There was an unexpected note of sympathy in his voice. "Don't exert your weary old bones too much over other people's affairs. Let 'em get on with it. It will probably be all right in the long run. If by any chance they do get caught out and there's a general *brouhaha*, it really isn't any business of ours. All we could really be blamed for is standing by an old friend in time of trouble."

"Time of trouble is the operative phrase," I said. "And it's no use pretending that I'm not a prey to hideous presentiments because I am."

"Don't be, it's bad for the acids," said Robin sleepily, and switched out the light.

I am confused about the substance of dreams. Some people say that a whole nightmare, however long it may have seemed to last, actually takes place only in the split second before waking. Others maintain that the moment your head touches the pillow your subconscious takes over and starts ploughing up all the memories of all the things that have happened to you since you sprang from the womb, which is a disagreeable thought because there are certain little wickednesses and shady doings in all our lives which it would be nice to think were dead and buried forever and not likely to be remembered even by oneself. However, there it is, whether we like it or not we have to carry about with us this perpetually expanding inner warehouse that goes on implacably hoarding away neither taste, selective discretion, nor even tact. I suppose that explains why, on this particular night when my mind was full of the Bunny-Eloise affair and the repercussions that might ensue, I should have an entirely irrelevant nightmare about my late aunt Cordelia. She was the one who left me the tiara, and I was very fond of her. She was a darling old lady, frail and sweet and overflowing with the milk of human kindness, and when I was young I used occasionally to go and stay with her in the Palace Hotel at Montreux and be stuffed with chocolate and taken on the lake in a green boat. In my dream, however, she was not frail and sweet at all but, inexplicably, a murderous harpy with bloodshot eyes and wild, flowing hair who was trying to push me over a cliff. As we struggled nearer and nearer to the edge I could feel the pebbles crumbling away under my feet, she gave an insane laugh, and shrieked, "You can have the use of my Chris-Craft whenever you want it but *not* for the Royal Shropshires!" With this she gave me a final push, and I felt myself falling through space with a shrill ringing sound in my ears. I woke, shaking with terror, to find myself on the floor beside my bed with the telephone ringing just above my head. I reached up blindly for it and sent a china cigarette box crashing to the floor. This woke up Robin.

"What on earth are you doing?" he enquired sleepily.

"Answering the telephone."

"Why are you on the floor?"

"I'll explain that later—just be quiet for a minute." I lifted the receiver and heard a clicking noise then Eloise's voice.

"Grizel—Robin—is that you?"

"It's me, Grizel . . ."

"Thank God. I've been trying to get through to you for ages."

"What's wrong?"

"Please either you or Robin come at once. Bunny's terribly ill. I found a thermometer in the bathroom and took his temperature . . . it's over a hundred and five and he's delirious." Her voice was frantic.

154

"Keep calm," I said, shocked into complete consciousness. "Wrap him in every blanket you can find, we'll be with you in half an hour."

"He ought to have a doctor."

"We'll deal with that, but we'll have to get you away first. If there's any aspirin in the house give him three tablets, if not, just stay put until we get there." I hung up and scrambled to my feet. Robin by this time had switched on the light and was sitting up in bed.

"Quickly," I said. "Bunny's ill with a raging temperature. We must get over there at once."

"Good God!" said Robin irritably, hopping out of bed. "I might have known something like this would happen. We'd better get Dr. Bowman at once."

"No. Not until we get there. We must get Eloise out of the way first. We'd better go separately. You take the station wagon, and I'll follow you in the Austin."

"Mistress of herself when china falls," said Robin, picking up the cigarette box.

A few minutes later, wearing bedroom slippers and coats over our pyjamas, we had got the cars out of the garage and were bumping along over the coast road. The moon had set and the night was pitch-dark except for the fireflies. I tried to remember as I followed the winking red lights of the station wagon whether or not Bunny had ever been to the Far East and contracted malaria. If so this could be easily explained and he'd be all right in a few days and there was nothing to worry about. But my heart misgave me. As far as I knew Bunny had never had a day's illness in his life, and suddenly to run a temperature of over a hundred and five was ominous to say the least of it. In my mind I ran through a depressing list of all the tropical diseases the flesh is heir to: polio, cholera, typhoid, bubonic plague, dengue, spinal meningitis, all the horrors. I had visions of poor Bunny dying and having to be buried immediately on account of the climate and Robin and me standing, with a few chosen friends, watching his coffin being lowered into a miserable little grave in the Pendarla cemetery. By the time we arrived at the house I was nearly in tears. There were no lights discernible in the front so we left the cars in the drive and went round to the back where we found

Eloise waiting for us on the verandah. She was smoking a cigarette and obviously making a gallant effort to be calm.

"He's quiet for the moment," she said, leading us into the bedroom. "But he was absolutely raving a little while ago."

She had certainly been thorough about the blankets. Bunny was lying on his back under a mountain of them. His face was very pink and he was breathing stertorously. When we came into the room he opened his eyes; they looked glazed and unnaturally blue.

"I wish to see the matron, please," he said huskily. "The food is quite uneatable. And please send the pretty nurse back." Then he shut his eyes again and I signed to Robin and Eloise to come into the living room. We all three crept out, and Robin quietly closed the door behind us.

"I found some brandy in a cupboard in the kitchen," said Eloise tremulously. "It's been rather a comfort. Would you like some?"

"Yes—I certainly would." I turned to Robin. "You'd better telephone to Dr. Bowman at once, darling. He looks pretty bad to me."

"Okay," said Robin. "I'd like a nip too while you're at it." He went out into the hall where the telephone was while Eloise produced two glasses and the brandy bottle.

"Would you like anything with it, or just neat?" she asked with studied politeness. I noticed that her hands were trembling.

"Neat," I said firmly.

"Good," she said. "Because I don't know where anything is." She looked at me miserably, poured out three glasses of the brandy with great care, then suddenly flung herself onto the sofa and burst into tears. I immediately sat down next to her and put my arm round her shoulders.

"Don't give way too much now if you can help it," I said gently. "Robin will drive you home in a minute, and I'll stay here and cope with the doctor."

"Do you think he's going to die?"

"Of course not," I said, with a cheerfulness that I was far from feeling. "He's probably in for a bout of malaria and will be right as rain in a day or two."

"But his temperature was over a hundred and five. That's terribly high, isn't it?"

"Not here," I lied. "In England it would be, but in this climate it doesn't mean nearly so much. Have another sip of brandy." I handed her her glass from the table. She took a swig and fumbled in her bag for her handkerchief.

"I feel so awful about dragging you both out of bed in the middle of the night, but I was in an absolute frenzy, I really was."

"I don't blame you. You did the only possible thing. You wouldn't have handled this on your own in any case."

At this moment Robin came out of the hall. "Bowman's coming right away, he'll be here in about a quarter of an hour. You'd better drive Eloise home and I'll wait here."

"I think I'd better wait here and you drive Eloise home."

"Why don't you both stay here and let me drive myself home?" suggested Eloise with a slight return of spirit.

"Because it's pitch-dark and you don't know the way," I said with firmness. "In any case women are more experienced in dealing with this sort of thing than men are."

"What extraordinarily inaccurate statements you do make, to be sure," said Robin equably, drinking some brandy. "However, as you seem to have placed yourself so very officially in charge of the situation, I will do whatever you say. . . . Come on, Eloise, let's get cracking."

I went with them into the hall, turned on all the lights, and watched them drive away in the station wagon, then I came back and went into Bunny's room. He was still moving restlessly under the blankets, muttering inaudibly to himself, and his eyes were closed. I tidied the bed as gently as I could without disturbing him and wandered about setting the room to rights. I noticed that he had taken my advice and removed all the snake and spider pictures, and the walls were now bare except for a rather spotted print of the old chain pier at Brighton. On the dressing table I discovered a small blue enamel wrist watch with E in diamonds and a coronet on the back of it, this I slipped hastily into my pocket. I looked around for other compromising objects, but there weren't any. Then I went out onto the verandah, lit a cigarette, and sat down and waited for Dr. Bowman.

It was still dark but lightening minute by minute, the tree frogs had stopped their trilling, and there was nothing to be heard but an occasional bird squawk and the far-off, muffled booming of the waves on the reef. Bunny's black and white cat appeared suddenly from the garden and stared at me. I said "Topsy Topsy" and "Puss Wuss" invitingly, but it turned its head away and proceeded to lick its stomach.

Presently I heard the noise of a car in the distance and saw the glow of headlights on the lower coast road tipping the black, silhouetted banana leaves with yellow, so I went back into the house and waited by the front door.

Dr. Bowman is a brisk, efficient man in his early forties, his wife is even brisker and a vet, which is very handy. She achieved considerable local fame by operating on Mrs. Innes-Glendower's Pekingese when all hope was despaired of and returning it as good as new. He greeted me cheerfully, and I led him into the sitting room.

"What's the trouble?"

"I don't know. He's running a high temperature—over a hundred and five."

"Did you take it?"

"No—I didn't really . . ." I hesitated. "He took it himself."

"And then he telephoned you?"

"Yes. So Robin and I got out of bed and came over as quickly as we could."

"Good. Is your husband here?"

"No. He went back."

"I thought that was his car I saw in the drive."

"No. That's mine. He went back in the station wagon."

Dr. Bowman looked puzzled. "You came over in separate cars?"

"Yes, we did," I replied firmly. "We thought that in case Bunny had to be suddenly carted off to hospital or something it would be better to be independent."

"Very sensible," said Dr. Bowman dryly with a slightly quizzical expression in his eye. "Let's have a look at the patient."

We went into the bedroom. Bunny was no longer lying on his back but sitting bolt upright against the pillows staring fixedly in front of him. "I'm a man of my word," he said distinctly. "And I swear on my honour as a frogman that she shall be safely back in her own bed before the staff are up."

"Hallo, old chap," said Dr. Bowman breezily. "Do you mind if I have a look at your chest?"

"If you must, you must," said Bunny wearily, closing his eyes. "But it's the thin edge of the wedge."

Dr. Bowman bent over him and deftly opened his pyjama jacket. Bunny's chest was covered with angry-looking red spots.

"I thought as much," said the doctor. "Chicken pox."

"Oh dear!" I stared at him blankly. "It can't be!"

"Look for yourself."

"But chicken pox is a child's disease—I had it when I was seven —Bunny's much too old to have it at his age."

"Nobody's too old to have it, and the older you are the nastier it is. Has he got anyone here to look after him?"

"No—only Cynthia. She comes in by the day. I'm afraid she isn't very bright."

At this moment Bunny opened his eyes again. "Hallo, Grizel," he said quite normally. "What on earth's going on?"

"You've got chicken pox," I said. "That's what's going on."

"I can't have. I'm far too long in the tooth to have chicken pox —it's a kid's disease."

"If you had it when you were a kid you probably wouldn't be having it now," said the doctor. "Can you remember whether you had it or not?"

"I must have," said Bunny. "Everything was lavished on me as a child, no expense was spared. My parents were immensely rich and, I'm afraid, rather vulgar."

"I'd better take your temperature," said Dr. Bowman.

After his temperature was taken Bunny slumped over on his side and started to mutter again. The doctor shook the thermometer down and signalled me to go into the sitting room; he followed me, closing the bedroom door behind him. I sat down and stared, horrified, at the three obviously used brandy glasses. Dr. Bowman looked at them too but made no comment.

"I think you'd better go home and get some sleep," he said. "I'll telephone for a nurse and wait here until she comes."

"There's nothing I can do?"

"Nothing at all. He'll have to have a night nurse and a day nurse for the next few days. He's got it pretty badly. But I can cope with all that. The telephone's in the hall, isn't it?"

"Yes," I said absently, and stood up.

"It's lucky your three youngsters have had it," Dr. Bowman

grinned, "otherwise I should have to put your house in quarantine."

"Yes, it is, isn't it?" I smiled rather wanly. "How long do you think it will take him to get over it?"

"He'll be a great deal better in ten days to a fortnight, but it will be longer than that before the spots disappear."

"Oh, poor Bunny "

"Yes, it's tough luck," said the doctor briskly, and ushered me into the hall and out of the front door. It was by now quite light, and I drove home thoughtfully under a violent pink sky that reminded me unhappily of Bunny's chest.

When I got home I found Robin and Eloise sitting on the back verandah drinking coffee.

"There didn't seem much sense in going to bed again," said Robin. "So we thought we'd wait for you and have a sort of pre-breakfast breakfast."

"What did the doctor say?" asked Eloise. She looked pale and anxious.

"Chicken pox," I said laconically.

"But he's grown-up," said Eloise. "Grownups don't have chicken pox!"

"Apparently they do." I sipped some coffee from Robin's cup. "Anyhow that's what he's got and he has to have a day nurse and a night nurse and he won't be convalescent under three weeks and even then he'll still be a bit spotty."

"This is awful!" said Eloise. "What *am* I to do?"

"There's nothing much any of us can do. We'll just have to rise above it." I fumbled in my coat pocket. "Here's your watch," I said, handing it to her. "You left it on the dressing table."

She took it from me. "Thank you," she said, her eyes filling with tears. "You really have been wonderful, both of you. I can never never tell you how grateful I am."

"Please don't worry about all that," I said. "Why don't you let me take you up to your room and give you a nice Seconal, you can sleep until lunchtime. The servants will be about soon anyhow, and it would muddle them to find you sobbing in a Balenciaga dinner dress at six o'clock in the morning."

"Actually it's only a copy." She rose with a deep sigh. "I found a marvellous old girl in Mount Street. She has no creative flair, but she can reproduce anything down to the last stitch. I'll give you her telephone number if you like."

"If she's still alive the next time we get to England I'll fly to her."

"We might stop off on the way from the airport," said Robin.

She turned her forlorn, tear-filled eyes on him. "You've been an absolute angel, driving me home like that and being so sweet and sympathetic. I shall never never forget it."

"Come along, dear," I said, and took her firmly by the arm and led her upstairs to the guest room. I stood about aimlessly while she undressed and got into bed and then went along to my own bathroom to fetch the Seconal. When I got back she was sitting up smoking a cigarette and looking exquisitely wistful. I poured out a glass of water and gave her a pill. She looked at it thoughtfully.

"Seconal's a lovely colour, isn't it? Much prettier than Nembutal."

"Much," I agreed. "But Sodium Amytal is the best of the lot, that vivid blue."

"Too strong for me," she said swallowing the pill. "They make me feel dizzy when I wake up." She put the glass of water carefully down on the bed table and took a puff at her cigarette. "I suppose the best thing really would be for me to go back home?"

"We'll discuss all that later."

"I don't see how I can immediately. It would look so silly."

"Relax," I said. "And don't bother about anything until you've had a good sleep."

"I wish I could remember whether I'd had it or not."

"Had what?"

"Chicken pox."

"I don't wish to sound prying or indelicate," I said. "But how far did you actually go with Bunny?"

"Quite far really. I mean we got into bed and all that, but nothing much happened because he kept on saying the most extraordinary things. I suppose he was delirious, poor darling."

"Can you think of anyone who'd *know* whether you had chicken pox when you were a child?"

"Nanny would of course, but she retired years ago. I think she's somewhere in Cumberland."

"We might cable her in the morning if you've got her address."

"I haven't," said Eloise hopelessly. "I don't even know her name any more, because she married somebody or other."

"Well, that rules her out. Your mother's still alive, isn't she?"

"She certainly is," Eloise spoke with feeling. "She's got a hideous villa in Cap Martin and never stops having rows with everyone. In any case she never paid the slightest attention to me when I was a child, she wouldn't have known if I'd had both my legs amputated."

"Then the only thing to do is to hope for the best and wait and see. At all events go to sleep now." I switched out the bedside lamp and pulled the curtains to shut out the daylight.

"I think the Seconal's beginning to work," murmured Eloise drowsily. "You've been divine over everything, and I shall never be able to repay you as long as I live."

I went out quietly and closed the door.

"Where's the duchess?" demanded Simon at breakfast.

"Where I should like to be," I replied. "In bed and asleep."

"Why is she in bed and asleep? Is she ill?"

"Not yet," said Robin.

"She had rather a bad night." I poured myself another cup of coffee. "I expect it was the excitement of the journey and sleeping in a strange bed."

"Strange beds can be very tricky," said Robin. I frowned at him, but he merely smiled innocently.

"I had a bad night too," said Nanny with a martyred expression. "I didn't close an eye until the small hours, and then when I did finally drop off I heard the cars starting up. I looked at my travelling clock and it was four fifteen."

"Mr. Craigie and I had to go over to Mr. Colville's. He was taken ill in the night and telephoned to us."

"Fancy that," said Nanny. "Nothing serious, I hope?"

"Not serious but uncomfortable," Robin said. "He's got chicken pox."

"You're pulling my leg again, Mr. Craigie." Nanny gave a little titter. "Mr. Colville's much too old to have chicken pox." She rose and dusted some crumbs daintily from the front of her dress. "Come along, children, it's time to go and I have to stop at the post office."

162

"Will he have jelly and cream like we had and that white fish?" enquired Janet.

"I expect so, darling, when he's a little better."

"I liked measles better than chicken pox," said Simon. "It wasn't so itchy."

When Nanny had finally disappeared with the children I rang for Tahali and ordered some more coffee. Robin was immersed in *The Reaper*.

"Your friend Mr. Seekala has certainly outdone himself this morning," he laughed. "Listen to this. The headline is 'Beautiful and Distinguished Visitant'—then he goes on—'Yesterday at Pendarla Airport Her Graciousness the Duchess of Fooey stepped radiantly from a B.O.A.C. Stratocruiser into the full glare of our famous Samolan sunshine. She posed with unutterable affability for our special photographers and was received by Mrs. Craigie with hom she is to make a tropical holiday. Her Graciousness is well known in England and Scotland and Ireland for her high and mighty entertainments and we Samolans in our far-away luxuriant paradise are most honoured and excitable to welcome her among our midst and we respectfully wish her the most rewarding and jolly times.'"

"Good for Mr. Seekala."

"There's a bit more," said Robin. "Which isn't quite so good."

"Go on," I said, with a sinking heart.

Robin continued to read. "'Mrs. Craigie and the Duchess of Fooey are lifelong chums of great intimacy and the very first thing Her Graciousness did after they had warmly embraced in the Customs house was to enquire with tenderness after Master Simon Craigie to whom she has given the pet name of Binny.'"

"Thank God the idiotic little man has an inaccurate ear at any rate."

"All the same," said Robin, "Binny *is* a bit near the knuckle if anybody happens to be in the know."

"It can't be helped," I said crossly. "I'm rapidly getting to a state when I don't care if everybody is in the know. I'm sick to death of the whole maddening situation, and if we both hadn't been so lily-livered and weak-minded none of it need ever have occurred."

"We're stuck with it now whether we like it or not," said Robin philosophically. "But the question is, how long, oh Lord, how long?"

"She'll have to stay on for a bit whatever happens, just for the look of the thing. Sandra's promised to have her for three days next week anyhow."

"I don't mind really," said Robin. "She probably won't be much trouble and she's certainly decorative. Perhaps you could suggest her for a part in the water pageant! She'd look smashing riding into Cobb's Cove on a dolphin or something."

"I'm sure she would, but we don't happen to have any dolphins available at the moment."

"That's the trouble with the Samolan Amateur Dramatic Society," said Robin. "They may be industrious but they lack imagination and foresight."

"Be quiet, darling," I said. "My head's splitting."

FOURTEEN

Later in the morning when Robin had gone off to supervise the
banana cutting I telephoned to Bunny's house for news. I expected
to talk to Cynthia, but a strange voice answered. "I am the nurse,"
it said. "My name is Nahoona Nahooli. To whom please may I
be speaking to?"

"Mrs. Craigie. I want to know how Mr. Colville is."

"He is sleeping."

"Good. Is his temperature still high?"

"That I would not be permitted to say, it is for the doctor to
tell."

"Is the doctor there?"

"Oh no. He is at the hospital, but in the afternoon he will come."

"Thank you," I said patiently. "I would have liked to know if
Mr. Colville shows any signs of improvement."

"He is sleeping."

"Perhaps you will be kind enough to ask the doctor to telephone
me after he has seen Mr. Colville."

"Perhaps I will," she said politely. "Bye-bye for now," and she
hung up.

I went out onto the back verandah, sat in the swing seat, and
stared listlessly at the view. I watched a mongoose run across the
lawn and disappear into the casuarina grove. There are actually
no dangerous snakes on the island, only a few somnolent grass
ones here and there, but several years ago someone misguidedly
imported a couple of mongooses—I cannot bring myself to write
"mongeese" because it looks so silly—and since then they have
multiplied by the million and steal eggs from chicken runs and
are a grave nuisance. The garden was shimmering in the heat and

I wished I had my dark glasses, but they were in my bedroom and I hadn't the energy to go and fetch them. Tahali appeared with the mail and I asked him to make me a horse's neck; he grinned sympathetically and withdrew. There were only two letters, one from Mother and the other, obviously a "Collins," from Molly Frobisher, whose wild, scrawly handwriting was unmistakable. I opened Mother's first.

My Darling Grizel,
    Your last letter arrived *quite* safely and I should have answered it before but I have been in bed for a few days with an absolute *streamer!* Fortunately it didn't go to my chest, which they usually do, and now I'm up and about again.
Fancy that horrid little Chalmers boy hitting poor Simon with a ruler! I sincerely hope he got a good wigging for it. I don't know what children are coming to these days, no discipline whatever. Only last week Jeannie brought her little grand niece to tea, she's seven and a half, very fat and a perfect horror. She gobbled up everything on the table without saying 'please' or 'thank you', knocked over the milk jug, fortunately not the Rockingham, and kept whining to be taken to the W.C. She went three times and she wasn't here more than an hour and a half. Imagine! I said to Jeannie afterwards that the child must have something *seriously* wrong with her but she said no, she just liked sitting in there! Eleanour Bartlett is going to have a baby *at last*. She's in the seventh Heaven. I do hope it will turn out all right, they've been persevering for so long and poor Walter had to have all those nasty injections. Grace Felstoad took me to a matinee of the new play at the Court Theatre last Thursday afternoon. All the papers had said it was wonderful but there was scarcely anybody there. Personally I didn't care for it much. It was all about the lower classes of course, everything is nowadays, and there was no scenery to speak of, just doors and windows, so one never knew where anybody was. The girl in it wasn't bad but she looked as if she needed a good scrubbing. Grace enjoyed every minute of it and cried at the end when the man was taken off to prison. I'm afraid I didn't because I thought he ought to have been there in the first place. I don't think I have any more news. Jeannie had to take Angus to the vet because he got a chicken bone wedged in his throat but

the man got it out all right. I really must stop now my pet because Jeannie has come in with the luncheon tray. Give my love to Robin and the dear children. Lots of hugs. Your loving Mother.

P.S. I read in the Daily Express the other day that Eloise Fowey was coming out to stay with *you!* I must say I was *astonished!* I had no idea you knew her that well. But it probably isn't true, one can never believe what one reads in the papers.

I put the letter back in its envelope with a sigh, reflecting grimly that for once the *Daily Express* had been impeccably accurate. Molly's letter was shorter and to the point.

Dearest Grizel,

We loved our stay with you and I do hope we weren't a nuisance. The flight home was perfect and Robin was so sweet to take us to the airport, please give him our love and thank him. We are now in a terrible upset because the most awful thing has happened. The very day after we got back believe it or not Mickey started running a high temperature. I was frantic thinking he'd got some terrible tropical fever but thank Heaven it's only chicken pox. Old Doctor Akunani has put the house in quarantine and now we're waiting anxiously to see if Timmy and Sylvia get it. Isn't it too maddening after that lovely restful holiday and everything? I really must stop now because I have to dab poor Mickey again with calamine lotion. Thank you again dear and our love to you all. Your affectionate—Molly.

I closed my eyes against the glare and thought sadly of poor Bunny. If only he hadn't invited us all over for the picnic and if only he hadn't hauled the wretched Mickey out of the water and carried him ashore, he would now probably be hale and hearty and enjoying his illicit love affair tiptop instead of lying sweating in bed, covered in spots, with a Samolan nurse twittering at him. It only went to show, I reflected, that good and kindly deeds do not necessarily bring their just reward. It seemed damned unfair that poor Bunny, who was not by any means an ardent child-lover, having, for my sake really, taken all that trouble to entertain the shrieking Frobishers, should be so disagreeably punished for it.

At this moment Tahali appeared with the horse's neck on a tray and placed it on a small table beside me.

"I have made it strong," he said, "because Mistress looks weary."

"Mistress *is* indeed weary," I said gratefully. "On account of having been up all night."

"That I already know." He gave a slight giggle.

"How did you know?"

"I come back from small jinks at my friend's house in the night and find garage doors open and both cars gone. Then I met my cousin Baiuna in Mrs. Ching Loo's store this morning."

"What on earth has your cousin got to do with it?"

"He is a fisherman," said Tahali cryptically.

"I still don't quite understand."

Tahali gave a knowing wink. "He was on the reef last night opposite to the bungalow of Mr. Bunny and he saw lights going on and off and cars going backwards and forwards and he said to himself there is something of great excitement happening."

"He was dead right," I said dryly. "There was."

"Now I hear from Clementine who herself heard it from Miss Nanny that Mr. Bunny has a chicken disease. Is that the truth?"

"Unfortunately it is."

"Is it something of which he might die?"

"Good heavens no. But he will be very uncomfortable for quite a while."

"It is most sad for him and I am upset."

"So are we all," I said. "Very upset indeed."

"The duchess is upset too," said Tahali. "She was weeping when Eulalie took her the coffee."

"Eulalie must have imagined it," I said sharply. "The duchess has nothing to weep about."

"Would she not also be weeping for poor Mr. Bunny?"

"Of course not, why should she? She only met him for the first time at dinner last night."

Tahali looked puzzled. "That is most surprising. I was thinking that they were the friends of long duration."

"Why should you think any such thing?"

"Because Cynthia, who works for Mr. Bunny and is the first cousin of my friend in the valley, has seen all the photographs."

"Which photographs? I don't know what you are talking about."

"The photographs Mr. Bunny keeps in his big desk. They are

taken of the duchess in many pretty poses, in one of them she has a little diamond hat."

"Now listen to me, Tahali," I said, grasping the nettle danger as firmly as I could, "you must promise me on your word of honour never to speak of this to a living soul."

Tahali smiled engagingly. "Then it is the truth?"

"Yes, in a way it is," I said. "But it is a deep secret, and if it were to be found out it would land Mr. Robin and me in the most dreadful trouble. No matter what Eulalie or Cynthia or your cousins and aunts and friends in the valley may say to you, you must solemnly swear to me here and now that you will pretend to know nothing whatever about it."

Tahali looked stricken. "You are angry with me?"

"Of course I'm not angry with you, but I will be unless you promise on your oath to do what I ask."

"I am not quite aware what is an oath, but I will promise on it with great willingness. I would not for the world be the cause of trouble for you." Tahali sighed unhappily.

"Good. Then it is a bargain between us." I rose to my feet. "And we will shake hands on it." Tahali, looking more stricken than ever, took my proffered hand and shook it with considerable fervour. At this moment Sandra walked, unannounced, onto the verandah. I had been so preoccupied that I hadn't heard the sound of her car. Tahali dropped my hand like a live coal, bowed deeply, and disappeared. Sandra looked at me askance. "What on earth were you shaking hands with Tahali for? Is he going away?"

"No," I said. "But I may be, I may be going a long long way away. This strain is driving me mad."

Sandra sat down on the swing seat. "These shoes are hell," she said, kicking them off. "They make me feel like a Chinese concubine. Where's the flighty duchess?"

"Upstairs. Sitting in tears among the alien corn."

"I think it's 'amid,'" said Sandra, "but I wouldn't bank on it. What's all this about Bunny having chicken pox?"

"Good God!" I sank back into my chair. "How did *you* know?"

"Everybody knows everything immediately on this island," she said. "It's far far too small. As a matter of fact the matron at the hospital told me—I had to go there this morning to see poor Letty Togstone, she's slipped a disc. I presume it's true?"

"Only too true," I said. "And what's more he's got it very badly. He's running a high temperature and his chest looks like a bad Matisse."

"Have you seen him?"

"Of course I have. Robin and I have been jolting back and forth along that ghastly road all night long. I'm worn out."

"Was Eloise there—in Bunny's bungalow I mean?"

"Yes. It was she who telephoned to us. She was in a frenzy."

"I don't wonder." Sandra giggled heartlessly. "Were they actually what's known as 'having a go'?"

"I think they were beginning to, but then he became delirious and burst out in spots."

"Oh Lord! You don't suppose she's infectious, do you?"

"We have no way of knowing. She can't remember whether or not she had it when she was a child and the only person alive who could possibly enlighten us is her old Nanny who's married someone whose name she's forgotten and is living in Cumberland."

"You're making me quite dizzy," said Sandra. "Anyhow I can't possibly have her at Government House until we find out for certain."

"Yes, you can," I said. "You promised."

"She may be one of those 'carriers' who just go about giving it to everybody without having it themselves."

"I suppose you've had it in your day?"

"Oh yes. I had the lot. My childhood was an endless series of thermometers, lozenges, steam kettles, and poultices. I was a frail little thing."

"Well, you've certainly made up for it since."

"I don't intend to *blame* you for being snappy," she said. "But I would like to remind you that you brought all this on yourself. However, I'll stand by my promise. She can come for three days, chicken pox or no chicken pox. There's always the chance that she might give it to Cuckoo, which would be heavenly."

At this moment Eloise appeared, wearing sapphire-blue slacks, silver sandals, and a cyclamen-coloured shirt.

"Well," said Sandra, rising amiably to greet her. "The hurrying years have certainly left you remarkably unscathed. You've hardly changed at all."

"How angelic of you to say so," Eloise smiled wistfully. "I feel a hundred." She turned to me. "I didn't know whether anyone was coming to lunch or not or what I ought to wear. If I look too casual like this I can easily change into something else."

"You look charming," I said, "and nobody's coming to lunch unless Sandra wants to stay. It's curry, I think, so there'll be quite enough to go round."

"I'd love to but I can't," said Sandra, sitting down again on the swing seat. "I've got old Sir Albert and his daughter, not the dotty one, thank God, and a couple of American congressmen who are on their way to Tokyo for some reason best known to themselves coming at one o'clock sharp, and then I have to go to the Institute to open an exhibition of art photographs at two-thirty. They've been taken by that dubious nephew of Lady Fumbasi's, and they're very fuzzy and inspirational. Personally I can't make head or tail of them and George says they look as if they'd actually been *taken* in a dark room instead of being developed in one, but I promised and that's that. In the meantime I wouldn't say no to a little nip of something."

I got up and rang the bell for Tahali.

"I'm expecting you to come to me for a few days next week," Sandra said to Eloise. "I can't say the exact date yet because we've got a Board of Trade man and his wife and some Burmese hovering over our heads, but I'll let you know definitely before Friday."

"That will be lovely," said Eloise. "It's terribly sweet of you."

I sensed between Sandra and Eloise that strained affability that occurs when two women don't really care much for each other. However, Sandra was really making a valiant effort and I was grateful to her. Eloise settled herself in the planter's chair and lit a cigarette. She looked pale and outwardly serene, but I felt sorry for her. She was, after all, in a disagreeable situation whichever way you looked at it. I had no way of knowing whether or not she really was as deeply in love with Bunny as she said she was, but at least she had obviously been keen enough to fly all the way out from England to be with him, well aware of all the dangerous social hazards entailed, and here she was stuck with Robin and me and the children with no hope of access to her paramour and no possible means of escape beyond a few days at Government House where she must know in her heart that she wasn't really wanted. As far as my own feelings for her were concerned I hadn't quite made up my mind. So far she had been in no way tiresome or demanding. She had been charming to the children and Nanny and the servants and seemed almost pathetically eager not to embarrass Robin or me or put us to the slightest inconvenience beyond the actual fact of her physical presence in the house. Whatever might be the outcome of these irritating circumstances, I resolved, in spite of my exasperation over the whole business, to keep her entertained as well as I could and try not to be put off by her continually calling Robin and me angels and telling us how grateful she felt. I also resolved, less kindly perhaps, to do everything in my power to prevent Bunny from marrying her. Beautiful and alluring and amiable as she was there was an inherent silliness in her character which I knew with all my instincts would never suit Bunny in the long run. He was an intelligent man despite his irrepressible dilettantism and not given to tolerating fools gladly, and the moment the hullabaloo over the divorce had died down and the first fine careless raptures were over he would find himself caught up in an oversocial married life for which he was temperamentally unsuited and probably be utterly miserable. I knew very little about the pattern of Eloise's life in England, but judging from press reports and photographs in the *Sketch* and *Tatler* her personal cronies were not of the type likely to appeal to him at all. They mostly, as far as I could gather, came under the ambiguous heading of "The International Set," who wandered aimlessly back and forth between London, Paris, Rome, Cannes, and Deauville, and wandered, equally aimlessly, in and out of bed with one another and in and out of the divorce courts with their lawyers.

Bunny, underneath his apparent insouciance, is of a surprisingly bookish turn of mind and is a partner, not a very active one, I must admit, in a rather *avant-garde* publishing firm. When in England he lives, in moderate discomfort, in a converted flat in Lowndes Square where he is cherished by a doting old housekeeper called Mrs. Turpin, who looks as though she had stepped straight out of Cranford. The last time Robin and I went home we lunched with him there. The food was adequate but unimaginative because, like Sandra, he has no gastronomic flair, but what struck us most was the all-pervading atmosphere of solid, sleek bachelorhood. It seemed to me inconceivable that he should seriously contemplate giving all that up and settling down with an ex-duchess whose spiritual home was the Oliver Messel suite at the Dorchester.

At this moment my reflections were interrupted by the appearance of Tahali with the drink tray. He put it down on the table beside Sandra, and she looked at it thoughtfully.

"I'm torn," she said, "between a pink gin which will probably give me a headache for the rest of the afternoon or straight vodka which will certainly give me hiccups."

"Plump for the vodka. It mixes with anything, and you're bound to have wine at lunch."

"I'm not bound to," she sighed, "but I expect I shall. I'll need something more than lemonade to support me with Sir Albert to the right of me and congressmen to the left of me."

When we had all decided what we wanted and Tahali had given it to us, he bowed, still looking a little glum, and withdrew.

"Tahali looks wretched," said Sandra after a slight pause. "You haven't been bullying him, have you?"

"Not at all. I've merely been giving him a brief lecture about not listening to gossip."

"It's no use telling Samolans not to listen to gossip, it's their lifeblood. The grapevine system on this island is more efficient than M.I. 5, and FBI, and the Deuxième Bureau rolled into one." She gave a sidelong glance at Eloise, who was sipping tomato juice and gazing into space. "What had he been gossiping about?"

"Actually he hadn't been gossiping at all," I said. "But his sisters and cousins and aunts had, and I was determined to nip it in the bud."

"I see." She shot another look at Eloise and raised her eyebrows questioningly. "I suppose that was why you were shaking hands with him so earnestly when I came in. I thought for a moment that you'd gone mad."

"It was a sort of 'honour-as-a-scout' pact. I made him promise to see no evil, speak no evil, and hear no evil."

"Let's hope it works," she said. "It's certainly depressed him for the time being. Personally I've long ago given up trying to impose Baden-Powell ethics on our sunny islanders. They just giggle at me uncomprehendingly and go their own sweet way."

"Tahali is loyal to the core, the only danger is that he might go off on one of his Saturday night binges. That, to quote Captain Hook, 'is the fear that haunts me'!"

"Oh, what a tangled web we weave, when first we practise to deceive." She winked at me shamelessly and proceeded to put on her shoes. "I must go now. The vodka's flown to my head and I shall probably be arrested for drunken driving." She turned to Eloise. "Why don't you and Grizel come in for drinks tomorrow evening? There won't be anyone there but George and me, but come early, about sixish, because we're dining out."

"I'd love to," said Eloise with a wan smile, "if it's all right with Grizel."

"We're dining out too," I said, "so that will be fine. Robin and I are taking Eloise to Kelly's Tavern. She hasn't met Juanita yet, and I think she ought to."

"A treat in store," said Sandra. "She's famous and full of rich, fruity oaths, you'll adore her." She rose to her feet and winced painfully. "It's no use, they'll have to go back and be stretched. I shall be crippled for life if I go on like this."

Eloise got up too and Sandra, surprisingly, gave her a peck on the cheek.

"It's lovely you being here," she said. "We'll show you all the sights and, between the lot of us, see that you enjoy yourself. I do think it's hard luck about Bunny being ill," she added. "But you must try not to let it get you down."

Eloise gave a sad little smile. "Thank you," she said. "You're all being angelic to me."

I took Sandra through the house and out to the front drive. "Poor beast," she said as we went. "I can't help being sorry for her. I do hope she'll have cheered up a bit by the time she comes to us. That beautiful bruised and broken look is liable to get on George's nerves. We must all rack our brains to try to find someone attractive to act as a sort of 'stand-in' until Bunny's got rid of his spots. Perhaps Hali Alani would do?"

"I can't see Hali as a stand-in. He's an 'all-or-nothing' boy if ever I saw one. Also"—I added—"I think that that suggestion, coming from the governor's lady, is a bit on the *louche* side."

"We must accept life as we find it," said Sandra, getting into the station wagon. "It's no use taking up moral attitudes. Anyhow you've cast yourself as the intriguing 'madam' in this rather be-

174

draggled little romance, and it's up to you to organize things and see that everyone's happy." She waved gaily and drove away and I went thoughtfully back to Eloise.

Lunch was a sore trial from the word go. Robin came back from the plantation obviously in a bad temper about something or other. Eloise picked her way mournfully through the curry which wasn't as good as it usually is and answered, when addressed, in monosyllables accompanied with a brave smile that only too palpably masked an aching heart. Nanny, who had been in the town and had coffee at Miss Banks's tearoom, was in an informative mood.

"The youngest Broomhead child was knocked off her bicycle by a milk van on the Narouchi Road yesterday," she announced brightly. "She had to be rushed off to the hospital, poor little mite. She had slight concussion, but fortunately there were no bones broken."

"What happened to the bicycle?" enquired Robin.

"Smashed to pieces, and she'd only had it for three days."

"In that case she shouldn't have been riding it on the Narouchi Road."

Nanny gave a little sniff and turned her attention to Eloise.

"The traffic on this island is getting worse and worse. I know it only too well because I have to drive the children back and forth to school every day. The natives have no road sense at all. All they seem to mind about is how fast they can go. It's quite terrifying, it really is. Do you drive a car, Duchess?"

"Yes," said Eloise dimly, as though she were being dragged awake from a tragic, private dream.

I glanced up at Tahali as I usually do when Nanny refers to the Samolans as "natives." It is a private joke between us, and he responds as a rule with a small grin. This time, however, there was no amused glint in his eye and he just stood staring in front of him with a resigned expression waiting for us to finish our curry. After a slight pause Nanny returned to the attack.

"I ran into poor Mrs. Elphinstone in Queen Street."

"I hope you didn't knock her off her bicycle," said Robin, helping himself to some more rice. I frowned at him but he paid no attention.

"She was just going into the post office," Nanny went on, ignoring his interruption. "Apparently her daughter has just run away from her husband. She was very distressed about it. After all they've been married for over twelve years. It does seem funny, doesn't it?"

"Hilariously," said Robin.

"Have a little more curry, Eloise," I said hurriedly.

"No, thank you," she said. "It's divine but I really couldn't."

"If she had been the flighty type it would be more understandable," continued Nanny undaunted. "But she isn't. She's quite a mousey little thing. They were both out here last year, she and her husband, and they seemed to be absolutely devoted. And now, out of the blue, off she goes to Kenya with a man years younger than herself. Mrs. Elphinstone simply can't understand it, and I must say I agree with her. It seems so callous, don't you think?" Again she turned sociably to Eloise.

"Very," said Eloise almost inaudibly, and took a sip of water.

"You can say what you like," said Robin. "But there's nothing to touch the English strawberry."

Nanny looked astonished. "How do you mean? I don't understand."

"Just that," said Robin. "The American ones are far too big, and the French ones are far too small."

"The French *fraise des bois* are delicious!" I turned to Nanny conciliatingly. "When we were home last time we spent two weeks in Paris and we absolutely gorged ourselves. It was summer of course, and they served them in dear little baskets filled with green leaves. I really think we ought to make an effort to grow them here in the garden. I'm sure they'd do all right on that flat bit by the water tank."

"Never," said Robin firmly. "It would be flagrantly unpatriotic."

Nanny gave him a pursed-up, offended look and lapsed into silence for the rest of the meal.

Later, when Nanny had disappeared and Eloise had gone upstairs to her room, Robin flung himself onto the swing seat and groaned. "This has got to stop once and all," he said. "The combination of Nanny's social vivacity and Eloise's lack of it is more than I can stand. A few more meals like lunch today and I shall institute divorce proceedings."

"On what grounds?"

176

"Mental cruelty of course." Robin groaned again. "The very fact that you allow Nanny to eat with us at all is calculated mental cruelty and you know it."

"It's only for lunches. She has her evening meal with the children. And it's only lunches when we're by ourselves. When we have guests she has a tray in her room."

"We were *not* by ourselves today," said Robin through clenched teeth. "And what is more it looks to me as though we were never going to be by ourselves again. We have with us, probably for months to come, a morose, frustrated nymphomaniac, and all because you let Bunny twist you round his little finger."

"That's not fair. You let him twist you round his little finger just as much as I did. And it's unkind to call Eloise a nymphomaniac. She may be a bit morose, I grant you, but who wouldn't be in her place? She'll probably snap out of it in a few days."

"I have nothing against a little light nymphomania in itself, but in its depressive form augmented by Nanny's inane chirruping, it is not to be borne."

"In any case," I retorted hotly, "it certainly doesn't help matters for you to bait Nanny incessantly as you do. You were horrid to her today and upset her thoroughly. She's probably upstairs in her room at this very moment sobbing her heart out. Why don't you try being nice to her for a change?"

"What form of niceness do you suggest?" he asked grimly.

"Charm her, pay her little attentions, draw her out of herself."

"Drawing Nanny out of herself presents no problem." Robin spoke in a tone of controlled exasperation. "It's getting her to keep her idiotic trap shut that is the difficulty." With this he got up and stamped off moodily into the garden.

I went slowly upstairs to my bedroom, took two aspirin, drew the curtains, and lay down wearily on the bed. My head was splitting and my heart heavy with foreboding. I was furious with Robin but I had, in fairness, to see his point. Nanny *had* been maddening at lunch, Eloise *had* been morose, even Tahali, my usual stand-by in time of stress, had obviously taken offence at what I had said to him about gossiping and withdrawn the light of his countenance. I felt thoroughly depressed and ready to weep. I foresaw that the presence of the wretched Eloise in the house was likely to be more disruptive than I had bargained for. It wasn't her fault of course, over and above her initial silliness in coming to Samolo at all, any more than it was Bunny's fault that he had chicken pox. She would probably, as I had said to Robin, snap out of her immediate gloom in the course of the next few days, but even if she suddenly became as merry as a grig and the life and soul of the party, the fact remained that she was a cuckoo in our domestic nest and, in spite of her beauty and affability, likely to remain so. As far as Nanny was concerned there seemed to be only two alternatives. Either I could suggest to her tactfully that during Eloise's visit it would be more convenient for her to lunch in her own room, which, however well or ill she took it, would assuredly hurt her feelings dreadfully. The other alternative was to invite different people to lunch every day so that there would automatically be no room for her. The prospect of either course filled me with despair. The next few weeks were bound to become increasingly hectic with the royal visit pending. I had promised to help Sandra in every way I could, and apart from attending committee meetings of the S.A.D.S. there were certain to be a whole lot of other things to do. I really couldn't, in the face of all this, undertake to give a series of luncheon parties merely because Nanny's conversation grated on Robin's nerves. I toyed wildly with the idea of working up a sudden nervous breakdown and moving into a private room in the hospital with a lot of books and crossword puzzles, but I knew in my heart that I should be unable to carry it through. In the first place Robin would see through it in a flash, and even if he didn't, such a drastic course, apart from going against my conscience, would entail Eloise being in the house alone with him which, although I am not of a naturally jealous disposition, I didn't fancy at all. I turned over on my side resenting bitterly Robin, Nanny, Eloise, Bunny, Tahali, the Frobishers, and the whole unkind and unfriendly world.

When I awoke at about four-thirty my headache was still lurking, but I felt a little more cheerful. I rang for some tea, and Eulalie later wandered in with it. She placed the tray languidly on my stomach with a sorrowful look.

"It is sad about Mr. Bunny," she said.

"Very sad," I agreed, with a slight pang of guilt because I hadn't rung up to enquire after lunch as I had intended to.

"His fever is better," she said. "But he is most angry."

"How do you know?"

"My cousin told me." She sighed a deep sigh and sauntered out.

I sipped my tea gratefully. It was the Earl Grey that Eloise had brought out and tasted smoky and delicious. When I had finished it I lit a cigarette and went out onto the verandah. The sun was still hot but not oppressively so, and the casuarina trees cast feathery shadows across the drive. Far away, from the direction of the Lailanu foothills, I could hear the faint throbbing of drums, which indicated a local celebration of some sort, a betrothal or a marriage or a funeral. How lovely, I thought enviously, to be a Samolan matron instead of a British matron and live a contented life free from social and moral inhibitions and untrammelled by the tiresome, overcivilized ethics which we, with our so-called enlightenment, so needlessly imposed upon ourselves. A Samolan woman of my age, married or unmarried, would by now have left all turbulence behind her and settled down to a cosy, vegetable existence with her children growing up and virtually no domestic problems to plague her. True, everything being relative, she would probably have a few ups and downs; there might not be enough rice to go round, or her man might come home drunk on Kala-Kala and knock her about a bit, but on the whole her life would proceed gently towards the grave with a great deal more serenity than mine showed any signs of doing. It was not that I actively yearned for Robin to come home drunk and beat me up, or welcomed the idea of there not being enough food in the house, but in my present state of depression I couldn't help feeling that such dramatic contingencies would be easier to cope with than having to decide whether or not Nanny should be banished to her room with a tray, and what I should do if, in a fit of tearful umbrage, she elected to pack up her things and go, leaving me with no one to look after the children, the water pageant and the royal visit pending and Eloise dolefully sitting about the house waiting to be cheered up.

At this moment the telephone rang and made me jump. When I answered it Daphne's voice boomed at me through the receiver.

"I didn't wake you from your beauty sleep, did I?" she asked breezily.

"No. I've just finished tea."

"Good for you. Personally I can't stand the stuff—too wishy-washy."

"It was Earl Grey," I said defensively. "Eloise brought it out to me from Jackson's."

"*Chacun à son goût.*" She gave a hearty laugh. "How's Eloise enjoying herself?"

"Very much," I said. "She's in her room at the moment. Would you like to talk to her?"

"I don't suppose she'd remember who I was, I haven't seen her since the good old M.T.C. days. But if you and Robin aren't doing anything tonight we thought you might like to bring her over. We're having a barbecue on the beach, not a party, only Peter and Esmond and us. I know it's short notice, but I thought I'd just ring you on the off chance."

"I think we'd love to," I said guardedly. "But Robin isn't back yet, and I don't know whether or not he's made any plans. Can I call you back?"

"Right," said Daphne. "But don't leave it too late because we've got to prepare the steaks. As a matter of fact you needn't trouble to call back. If we don't hear from you by six o'clock we'll forge ahead."

"Lovely," I said. "What time would you like us to come?"

"Any time between seven and eight. For God's sake tell Eloise not to doll herself up. Just slacks and a shirt."

"All right," I said. "It sounds wonderful."

"Good show!" said Daphne and hung up.

I went, with a lighter heart, to turn on my bath, determined, that even if Robin refused to come, I would take Eloise on my own. The evening might turn out to be a bit boisterous, particularly if Daphne decided to take to the bottle, which she usually did, but anything, I felt, would be preferable to dining at home, with Robin and me making gay conversation while Eloise fought back her tears.

FIFTEEN

Fisherman's Hole is in my opinion one of the most attractive places on the island. It is a long, one-storied wooden building which used, in the old days, to be a wharf for storing copra. It stands on the edge of a secluded bay and has its own little crescent of white sandy beach and an old stone jetty from which you can dive into deep water. Daphne and Lydia between them have made it quite enchanting. There are four bedrooms and bathrooms, a large kitchen fully equipped with every "ideal home" gadget imaginable and a long, low-ceilinged living room opening onto a wooden verandah which is built on coral rocks and from which flat stone steps lead down to the beach. In order to get to it you drive through the tail end of the Stirling sugar plantation, across a disused railway line, and through a grove of ironwood, breadfruit, and casuarinas.

Robin had been more tractable than I had anticipated and Eloise had accepted the idea of dining out with listless resignation, and so we left the house at half past six and made a slight detour to call on Bunny on the way. This visit, although well intentioned, was not an unmitigated success. The Samolan nurse received us rather suspiciously, ushered us into the living room, and retired into the bedroom from which she emerged after a few moments with the information that Mr. Colville wished to see Mrs. Craigie, but no one else. This, not unnaturally, reduced Eloise to immediate tears and Robin, with a cheerful nod to the nurse, hurried her out into the garden. I went into the bedroom and found poor Bunny sitting up in bed looking truly dreadful. His face was covered with large angry red spots which had been plastered generously with calamine lotion, giving an over-all mauve patina through which his very blue but bloodshot eyes looked at me balefully.

"For God's sake don't let Eloise in," he said hoarsely. "If she saw me like this she'd never speak to me again."

"It's all right. She's in the garden with Robin." I smiled at him sympathetically. "There's no need to work yourself into a state, we'll head her off. How's your temperature?"

"Frankly," said Bunny, "I neither know nor care. I don't give a bugger if it's high or low or medium. And I don't give a bugger if I live or die either."

"Come, dear," I said. "That's no way to speak. I hope you don't use that sort of language in front of that pretty little Samolan nurse."

"That pretty little Samolan nurse is a fiend incarnate. She is bright, cheerful, efficient, and entirely intolerable. She does nothing but frig in and out with trays and lotions and thermometers until I want to kick her pretty little Samolan teeth down her pretty little Samolan throat!"

"You really must try to keep calm," I said soothingly. "You'll only upset all your acids and make yourself worse."

"I couldn't be worse. I feel perfectly bloody and look like an elderly French character actress."

"It's the calamine that gives that effect," I said. "But you really must grin and bear it and try not to be too cross. I know it's beastly for you, but there's nothing whatever to be done except give up to it and wait until it gets better."

Bunny shifted miserably on his pillows. "How's Eloise? Is she all right?"

"Perfectly," I replied. "She's naturally upset about you being ill, as indeed we all are. She's being a darling and no trouble at all. All you have to do is just to relax and not mope and moan too much."

"That silly sod of a doctor says I shall have to stay in bed for another week to ten days."

"Well, you'd better do as he says. He knows what he's talking about."

"To hell with him," said Bunny closing his eyes. "To hell with everybody and everything in the whole Goddamned world."

182

"Now you really have sworn quite enough for one day. I think you'd better try to go to sleep."

He opened his eyes and looked at me appealingly. "You won't let her see me—promise me you won't!"

"I think it's rather unkind not to let her see you if she wants to," I said. "But if you feel so strongly about it I'll explain as tactfully as I can."

"You're a real pal." He gave a ghost of a smile. "And if I ever recover, which is most unlikely, I shall give you a handsome present."

At this moment the nurse came in. She flashed Bunny a sharp, professional smile and turned to me with unmistakable disapproval.

"The patient is by now most tired," she said. "He should by orders have no visits."

"I'm leaving now anyhow," I replied coldly. I waved good-bye to Bunny and went out. The nurse followed me into the living room.

"My name is Nahoona Nahooli," she began.

"I know. We went into all that on the telephone. My name is Mrs. Craigie, and I intend to visit the patient whenever I wish to. What is his temperature today?"

"That I am not permitted to be telling."

"Nonsense," I said with an edge in my voice. "It's not a state secret, and it's unlikely to be of the faintest interest to anybody who isn't personally fond of him. I happen to be one of his closest friends and so kindly tell me what it is immediately and don't be so silly."

Cowed by my tone, she backed away a few steps. "It was a hundred and one point four when I took it at three o'clock," she said sulkily.

"Good." I rewarded her with a brusque smile. "I shall probably be calling again sometime tomorrow. Thank you very much."

With that I left her and went out onto the verandah where I found Eloise and Robin smoking cigarettes and staring glumly at the sea. While we walked slowly round the house to the car I explained to Eloise that Bunny was much better in himself but that he really didn't want her to see him in his present state. She accepted this, but there was a petulant note in her voice.

"If he was willing to let you see him, I can't see why he shouldn't have wanted me to."

"Our relationship is on rather a different footing," I said. "His male vanity would not be upset by me seeing him looking like an elderly French character actress, but for you to do so would be humiliating for him. You must see that."

"How do you mean—an elderly French character actress?" Her exquisite face puckered with bewilderment.

"It's the calamine lotion," I explained. "It makes him look heavily powdered and bright mauve."

"Poor angel," she said with a deep sigh, and we got into the car and drove off.

As the crow flies it's only a few miles from Bunny's bungalow to Fisherman's Hole, but the road turns inland and twists about a lot so it takes longer than one would think. During the drive I thought it wise to brief Eloise a little about the Daphne-Lydia setup.

"It's a fairly eccentric menage," I explained. "But they are both great fun really. You probably remember Daphne, the elder one, in the M.T.C."

"I should just think I do," said Eloise. "She once threw a spanner at me. But I expect it was only because I got on her nerves. I seemed to get on everyone's nerves in the M.T.C."

"You were a good deal younger than most of us," I replied gallantly.

"It wasn't only that." She gazed pensively out of the window for a moment. "It was that I never seemed to be able to do anything quite right, did I? And I was always forgetting to call people 'madam' when I should have. I remember Mimsy Wargrave being absolutely livid with me one day outside Claridge's because I didn't salute her. But it seemed so silly when we had been up until five o'clock in the morning at the same party and both had hangovers."

"She was your superior officer," I said loyally.

"Everybody was my superior officer. That's what was such hell."

"I'm on your side," said Robin. "I once got a bad ticking off for not saluting my aunt in Sloane Square. She came striding round the corner, squeezed into a Sam Browne belt, and took me completely by surprise. I said 'Christ!' dropped my gas mask, and bolted into Peter Jones. But she was after me like a flash, and there was a ghastly scene in the china department. She left me, shaking like a leaf, surrounded by breakfast sets."

"I don't believe you could get breakfast sets during the war. Even at Peter Jones."

"There you go," said Robin. "Trying to undermine me as usual."

"At all events," I said, getting back to the subject of Daphne and Lydia, "the house is really very attractive and the food's sure to be good because it always is, but be prepared to leave when I tip you the wink. After a certain hour in the evening Daphne is liable to get a little out of hand."

"Are they mad about each other?" enquired Eloise.

"I think they must be, they've been together for years."

"It's funny," said Eloise thoughtfully, "I've never had any leanings in that direction. What do you suppose they actually do?"

"We might bring that up at dinner," said Robin, as we bumped across the railway line.

"What I mean is"—Eloise went on—"I can't see how it could be really satisfactory, physically. I mean it must be rather dull not having anything to put anywhere."

"You delicacy does you credit," said Robin.

Eloise, for the first time that day, gave a little giggle.

We turned into a little drive fringed with hibiscus and poinsettias and drew up before the front door which was opened immediately by Daphne herself wearing bell-bottomed sailors' trousers, a striped fisherman's vest, and pearl earrings. She was holding a carving fork in her left hand and greeted us enthusiastically.

"Jolly good timing," she said. "We're just going to put the steaks on." She turned to Eloise and shook her hand breezily. "Blow me down!" She stared at her admiringly. "You certainly do look smashing!"

Eloise, wincing a little from the handshake, switched on charm like a neon light. "How lovely to see you again after all these years."

"I doubted if you'd even remember me," said Daphne, ushering us through the house and onto the verandah. "It's been the hell of a long time."

Lydia greeted us next, in lime-green slacks and a pink shirt, and introduced us, in her pretty fluting voice, to their house guest, Ursula Gannet, who was wearing skin-tight black velvet pants, a black bolero coat over a white shirt, and a red scarf round her neck. Her jet-black hair was scraped back from her forehead and glinted in the lamplight like patent leather. She had a charming smile, perfect teeth, and looked like an only slightly effeminate matador. Peter and Esmond, in beige and navy blue, respectively, were presented to Eloise, and we all sat down while Loo Chung, Daphne's Chinese houseboy, handed round a tray of rum punches.

"I don't know whether you care for that sugary stuff," Daphne said to Eloise. "It's a speciality of the house and Loo Chung's pride and joy, but personally I prefer to stick to scotch."

"I'd rather have this." Eloise gave a ravishing, indiscriminate smile to everyone. "It looks divine." She took a glass from the tray, and Loo Chung gave a little hiss of pleasure.

Robin and I took one too and relaxed. Peter and Esmond fluttered round Eloise offering her cigarettes and olives and little pretzels.

"I shouldn't waste time on those," said Daphne. "There are some hot cheese things on the way. They're another of our specialities but they're stiff with garlic. I hope you don't mind garlic?"

"I adore it," said Eloise radiantly. "As long as everyone else has it."

"There's no need to worry about that in this house," cried Lydia. "We all absolutely live on it."

"They certainly do," Ursula Gannet hissed at me in a deep contralto. "I'm constantly waking up in the night and having to drink gallons of water."

"It's supposed to be very good for one," I said. "But I'm never quite sure."

"You're not a bit like I thought you'd be," she said abruptly. "The girls have talked about you a lot, but you're not at all what I imagined." She leaned close to me and stared into my face as though searching for some special birthmark by which she could identify me; her eyes, under plucked and painted black eyebrows, had an intense, amost hypnotic quality, and she'd put on a little too much Arpège.

"What on earth *did* you imagine?"

"I don't quite know, but someone more *matte*, less vibrant."

I gave a self-conscious laugh and took a swig at my rum punch. "I'm afraid I'm not feeling particularly vibrant tonight," I said.

"I've had quite a tiring day, what with one thing and another."

"It's not what you feel, it's what you are." She gave me a piercing smile. "We all of us have certain qualities, paradoxical though they may be, which lie dormant in our inner selves like coiled springs waiting to be released. Some people can sense them, some people can't, but they're there all the same, however much we try to hide them."

"I really don't think there's much in my inner self that I am trying to hide," I said. "On the contrary I'm generally accused of being too extrovert. I'm given to talking too much at the slightest encouragement, and I frequently get carried away by my own verbosity and say things which, afterwards, on sober reflection, I wish I'd kept to myself."

"I understand all that perfectly," she smiled again. "But it's not what I mean at all. What month were you born?"

"December."

"Aha!" she said triumphantly. "Sagittarius! That explains a lot. I have a feeling that we're going to be friends."

"I hope so, I'm sure. You must come over and see the house sometime. It's not nearly so attractive as this, but it has its points."

"Your husband has beautiful hands," she said, after a slight pause. "I noticed them the moment he came in. Does he play any sort of musical instrument?"

"I'm afraid not," I replied. "I believe he tried to learn the saxophone once when he was young, but that wouldn't have much to do with his hands, would it?"

At this point we were interrupted by Daphne whacking her glass down on the table. "Goddamn it!" she cried. "I'd forgotten all about the steaks. Come on, chaps, and give me a hand. You can bring your drinks with you." She picked up the carving fork from the verandah rail and disappeared down the steps to the beach. Esmond and Peter followed her, and Robin remained firmly where he was.

By this time the last glow of daylight had left the sky and the fireflies had come out.

Loo Chung emerged from the house with another tray of rum punches followed by a pretty Samolan maid bearing two covered dishes. Lydia jumped up and took one of them from her. "At last," she said. "I thought something dreadful had happened." She brought the dish over and proffered it to Eloise. "Be careful. They're probably very hot." Eloise took a small cheese tartlet and bit into it warily. "You were right about the garlic," she said gaily. "But it's absolutely divine."

We all helped ourselves and Ursula Gannet leaned across to Robin. "I've been talking to your wife," she said earnestly. "She's a rare person."

"Everyone says that when they first meet her," said Robin with his mouth full. "But they soon change their tune."

"She's the rarest person I've ever met," said Eloise, on whom the rum punches were obviously having an effect. "She's been an angel to me ever since I arrived."

Lydia turned to Robin and me. "I quite agree. We see far too little of you both. You must come over far more often."

"We'd love to." I repressed a giggle of embarrassment. I always feel ill at ease when compliments are paid me. It's not that I don't enjoy them, but they make me self-conscious. During the last quarter of an hour I had been told that I was vibrant; that I had hidden paradoxical qualities deep within me which were waiting like coiled springs to be released, and that I was a rare person and an angel. All of which, together with the very strong rum punches, was going to my head and making me feel rather flustered. Determined to edge my way out of the limelight as quickly as possible, I was racking my brains to find a change of subject that was not too arbitrary when there was a loud "halloo" from the beach and Lydia rushed to the verandah rail and yelled, "All right—all right —we're coming." She turned to Eloise. "Daphne's liable to fly into a passion if we're not on time for her precious steaks," she said. "Would anybody like to go to the loo or anything before we go down?"

Eloise said that on the whole she really thought she'd better and Lydia signalled to Ursula Gannet. "You show her the way," she said, "while I go and placate Madame Boulestin."

Ursula Gannet led Eloise into the house, and Robin and I followed Lydia down the stone steps to the beach. It looked highly romantic, with little hurricane lamps sunk in the sand and a table spread beneath a wild almond tree. Daphne and Peter and Esmond were hopping round a large barbecue grill like dervishes.

I suddenly gave way to the giggles that had been threatening me for a long time.

"Do stop for a moment," I said to Robin weakly. "I'm feeling hysterical."

Robin stopped obligingly. "Pull yourself together, old horse," he said. "We've got a long way to go yet, the evening is only just beginning."

Lydia skipped on ahead of us, and I leant against a rock and thought of sad things but they only made me laugh more. I scrabbled in my bag for a handkerchief. Robin lit a cigarette and handed it to me. I puffed at it gratefully, wiping my eyes at the same time.

"Who's the bullfighter?" he asked. "She frightened the life out of me."

"I don't know. A friend of Lydia's, I think. She told me I was vibrant."

"I expect she says that to every girl she meets."

We walked on slowly down the steps and onto the beach.

"Everybody sit where they like," shouted Daphne, who was looking flushed from standing over the grill. "There's no protocol here."

When Eloise and Ursula Gannet had reappeared and we had all finally settled ourselves I found myself between Lydia and Esmond Templar. The moon had just risen over the horizon and was making a path of golden light across the lagoon. Far out, on the reef, a few torches were flickering, which meant that the indefatigable Samolan fishermen were spearing octopus. I've done this with Robin once or twice and it's fun, but rather agitating, because I am always terrified that a moray eel might pop out of a hole in the reef and attack me, which they are liable to do when irritated. Also there's the horrid business of killing the wretched octopus when you've speared it. This I can never bring myself to do and generally hand my catch gingerly to the nearest Samolan and then turn away and stare fixedly in the opposite direction, for their method of dealing with them is swift, efficacious, and quite revolting. They seize them firmly and, regardless of their tentacles squirming and flaying about, proceed, with gleeful insouciance, to bite their eyes out. This, however, does the trick in an instant and the writhing corpse is flung into a pail and on we go. Octopus, and—or—squid, I can never quite tell the difference, are considered a great delicacy by the islanders. I have eaten it occasionally, buttered up *à la meunière* or mixed with rice in a sort of kedgeree, but never with wholehearted enjoyment on not caring for the taste of hot india rubber.

I have never, in all the years I have lived here, really reconciled myself to the standard native dishes, some of them, such as banana purée, roast breadfruit, and paupis, which are little flat cakes of *langouste* and coconut, are delicious, but the majority are disgusting. Robin often lectures me about this and accuses me of being insular and suet-pudding minded, which indeed I am, but I have noticed that whenever he is faced with anything particularly local, he invariably asks for cold ham.

The food on this evening had no outlandish overtones and was beyond praise. The steaks were perfectly cooked, and Daphne had concocted a special, rather sharp sauce to go with it which was delectable. The salad, mixed expertly by Lydia, the vegetables, breadfruit purée and fresh peas cooked in mint, the sweet, a compote of iced pineapple and bananas soaked in cherry brandy, the cheese, and the wine were all ambrosial, and I sat back at the end of it, replete, benevolent, and a trifle sleepy.

The conversation during the meal had been general and had covered a great deal of ground. Esmond and Peter had questioned Eloise eagerly about the current London theatrical season, on which subject she was not very informative, only having seen *My Fair Lady* and something at the Lyric, Hammersmith, the name of which she couldn't remember. Then there was a heated discussion about the latest best-selling sex novel from America which was called *The Lute String Breaks* and described the erotic reveries of a New England spinster who falls in love with a basset hound. This had apparently received ecstatic reviews, a critic's award, and been banned in Boston. Peter and Esmond and Ursula Gannet were the only ones at the table who had actually read it, although Lydia remembered seeing a notice of it in *The New Yorker*.

"It has dimensions," announced Ursula Gannet in an oracular tone. "And there were moments in it that moved me profoundly."

"We loathed it, didn't we, Peter?" said Esmond. "A friend of ours in New Orleans sent it to us for Christmas."

"I must say," boomed Daphne from the end of the table, "it

sounds a bit rubbishy to me. I can't see why people want to write about that sort of thing anyhow."

"That sort of thing is love." Ursula Gannet fixed her with a cold eye. "It is a brilliant analysis of the loneliness of the human heart."

"Well, we found it gruesome," said Esmond undaunted. "That sinister old woman and that poor dog!"

"The dog was merely a symbol," said Ursula Gannet crushingly.

"Symbol or no symbol it had a beastly time, you must admit."

"It isn't who you love or what you love that matters," said Ursula. "It is the *capacity* for loving that counts."

"Even so," interposed Robin, "I think I'd draw the line at basset hounds. Unless of course I happened to be a basset hound myself," he added.

"Are basset hounds those ones with little knobs instead of tails?" enquired Eloise.

"No, dear," I said. "You're thinking of corgies."

"Americans seem to go in for all that sort of thing more than we do," said Lydia. "I mean all the books they write nowadays seem to be absolutely crammed with sex."

"We are all crammed with sex, I suppose, in one way or another," said Peter. "But I don't think we go on about it quite so much as the Americans. This friend of ours in New Orleans is an absolute martyr to it. Every time he has a little boozle he gets into a terrible state and rushes off to his psychiatrist. It costs him a fortune!"

"I presume he's an invert?" enquired Ursula Gannet.

"Aren't we all?" cried Esmond, and went off into gales of laughter.

"Not quite all," I interposed mildly.

"You're getting drunk, sugar," said Peter to Esmond. "Try to remember you're in mixed company."

At this point I inadvertently caused a diversion by swallowing the wrong way and choking. Daphne sprang to her feet and advanced towards me.

"Would you like me to slap you on the back?" she asked.

"Not very much," I gasped. "I'll be all right in a minute."

"Drink some water," said Daphne.

"Eat some bread," said Lydia.

"Go on choking," said Robin. "It'll clear the air."

This sent me off into a fresh spasm which lasted convulsively for several minutes. When I had finally got control of myself and was dabbing at my streaming eyes Ursula Gannet leaned across the table to me.

"Bravo!" she whispered with a cryptic smile. "The more I know of you the more I admire you!"

I smiled back at her weakly and glanced at Robin who was gazing innocently out to sea and humming the "Toreador Song" under his breath. Fortunately at this moment· Daphne suggested that we all move onto the beach to have our coffee so that the servants could clear the table. A semicircle of chairs had been arranged on the sand a few feet above the water line. In the centre of the semicircle was a low bamboo table on which were two hurricane lamps and the coffee tray. By this time the moon was high in the sky and the shadows of the wild almond trees and coco palms were inky black on the sand. There was not a breath of wind and the candles, in their graceful glass shades, burned steadily without a flicker. The bay and the headlands and the distant mountains looked luminous against the darker sky, and in the small waves that lapped at our feet there were vivid streaks of phosphorous. I sat down next to Eloise, who was scrutinizing her face anxiously in her hand mirror, and lit a cigarette.

"You must admit," I said, "Samolo is really doing its best for you."

She smiled absently. "It's all perfectly divine," she said. "And everyone is being angelic."

I looked at her sitting beside me in the moonlight and reflected, without rancour, on the curious impartiality of nature. Why should Eloise Fowey, nee Eloise Fox-Barron, have been endowed from the outset with every conceivable physical attribute that the female heart could ever wish for? Her figure was prefectly proportioned, slim where it should be slim and plumpish where it should be plumpish: her legs were long and *racée*, her hands elegant, and her skin impeccable. The bone structure of her face was clearly designed to withstand the ravages of time indefinitely. Her lovely *cendré* hair would silver becomingly with age, her skin would wrinkle, but the indelible beauty would remain basically unimpaired until she was a hundred. I hoped, a trifle maliciously, that by then perhaps the passing of years might have enlarged her vocabulary a little, but as she was now in her late thirties or very early forties and no apparent improvement was discernible, I foresaw little chance of it. It wasn't that she was entirely a fool. There was a gleam of shrewdness occasionally in her lovely eyes and she was capable, from time to time, of saying quite amusing things, but this, I realized, was largely a question of acquired jargon. Her humour, what there was of it, was imitative rather than inherent. She had moved among people for so long who talked and joked in a particular way that she had assimilated, with neither thought nor intention, their special clichés, exaggerations, and verbal idiosyncrasies. I wondered, if Bunny should eventually be foolish enough to marry her, how long it would take him to discover this, how long his alert and questing mind would remain subjugated by his physical desire for her? There was no knowing of course. Throughout the history of the world highly intelligent men had been enslaved far longer than they should have been by beautiful but silly women. There was Nelson and Emma Hamilton, Napoleon and Josephine, Bothwell and Mary Stuart, although of course that packed up fairly quickly. I discarded Antony and Cleopatra from my list because nobody could describe Cleopatra as silly. She was a "lass unparalleled" and sharper than her own needle. I also discounted Pelléas and Mélisande on the ground of their being fictional, although for sheer unadulterated silliness poor Mélisande undoubtedly took the prize. Compared with her, Eloise automatically became Germaine de Staël and Madame Curie rolled into one.

Ursula Gannet came up to me and handed me a cup of coffee.

"You are looking pensive," she said. "I wonder what you are thinking about?"

"Beautiful women," I said, and wished immediately that I hadn't.

She handed me the sugar bowl like an accolade, and I helped myself nervously to two lumps. "You and I must have a long talk one of these days." She flashed me a secret smile and moved away.

"That one gives me the creeps," said Eloise. "She has such a funny way of looking at you. Where do you think she comes from?"

"I believe she has a cottage in Kent."

"There are lots of them in Kent," she gave a little laugh. "I spent a weekend with Marjorie Pratt at Lyminge a short while ago and she took me to the local races and my dear the paddock was full of them, stamping about in corduroys and slapping each other on the back. Marjorie was terribly funny about it—you know Marjorie, don't you?"

"No, I'm afraid I don't."

"She's an angel. You really must meet when you come back to England. You'd get on like a house on fire. She was the one who rushed off to Venice with Bogey Pickard a few years ago, and there was all that fuss in the papers. Droopy doesn't approve of her because she teases him unmercifully and is inclined to get a bit fried after dinner."

"She sounds charming," I said mechanically, noting that it was the first time she had mentioned the deserted duke since her arrival on the island. "How is Droopy, by the way?"

She gave a little *moue* and shrugged her shoulders. "The same as usual," she said with a sigh. "That's the trouble with the poor angel, he's always the same as usual."

"What did he say when you told him you were coming all the way out here to stay with me?"

"Nothing much." She stared vaguely at the sea. "He never does say anything much about anything."

"He had no suspicion that it was really Bunny that you were coming to see?"

"Oh no. He'd never suspect anything in a thousand years."

"Is he still in love with you?"

Eloise gave a small frown. "Madly," she said. "But don't let's go on about it, because it makes me feel beastly."

"Have you made up your mind what you're going to do—eventually I mean?"

"No." She stirred her coffee and assumed a slightly sulky expression. "Bunny and I did start to talk about it the other night, but only sort of vaguely because you see we hadn't seen each other for a long time and it somehow didn't seem the right moment to begin plotting and planning. Also he had that fever although we didn't know it at the time, and he wasn't making much sense."

"It's all been most unfortunate," I said sympathetically.

"Yes—it has, hasn't it?" She lapsed into silence. "I don't know what I'd have done without you and Robin, you've been——"

I leant over and gripped her hand firmly. "Don't . . ." I said. "Please don't. I know perfectly well what we've been. We've been absolute angels."

She looked surprised. "That's exactly what I was going to say."

"I know it was. But don't say it because it really isn't true. All we've done is to behave normally in rather unexpected circumstances. Anyone else would have done the same."

"No, they wouldn't," she said. "You've been angels and it's no use pretending you haven't."

At this moment Ursula Gannet passed by carrying a cup of coffee to Robin. I withdrew my hand guiltily from Eloise's, but it was too late. She noted my furtive gesture with a slight lift of her painted eyebrows and shot me a look of such intensity that I dropped my coffee spoon onto the sand.

When I had retrieved it and she had moved away I started to laugh.

"What's the matter?" enquired Eloise.

"Nothing really. Just the wine and the lights and the music."

"But there isn't any music."

"There is if you can only hear it," I said a trifle wildly. "There's the music of the spheres to start with. Then there's the pounding of the surf on the reef and the tree frogs and the cicadas to say nothing of the high-pitched twanging of everyone's emotions."

"You simply must meet Marjorie Pratt," said Eloise. "She'd adore the way you put things."

Daphne left the coffee tray and came and sat cross-legged at our feet.

"Who's for a whizz round the bay in the Chris-Craft?" she said. "Just to blow the wine leaves out of our hair."

"Shouldn't we get rather wet?" Eloise looked doubtful.

"You'll be dry as a bone in the front seat and the sea's as flat as a pancake."

"Oh, Daphne, not *now*," cried Lydia petulantly. "For heaven's sake let's digest our dinner and relax."

"*You* needn't come if you don't want to." There was a dangerous note of irritation in Daphne's voice. "I was asking Eloise and Grizel."

"I think I'd rather stay where I am for the moment," I said. "I'm feeling overfed and rather somnolent."

Daphne placed her hand on Eloise's knee and looked up at her appealingly.

"Do come," she pleaded. "Just for ten minutes."

"All right." Eloise got up reluctantly. "But I'll have to put something round my hair."

"Bully for you!" cried Daphne, leaping to her feet and shaking the sand off her slacks with the violence of a sheep dog emerging from a pond. "You can have my scarf." She seized Eloise's hand and led her away along the beach towards the jetty. I noticed out of the corner of my eye that Ursula Gannet was casting a determined look at the vacant chair beside me, and so I hurriedly beckoned to Peter Glades, who moved over and sat down before she had time to get to it.

"What news of the water pageant?" I asked.

"Chaos at the moment." He giggled. "Kerry Stirling has already written yards and yards of the blankest possible verse and Inky Blumenthal, who's been clamped to that tinny old Bechstein of his for days, says it's all in the wrong rhythms for the background music he's writing. Apparently they had a terrible scene about it at Alma's on Sunday night and Inky slammed out of the house in a fury. But since then Alma and Ivy have been pouring gallons of oil in all directions and there was a grand reconciliation and now they're working away together as cosily as Rodgers and Hammerstein. I doubt if it will last, and personally I've never thought that Kerry was the right choice. The fact that he's written a few rather amateurish 'whodunits' and that dreary history of Samolo that nobody's ever been able to get through doesn't really qualify him for writing verse. Pico Whittaker would have done it much better. At least he's young and has modern ideas, and he is a genuine poet."

"There I really can't agree," I said. "Pico's a nice boy and I'm quite fond of him, but I've never been able to understand a word he writes. You must admit that those little snippery poems he contributes to *The Reaper* without any capital letters and with no scansion are completely incomprehensible."

"They're full of atmosphere."

"Atmosphere's not enough. You're quite right about his being young, and he may turn out to be a genuine poet in time, but at the moment it seems to me that he's absorbed too much of the moderns and not enough of the ancients."

"Good old Wordsworth, I suppose?" There was a note of contempt in Peter's voice.

"Certainly good old Wordsworth, and good old Keats and Shelley and Milton and Pope and Shakespeare while he's about it."

"You're a dear old-fashioned thing," said Peter. "But Time is marching on, you know!"

"That's one of the sillier catch phrases of our slogan-ridden era. We have no guarantee whatever that Time is marching on. For all we know it may be standing stock-still. Indeed there are many highly trained scientific minds that claim that it is actually going backwards. None of which"—I added—"has anything to do with who should write the water pageant."

Peter gave a bray of laughter. "You really are wonderful when you get going. I could listen to you talking for hours."

"So apparently could Marjorie Pratt."

"Who on earth's Marjorie Pratt?"

"I don't know her personally, but she ran off to Venice with Bogey Pickard and is inclined to get fried after dinner."

At this moment the quiet of the night was shattered by a loud roar as the Chris-Craft shot away from the jetty and headed out into the bay leaving behind it a wake of phosphorescent foam. Within only a few seconds it became a black speck in the path of the moon.

"My! My! That poor duchess!" said Peter. "She won't have a bone left in her body. Daphne once took Esmond and me to Noonaeo and back in that frightening little boat and we couldn't move out of bed for three days afterwards."

"She's offered to lend it to us for the water pageant."

He looked at me aghast. "What on earth could we do with it?"

"I don't know. It might come in handy at the end to epitomize the brave new world when the Royal Shropshires are tramping up and down on the beach and the church choir is belting out 'Land of Hope and Glory.'"

"My dear, it would be *too* distracting. It makes such a ghastly noise."

"So does the church choir."

Esmond wandered up and sat on the sand at our feet. "What are you two giggling about?"

"The water pageant."

"Don't!" Esmond gave a shudder. "That bloody water pageant is going to drive us all round the bend."

"You were madly enthusiastic about it at the committee meeting."

"Well, I'm not any more. Alma keeps on ringing us up at all hours of the day and night with new ideas. The last one was that poor Keela should suddenly appear out of the sea stark naked as the Spirit of the Island."

"Not quite stark naked," said Peter. "The essentials would be suitably veiled."

"I think it's a splendid idea. He's got a body like a Greek god. But I don't quite see how he could stay down long enough to pop up at the right moment."

"An Aqua Lung," said Esmond. "Alma's got it all figured out. He's to lie doggo under that rock that juts out to the right of the cove and shoot up to the surface when he gets his cue."

"How will he possibly know when it *is* his cue?"

"We haven't actually gone into that."

"What does Keela himself think about it?"

"Oh, he's quite willing. You know how sweet and obliging he always is, and of course, being a skindiver, he's mad about the Aqua Lung part of it."

"I don't quite envisage the Spirit of Samolo appearing in an Aqua Lung."

"Oh, he's going to discard that just before he shoots to the surface. The only thing that's really worrying him is the idea of being practically naked in front of the Queen."

"I'm sure she wouldn't mind about that," I said. "She's well used to watching war dances, and tribal dances, and curious native junketings all over the globe. I should think just one nude Samolan would be a positive relief to her after all those gibbering aborigines."

At this moment Loo Chung appeared staggering under the weight of an enormous drink tray which he placed carefully on the coffee table. Robin, who had been trapped into a deep heart-to-heart conversation with Ursula Gannet, sprang eagerly to his feet. "Let me deal with this, Lydia," he said. "Who wants what?" Everybody wanted something different and in the ensuing babel I shot a glance at Lydia, who was lying back staring out to sea with some intensity. I noticed that her fingers were drumming nervously on the arm of her chair. Peter followed my glance and noticed it too.

"Oh dear!" he said softly. "If Daphne doesn't bring that glamorous duchess back soon, the evening may end in tears."

Robin brought me over a mild whisky and soda, glanced furtively at his watch when he had handed it to me, and raised his eyebrows questioningly.

"I know," I said with a sigh. "But we can't possibly leave yet, can we?" Robin sighed too and moved away.

"Have you known her long? The duchess I mean," asked Esmond.

"Oh yes, for years and years, ever since the beginning of the war."

"She certainly is ravishing." He gave a little chuckle. "I must say it is hard luck on her Bunny Colville having chicken pox."

"Why on earth should it be?" I sipped my whisky and soda with what I hoped was disarming nonchalance.

"They're *mad* about each other. Didn't you *know*?" Esmond looked at me with genuine surprise.

"I certainly didn't," I said rather sharply. "And what's more I never listen to idle gossip."

"It isn't idle gossip, it's true. It's been going on for ages. They were in Capri together last August. Angus and Ian were there at the same time and wrote and told us all about it. Cooing away like turtledoves, they were, all over the Piazza."

"I don't know who Angus and Ian are, but they ought to be ashamed of themselves for spreading malicious slander."

"Angus and Ian couldn't be nicer and you'd adore them if you knew them, they're just your cup of tea," said Esmond, obviously unmoved by my disapproving tone. "They've been together now for fifteen years and it doesn't seem a day too much. They've got a divine villa in Florence filled with the most fabulous cinquecento."

"Then they should stay in it and not go wandering about making mischief."

"Hoity-toity!" Esmond laughed. "Some of us *are* getting crotchety, aren't we?"

"I'm not in the least crotchety."

"Oh yes you are," he said gleefully. "You're thoroughly on the defensive which proves that you know all and are determined to conceal it."

"It doesn't prove anything of the sort. I'm certainly on the defensive because I despise scandal-mongering. And if you and Peter spread this idiotic nonsense about Eloise and Bunny all over the island I shall never speak to either of you again."

"Darling Grizel——" He patted my knee affectionately. "It's no use taking up that governessy attitude with me. The damage is already done, and it was nothing to do with Peter and me either. Old Mother Innes-Glendower heard about it from her sister in Ennismore Gardens. Maisie Coffrington and Michael got it from Lulu Bailey, who runs a sinister little restaurant in Davies Street and knows everything about everybody. The only thing that surprises me is that it hasn't been announced over the Pendarla radio."

"I find all this very boring." I spoke with an aloofness that I was far from feeling. "And I really don't wish to discuss the matter any further."

Esmond gave a crow of laughter and sprang to his feet. "Cowardy Cowardy Custard!" he said. "Let's have another little drinkie." He took my glass from my hand and went over to the drink table leaving me in a state of quivering exasperation, with myself in particular, with Bunny and Eloise, and with the world in general. I longed to get at Robin, but he had got himself into a group with Peter, Lydia, and Ursula Gannet. I had been a double-dyed, gullible ass to have imagined for one moment that anyone as flamboyant as Eloise could conduct an extramarital love affair without a lot of people being aware of it. I had realized from the outset that it was a fairly open secret in London, but what I had not bargained for was that the news should have penetrated so swiftly to our own faraway colony. I cursed myself for this ostrichlike obtuseness and wished ardently that Eloise was at the bottom of the sea. With any luck, I reflected grimly, she well might be by now, but at this moment my hopes were dashed by the distant roar of the Chris-Craft coming round the headland.

"Here come those naughty runaways," said Esmond, returning with my drink. "I think the moment has come for us to put out our cigarettes and fasten our seat belts."

The conversation of the others died away, and we all watched in silence while Daphne, with admirable nautical skill, brought the speedboat alongside the jetty, sprang out of it with a rope and made it fast, and then, with the old-world gallantry of an eighteenth-century admiral, helped Eloise to alight. Lydia jumped up and strode off along the beach to meet them. A flurry of general conversation broke out again, but this time my ear detected a nervous strain underlying it.

Lydia, Daphne, and Eloise met and stopped at the foot of the steps leading down from the jetty. They were too far away for us to hear what they were saying, and we all made a valiant pretence of not trying to. They stayed there for what seemed like ages, and at one moment Lydia's voice, which is naturally high-pitched, rang out rather shrilly.

"That's Nana's bark when she smells danger," whispered Esmond.

Presently we saw Eloise detach herself from Daphne and Lydia and come slowly towards us untying a scarf from her hair. She sank gratefully into the chair that Robin pulled forward for her and looked at us all with a celestial smile.

"That was sheer heaven," she said. "It was a little bumpy when we got out beyond the reef, but I adored every minute of it."

"Have a whisky and soda," said Robin. "I should think you could do with it."

"I'd adore it," said Eloise. "One does get the teeniest bit chilly going so very fast in the middle of the night."

While Robin was mixing her drink Daphne came up, followed a few paces behind by Lydia. "Lydia says I've been damned rude and neglected all my guests," she said gruffly. "If that's the case I can only say I'm bloody sorry."

We all made appropriate sounds of denial and said that it didn't matter a bit and that we'd had a lovely time. Lydia flung herself into a chair and lit a cigarette with a shaking hand. She was obviously in a towering rage.

"I only said that if you intended to stay out for half the night,

you might at least have warned us beforehand." She gave a petulant little sniff.

"That's not all you said by any means," replied Daphne. "And
you damned well know it."

"It was really my fault that we were away so long," said Eloise
conciliatingly. "It was so divine out there with the moonlight and
everything, and I wanted to go on round the next headland, the
one beyond this one, and see the lights of the town."

"You must be black and blue," said Peter.

"Oh, we didn't go fast *all* the time," replied Eloise, unwisely, I
thought. "At one moment Daphne switched off the engine entirely,
and we just sat there in silence gazing up at the stars."

"Highly romantic!" said Lydia with an unpleasant little laugh.

Robin handed Eloise a whisky and soda and turned to Daphne.
"Can I mix you a drink?" he asked with a cheerful smile.

"You certainly can," said Daphne ominously. "And a stiff one at
that."

"I shouldn't if I were you." Lydia laughed again. "You had a lot
of wine at dinner, and you know it never suits you to mix alcohol
with the grape."

"I know what suits me and what doesn't suit me without any
advice from you, so you can just shut up, can't you!"

"There's no need to lose your temper."

"I apologize for Lydia," said Daphne to Eloise. "She loves making scenes over nothing."

"I'm sure I don't know what everybody's going on about," said
Eloise.

"Why don't we all move up to the house?" suggested Ursula
Gannet.

I rose to my feet hurriedly. "I'm afraid we must be going now
in any case," I said, shooting Robin a warning look. "Finish up
your drink, Eloise, it really is getting terribly late."

"For God's sake stay a little longer," said Daphne, taking a
heavy gulp of the drink Robin had handed her. "The night is
young."

"It may be," I said. "But I'm not, and I have a heavy morning
tomorrow. We've got a committee meeting, haven't we, Peter?"

"Eleven o'clock on the dot," said Peter.

Eloise finished her drink and rose gracefully to her feet. "Thank you for a perfectly divine evening," she said, taking Daphne's hand. "You've been an angel—you've both been angels." She included the smouldering Lydia in her all-embracing smile.

I shook hands politely with Ursula Gannet. "It's been lovely meeting you," I said. "And you really must get Daphne and Lydia to bring you over to see us one day."

"When I come to see you I shall come alone," she said intensely.

"In that case I shall have to send you a little map. It's rather difficult to find, once you have turned off the main road."

"Thank you for everything," she said. "And above all for being You." She turned away from me and walked slowly and majestically down to the edge of the sea. At this moment Daphne, who had swiftly drained her drink, exploded like a bomb. "Goddamn it!" she cried, advancing menacingly towards the still recumbent Lydia. "You've ruined the whole evening like you always do. And I'll tell you here and now I'm fed up with it."

"*I've* ruined the whole evening!" Lydia bridled. "I like that, I *must* say."

Daphne, breathing heavily, moved up to Lydia with the obvious intention of striking her, at which moment, Esmond, with laudable presence of mind, sprang forward and flung his arms round her.

"Now now now . . . !" he said, struggling with her. "We don't want any more of this nonsense. Remember what happened last time."

"Leave me alone and mind your own business." Daphne pushed him away from her with such force that he almost fell down. "I'm damned if I'm going to be dictated to in my own house!"

Lydia jumped up. "And I'm not going to be insulted and humiliated in your house or anyone else's. You're making a disgusting scene again and you ought to be ashamed of yourself."

"You started it, dear," said Peter. "You know you did. Fair's fair. You've been teasing Daphne like a naughty little mosquito for hours. Now come along and kiss and be friends for heaven's sake. It's terribly late and we've all got to go home." He turned to Daphne. "Please, darling—you really must stop getting so very cross so very quickly, it's *so* bad for your metabolism."

Lydia chose this moment to burst into floods of tears. "This is always happening," she sobbed. "And I can't bear it any more, I just can't." With this she turned, ran up the steps still weeping audibly, and disappeared into the house.

After a moment or two of embarrassed indecision Robin, Eloise, and I followed her silently, leaving Peter and Esmond to deal with Daphne. Ursula Gannet was still standing majestically at the water's edge gazing out to sea.

"Well!" said Eloise, when we had got into the car and were driving away. "That was all very peculiar, wasn't it?"

"The trouble with girls-who-would-be-boys," said Robin, "is that they so seldom behave like gentlemen."

SIXTEEN

The next ten days, between the Fisherman's Hole dinner party and Eloise's visit to Government House, passed without particular incident, but for Robin and me they were exhausting in the extreme. Eloise gave two press interviews, one to Mr. Seekala for *The Reaper* and the other to a dreary half-breed lady for the *Evening Argus*, which is the opposition paper. She was also photographed, smiling radiantly, all over the house and garden, which thrilled the children and fused the entire lighting system for three hours. The interviews and photographs duly appeared and were, fortunately, innocuous. Mr. Seekala, palpably infatuated, went too far with the superlatives and bogged himself down in a sea of exuberant metaphors. The lady from the *Argus*, although forced by the policy of her paper to make a few disparaging remarks about the "idle rich" and the "decadent aristocracy," was obviously almost as much a pushover as Mr. Seekala. So indeed, it seemed, was everybody else. In duty bound we took Eloise out practically every night: to Kelly's Tavern, where Juanita was enchanted with her and showered us with champagne and caviar: to Buddha and Dusty's: to Bimbo and Lucy's: to old Mrs. Innes-Glendower, who gave a dinner party for twenty people in her honour: and last, but by no means least, to an excruciating "gala" at the Royal Samolan where dear Siggy Rubia greeted us on a red carpet and presented Eloise with an address of welcome and a vast bouquet of lilies, after which we were forced to sit through a deafening Samolan cabaret which lasted until two in the morning. Eloise sailed through all this effortlessly and triumphantly and, within a very short space of time, became the toast of the island. Poor Bunny, whom I visited whenever I had time, read of all these social junketings in *The Reaper* and became increasingly gloomier and gloomier. His temperature was normal, but he was not allowed to swim or lie in the sun and he was still a really horrible sight to look at, and still determined that Eloise shouldn't see him until his spots had vanished. They talked to each other on the telephone from time to time, but as I had made them both swear to be discreet and only discuss general topics, these conversations were not a great comfort to either of them.

Meanwhile the water pageant was lumbering heavily towards its first rehearsal. Kerry Stirling had finished the libretto, which he read to us at a special meeting convened for that purpose. It was received with only moderate enthusiasm by the committee with the exception of Alma, who appeared to be wholeheartedly delighted with it. Personally I thought it banal in the extreme, but as the only constructive suggestion I could think of was that it should be rewritten from beginning to end and by somebody else, I thought it wiser to keep my mouth shut. Time was running out and the royal visit would be on us in just over three weeks, so the only possible course was to press on and hope that the beauty of the setting and the historical glamour of the occasion would compensate for the mediocrity of the actual writing. There was also the hope that Inky Blumenthal, who had sat silently despondent throughout the reading, might save the situation by composing some genuinely attractive music. He had apparently completed nearly three quarters of the score, but we were none of us to be allowed to hear it until the last note was written. Having heard some of Inky's compositions at various local entertainments over the years, I was not too sanguine about this. He had a genuine gift for melody but at the same time a sort of pseudointellectual distrust of it, so that just when you thought you were embarked on a nice mounting flight of sound there would be a sudden, self-conscious dissonance which shattered the tune and took it wandering off in a totally different direction. I make no claims to musical knowledge and my appreciation is only one cut above liking "something that I can hum," but in these particular circumstances I felt strongly that what we should need would be dramatic, sweeping melody and as few harmonic tricks as possible. Whether or not Inky was willing or capable enough to supply it remained be seen, or rather heard, and this we would none of us be able to judge until nearly the last moment when it was orchestrated and played by the Royal Shropshire's band.

I duly reported all this to Sandra on the evening of the Innes-Glendower party for Eloise. We had wandered off into the garden together after dinner when the rest of the women were on the verandah and the men were still in the dining room.

"If you felt as strongly as all that about it why on earth didn't you say something? It's no use being on a committee and just *sitting* there."

"What could I have said that would have been of the faintest constructive value?"

"Exactly what you said to me just now; that the whole thing was dull as ditchwater and should be rewritten from start to finish."

"There isn't *time* for it to be rewritten from start to finish. Not only that but there isn't anyone to do it."

"You have absolutely no moral courage," said Sandra. "That's what's the matter with you. You allow yourself to be intimidated and overruled by everybody you meet."

"That's unfair and you know it," I replied with heat. "I can be as brave as a lion if called upon, but I wasn't called upon, I'm never called upon to open my mouth at those idiotic meetings. They all know perfectly well that I'm only there because you insisted. Also amateur theatricals are not my dish and they never were."

"You were wonderful as Lady Macduff. I haven't laughed so much for years."

"I only played Lady Macduff at the last minute because Jane Yalding was carted away to the hospital with appendicitis at the dress rehearsal. I wasn't as funny as all that anyhow."

"It was the scene with the boy that really set me off," went on Sandra reminiscently. "You looked so awfully *cross!*"

"I was. I was also petrified."

"Then you shouldn't have done it in the first place."

"There was nobody else available. Alma implored me to do it."

"There you are, you see. Overruled and intimidated as usual."

"Have it your own way," I said. "I'm a spineless mollusk. And the next time you ask me to act as an underhand, Government House spy on a committee, you know what my answer will be."

"Of course I do," said Sandra patting my arm affectionately. "It will be 'yes.'"

I accepted the pat with a small sigh of resignation because I knew beyond the shadow of a doubt that she was dead right, at least insofar as she was concerned. Sandra, to me, had more imperishable charm in her little finger than all the lovely Eloises of the world lumped together. She was one of those rare women who could exercise authority without seeming to do so; who could gaily exact allegiance, devotion, and service from her friends without appearing to be in the least demanding or tiresome. She was a benevolent autocrat and had been, I suspected, from her babyhood. I knew also that at any moment of personal crisis or tribulation she would be the first I would turn to. We started to saunter back to the house.

"You seem a little pensive," she said. "What are you thinking about?"

"You," I replied. "And the shameless way you use people."

"Nonsense! You're just as bad as I am. What about you foisting Eloise off on me for three whole days and nights? If that's not 'using' people I should like to know what is."

"It won't be so bad as you think. She's quite well disposed and hardly any trouble." I laughed. "Of course since she's become the belle of the ball you'll find Government House inundated with followers, but after all that's what it's there for, isn't it? In any case in her position it is only correct and proper that she should stay with you."

"I don't see why Government House should be considered an official refuge for adulterous duchesses. If she'd arrived here respectably, accompanied by poor Droopy, it would be quite a different matter. I should have invited them to stay as a matter of course. But as she's come beetling out all this way with the sole object of rolling about in the arms of her paramour I think it's exceedingly improper for me to offer her so much as a tomato juice. And if it hadn't been for you bullying me I shouldn't have."

"The trouble with you," I said, "is that you're too easily overruled and intimidated. You should put your foot down and display a little more moral rectitude."

"You win," said Sandra. "But it was a tawdry little victory."

We walked up the verandah steps and joined the others.

Two days after this conversation Eloise moved into Government House and my own house became, briefly, normal again. The first morning after her departure was blissfully routine and ordinary. The children chattered away at breakfast and made no effort to show off, which they had been given to doing of late in order to impress Eloise. Nanny's conversation was pleasantly muted and mercifully free from inaccurate gossip about the International Set with which she had recently been regaling us, and the telephone, from eight o'clock until lunchtime, only rang once, and that was only Lucy Chalmers inviting the children to a beach picnic on the following Sunday. Robin and I lunched peacefully alone together. In the afternoon I had my hair done at the Royal Samolan because Robin and I were dining at G.H. in the evening and it looked—my hair, I mean—as though I had been living in a wet cave for three weeks. I then went to Madame Alice's in King Street for a fitting, having recklessly ordered three new dresses in honour of the royal visit. Madame Alice is the most unabashed pseudonym I ever encountered. She is a full-blooded Samolan, born and bred, and has never got nearer to France than the far-thermost tip of Bakhua Point. Her real name is Lalua Nalikowa, which means "Flower of the Valley." However, pseudonym or no pseudonym, she is smart as a whip and is an expert needlewoman. She is also an unscrupulous copier, and all the lush fashion maga-zines from Paris and New York arrive at her shop weeks before anyone else on the island has a chance to see them. I will not go on about the dresses I was having made because there is nothing duller than reading about what someone is wearing thousands of miles away, particularly when you haven't the faintest idea what that someone looks like. Suffice to say that two of them, one for the royal arrival and one for the garden party, were Balmain (*soi-disant*) and the evening one was pure Balenciaga (also *soi-disant*). After my fitting, which was hot and exhausting as fittings always are, I drove quietly home and slept soundly for an hour. Robin and I had a cocktail by ourselves on the back verandah and watched the fireflies and the early stars, then we went, rather re-luctantly, to Government House. We arrived early and found Eloise sitting with Chris Mortlock in the drawing room. She was wearing madonna blue and was stitching away happily at her petit point. Chris was staring at her with the besotted expression to which we had, of late, become so well accustomed. Presently Sandra and George appeared and then the rest of the guests— Maisie Coffrington, Michael Tremlett, Juanita, and an American couple whose name I didn't catch. Sandra was gay and delightful to everyone as usual and the actual dinner was, surprisingly, quite good. After it we all sat about on the terrace until it was time to go home. Altogether an agreeable and uneventful evening. Nothing embarrassing had happened, nothing significant had been said, and Robin and I drove home relaxed and sleepy after one of the first peaceful days we had had for weeks.

The next day was also happily uncomplicated. It was a banana day, and I drove down to the wharf early in the morning with Robin to watch the loading. This always enchants me, and although by now I must have seen it hundreds of times I never tire of it. To begin with it usually takes place at first light or just after when the sea is pale opal colour and the coco palms still look black against the glowing sky.

Throughout all my childhood, youth, adolescence, and early adulthood I had always regarded bananas with apathy. I remember that when I was very young I used to enjoy peeling them slowly strip by strip, but after that, disillusion. A dull fruit, yellow with brown stripes outside and pale and dry and stuffy within. If anyone had told me in those early days that in my later years bananas would become an integral part of my life I should have laughed them to scorn. But then of course we, on our lovable but rain-sodden northern island, have no conception of what a banana is really like. To us it is little more than a comical fruit, a slip-on-the-peel, Let's-all-go-down-the-Strand music hall joke. But in a far-flung outpost of Empire like Samolo, it is far from being a joke of any kind. It is of immense and awe-inspiring significance. The banana plays an important part in our destinies. If the crop is healthy and good and fetches the maximum price our spirits soar, but when some small unaccountable insect appears from nowhere and lays waste the whole plantation, or when a typhoon suddenly comes screeching across the sea and murderously flattens our whole growing world, then down we go into the depths of despair and life is absolutely beastly for quite a while until the next crop emerges from the debris, young and green and hopeful. Another thing about the despised banana in its natural habitat is that it is the most lovely colour imaginable, a vivid emerald green. It also has an obscene, inverse phallic flower of bright magenta, blue, and Schiaparelli pink which hangs upside down and is not all that difficult to paint because I have tried. At certain times of the year it is necessary to spray the whole crop with hyacinth-blue insecticide. Layers and layers of this colour against the various lush greens of the vegetation dazzle the eye and lift the heart. If I appear to be a trifle too romantic about bananas it must be remembered that my husband plants them and nurtures them and ultimately sells them, and they are therefore very important to me in more ways than one. However, even if I had nothing to do with them whatever and loathed the taste of them into the bargain, I could never resist the spectacle of them being loaded, in the early morning light, onto red painted barges, and being rowed out by handsome young Samolans to a stocky white ship standing out in the bay in the shining sun.

When the loading was over on this particular morning we drove back to breakfast. The children and Nanny had had theirs and gone off to school, and so we had the back verandah to ourselves.

Later on in the morning, when Robin had disappeared with Jock in the station wagon and I had had a more or less tranquil discussion of meals with Clementine in the kitchen and was preparing to put my feet up for a few minutes and begin the *Times* crossword, I heard the noise of a car in the drive and Bunny walked in. He looked pale and a little drawn, but his face was clear of spots. He kissed me absently on the cheek and flung himself onto the swing seat, which gave a terrible shriek.

"This thing needs oiling," he said.

"I know it does." I put down my *Times*. "And one of these days it's going to be. In the meantime it will make less noise if you stay still on it and don't bounce about."

"The whole point of a swing seat is that you can rock yourself gently to and fro on it and soothe your jangled nerves."

"You can soothe your jangled nerves in that rocker by the lamp. It's comparatively soundless."

"As a matter of fact nothing could soothe me this morning," he said. "I'm in a bloody rage."

"You've been in a bloody rage for over two weeks. It's high time you snapped out of it."

"I'd like to strangle Sandra with my bare hands!"

"Why—what on earth has Sandra done?"

"She's pompous and tiresome and far too pleased with herself. This damned royal visit must have gone to her head."

"She's none of those things, and nothing ever goes to her head, so don't be silly. Have a drink and calm down." I got up and rang the bell for Tahali.

"I'll accept a horse's neck in the spirit in which it is offered, but I can't promise to calm down." He lit a cigarette and stared moodily at the garden.

"You'd better tell me quietly what's the matter," I said, and sat down again.

"I telephoned her and asked her sweetly and civilly if I could come to dine at Government House tonight and, believe it or not, she flatly refused me!"

"Are you in the habit of ringing Sandra up and inviting yourself to meals?"

"Of course I'm not."

"Then don't you think it was a little obvious to do it now when Eloise happens to be staying there?"

"Maybe it was, but she's perfectly aware of the situation. She knows I'm in love with Eloise, and that I've had a beastly, frustrating, miserable time."

"Everybody knows you're in love with Eloise," I said grimly. "The whole island's ringing with the glorious news."

"It can't be." Bunny looked startled. "We haven't been seen together once since she arrived here."

"You forget that you've been seen together a great deal before she arrived here. You were seen mooning about Capri with her last summer by Angus and Ian."

"Who the hell are Angus and Ian?"

"They're friends of Esmond Templar's and are apparently keen letter writers. Then there's Mrs. Innes-Glendower's sister who lives in Ennismore Gardens, to say nothing of a dubious lady called Lulu something-or-other who runs a restaurant in Davies Street. They've all been at their desks scribbling away like Madame de Sévigné. In addition to which, your Cynthia, who happens to be a cousin of a friend of Tahali's who lives in the valley, has been broadcasting vivid descriptions of all those photographs of Eloise that you keep in the drawer of your desk. All of which adds up to one salient fact, which is that your love affair is about as *sub rosa* as the Nuremberg trials."

"I can't believe it," said Bunny. "You're making it all up."

At this moment Tahali appeared bearing a tray on which were two glasses of brandy and ginger ale. He placed the tray carefully down on the table beside me.

"I know Mr. Bunny like the horses' necks," he said with a beaming smile. "And so the moment I hear his voice and the bell ring I make them double quick." He turned to Bunny. "Mr. Bunny is gay and cheery with no more of the chicken spots?"

"Thank you, Tahali, I'm much better," said Bunny gloomily, "but there are still one or two left on my back."

"That I know already because my friend in the valley told me, but he said they were clearing well."

"That will be all for the moment, Tahali," I said, on which he bowed and went away.

"Well I'll be damned!" Bunny got up and began pacing up and down the verandah.

"Here's your drink." I handed him a glass. "Actually you can have them both because I don't want one."

He took it from me and went on with his pacing. "Who the devil is this friend in the valley?"

"I don't know, but whoever he is someone ought to give him a letter of introduction to Lord Beaverbrook. He's wasted here."

Bunny sat down again, this time in the rocking chair. "Does Sandra know that all these other people know?"

"I expect so. I haven't asked her. In any case I think you must see her point in not having you to Government House while Eloise is there. If the balloon goes up and Droopy finds out everything, which I should think he is bound to do soon, it would be very bad for Sandra to be implicated in any way. Personally I think she's been a darling to have Eloise to stay at all in the circumstances."

"Goddamn everything! I wish I were dead and at the bottom of the sea!"

"Why don't you try going down to the bottom of the sea for a little?" I suggested. "You know it always cheers you up."

"I think it's unkind of you to try to be funny when you know how wretched I am."

"I'm not trying to be funny. I mean just exactly what I say. You're quite well enough now to do a little skindiving. On with your Aqua Lung and go and have a look at a few nice barracuda. That would really be far more sensible than moping and moaning and inveighing against poor Sandra. Anyhow Eloise is coming back here tomorrow."

"I know." Bunny sipped his drink. "That's really what I came to see you about."

"How do you mean?"

"I want you to let her come to me tomorrow night."

"The whole night? Oh, Bunny—really!" I felt suddenly exasperated.

"It's no use looking cross and disapproving. I'm in love with her and I want her. That's natural enough, isn't it?"

"Yes," I replied wearily, "I suppose it is."

"Then you will let her come?"

"I've no way of preventing her if she wants to. I'm not her gaoler. But with the whole island buzzing with your illicit romance I think it's indiscreet, to say the least of it. Can't you wait a little longer?"

"If I wait a little longer I shall go mad."

"I think you've already gone mad!" I spoke sharply, aware that I was on the verge of losing my temper.

Bunny flashed me one of his charming smiles, but it was forced and unconvincing.

"I seem to have caught you in a bad mood."

"Bad moods are catching. I was perfectly cheerful until you stamped in and began sounding off against Sandra. But there is one thing that I would like to explain to you here and now and it is this. It is my considered opinion that you are making a cracking ass of yourself. Eloise may be beautiful as the day and enchanting in the bed, but she isn't your cup of tea really, and never could be, and for you seriously to consider spending the rest of your life with her is sheer idiocy. I know I shouldn't be saying all this to you and I also know that it won't have the slightest effect, but I must get it out of my system or I shall burst. I realize that everything's gone wrong for you and that you've had a frustrating, beastly time, what with the chicken pox and one thing and another, and I'm sorry about all that, of course; but I had hoped that during some of those hours when you were thrashing about in your lonely bed, covered in spots, you might have looked at the situation clearly for a moment and managed to get your emotions into the proper perspective. As you obviously haven't, I will say no more. It's none of my business, and you should never have involved me in it in the first place. Since you have, and I'm in it up to the neck, I will keep my promise and continue to help as much as I can. Eloise is coming back here after lunch tomorrow. I suggest that you come about six o'clock and fetch her. You needn't even trouble about bringing her back in the early morning; all the servants are perfectly aware of the situation and there's nobody left to deceive. I'll explain to her when she arrives that there is no need for her to unpack. I only suggest six o'clock because she might fancy a little snooze before flying eagerly into your arms. However, if she should want to go earlier I'll telephone you. If you would care for one final word of advice it's this. Give her as edible a dinner as possible. She's been wined and dined fairly luxuriously during the last weeks, and the shock of meeting Cynthia's cooking for the first time might discourage her."

"I've never known you to be really nasty before," said Bunny. "It's very disillusioning."

"I wish you'd go away now." I rose to my feet. "It's disillusioning for me too, and I feel horrid."

Bunny got up too and put his hands on my shoulders. "Forgive me," he said, rocking me gently to and fro. "I feel ashamed, honestly I do, for having let you in for all this."

"Now then—none of that . . ." I tried to wriggle away but he held me tight.

"What can I do to win you round, to get you into a better frame of mind?" he said gently. "Perhaps you'd like to see the remaining spots on my back?"

"Go away, Bunny, and leave me alone."

He let go of my shoulders, kissed me lightly on the cheek, and went into the house whistling. A moment later I heard the noise of his car starting.

At three-thirty the next afternoon when I was trying to squeeze some datura lilies into a vase that was much too small for them Eloise arrived back from Government House.

215

"How lovely it is to be home again," she said, embracing me. "I feel as if I'd been away for years."

"Did you enjoy yourself?"

"Oh yes—in a way. Sandra was awfully sweet; she's not nearly so snappy as she used to be, is she? And H.E. was an absolute angel. But still I'm glad to be back."

"I'm afraid you're not going to be back for long. Bunny is calling for you at six o'clock."

"Tonight?" She opened her eyes to their fullest extent, and I noted in their azure depths a fleeting gleam of apprehension.

"Yes. I fear he's in rather a 'Young Lochinvar' mood. You'd better unpack and then repack a small suitcase."

"What about Hali Alani's cocktail party?" Her voice was a trifle plaintive.

"I'll make excuses for you. I'll say that you are worn out after three hectic days at Government House and are going to have something on a tray in bed."

"Won't he be dreadfully upset? . . . Hali I mean?"

"Not nearly so upset as Bunny, if you renounce his longed-for, passionate reunion for a mere cocktail party."

"Yes—I suppose you're right." She sighed and a small frown puckered her forehead. "Oh dear . . ."

"Don't you *want* to go with Bunny?"

"Of course I do. I've been counting the days—but . . ."

"But what?" I asked relentlessly.

"Well, it is all rather sudden, isn't it? I mean I had no idea that Bunny would be well enough—quite so soon. Do you really think he *is* well enough?"

"He seemed hale and hearty yesterday afternoon. He still has a few spots on his back, but Tahali's friend from the valley says they're clearing up rapidly."

"Tahali's friend from the valley?" Eloise looked bewildered.

"I'll explain all that later," I said. "In the meantime I told Bunny that if you wanted to go earlier than six I'd ring him up. He's probably sitting by the telephone this very minute, biting his nails and groaning."

"You *are* in a funny mood today. You're not cross about anything, are you?"

216

"Of course not," I smiled. "I've nothing to be cross about. Do you want to go earlier or will six o'clock be all right?"

"Six o'clock will be perfect, and you're an angel!" She kissed me again absently and went into the house.

I continued my unequal struggle with the datura lilies until I at least managed to get them all into the vase. The result was not what I would have wished. They looked crushed and uneasy, and I was sadly aware that Lucy or Dusty or almost anyone I knew could have achieved a far more attractive arrangement in a quarter the time. However, they were done and that was that, and I took them firmly into the sitting room and left them there with a faint shudder.

Back on the verandah I settled myself comfortably in the planter's chair, lit a cigarette, and gave myself up to a session of sweet silent thought which was made all the sweeter for me by the remembrance of that reluctant look on Eloise's face when I told her that Bunny was coming for her at six o'clock. I had been watching her carefully ever since the debacle of the chicken pox and had observed that although at first she had, understandably, been disappointed, fretful, and even genuinely unhappy for a little, the intensive social campaign Robin and I had launched on her behalf had done a lot to revive her flagging spirits. Everyone had fussed over her and made much of her, and she had the satisfaction of knowing that she had been an unqualified success wherever she went. She was not, I was fairly certain, capable of very profound emotions, and although I was quite prepared to believe that she was as much in love with Bunny as she could be with anybody, I was willing to bet that if it came to a showdown and she was forced to make a decision one way or the other, that Bunny would be the one to be sacrificed. This, to me, was a comforting theory as far as it went, but the trouble with it was that by the time such a moment of crisis was reached, it would probably be too late. I had never met Droopy personally, but judging by all accounts he was solid, unimaginative and inclined to be pompous. I had no way of knowing whether or not he was as devoted to Eloise as she claimed he was. If he *really* had no suspicion of her affair with Bunny, which seemed inconceivable with everybody discussing it in all quarters of the globe, the shock of finding out about it suddenly might very possibly make him vindictive. In any case there was nothing further that I could do about it beyond keeping my promise to Bunny and continuing to provide a smoke screen even though I knew that sooner or later the sharp winds of gossip were likely to blow it away entirely.

At this moment the telephone rang and I went indoors to answer it. It was Sandra.

"Well, I've done my duty," she said. "And I hope you're duly grateful."

"Of course I am," I replied in a passable imitation of Eloise's voice. "And you've been an absolute angel."

"I don't ever want to hear that word again. I even found myself shuddering in church on Sunday morning. Did she get back all right?"

"Yes. About half an hour ago."

"She's not there now? With you I mean?"

"No. She's upstairs packing."

"Packing? You mean she's going away?"

"Yes, but not very far. Only seven miles."

"Oh, I *see!*" Sandra chuckled. "Tell her from me not to forget her petit point. It came in very handy here."

"How did the visit go off on the whole?"

"Not bad. Better than I expected actually. Chris went down like a ninepin of course, as I knew he would. He followed her about everywhere like a dazed red setter and kept on bringing her things. Hali came to dinner the night before last, and the effect was instantaneous. She really does know how to do it, doesn't she?"

"It's instinct more than knowledge. I don't think she really knows how to do anything."

"Nonsense. That's applied technique if ever I saw it. And of course the petit point is masterly. It gives her the opportunity to lift her eyes slowly to whoever is speaking to her, and believe me, when she lifts those great eyes slowly, the boys have had it."

"How did George react?"

"Sardonically. He's a wily old bird. But I did notice once or twice a faintly lascivious gleam in his eye."

"Robin's been all right so far, but I'm watching like a lynx."

"I must say"—Sandra went on—"she wasn't as morose as I expected her to be considering her ill-starred romance. How long is she going to be—you-know-where?"

"Only tonight. We must go on keeping up pretences."

"If I were you I should just let them get on with it. Everybody knows anyhow."

"Oh, Sandra—not *quite* everybody!"

"Enough to be going on with. Esmond Templar and Peter Glades are dining out on it. Apparently they have some dubious friends in Capri who——"

"I know all about that," I said irritably. "I also know about Mrs. Innes-Glendower's sister and Lulu Thingumajig in Davies Street."

"You needn't snap at me. I was only warning you."

"I know you were, dear, and it's very considerate of you, if a little redundant. I'm perfectly aware that I shall probably emerge from the whole business in the worst possible light and become the laughingstock of the entire island. However, it's far too late now to do anything about it. I should like to murder Esmond Templar and Peter Glades. I should also like to crack Bunny's and Eloise's heads together. But as I can do neither of these things without looking a bigger fool than I look already, the only course open to me is to press on to the bitter end and behave as though everything was clear and innocent and aboveboard."

"Bravo!" said Sandra. "Roedean forever. 'If you can keep your head when all about you are losing theirs and blaming it on you.'"

"Rudyard Kipling," I said wearily. "Born 1865. Died 1936."

"Correct. Come to lunch tomorrow and I'll comfort you with apples and stay you with flagons."

"All right. That at least will be one up on the macaroni cheese."

"*Touché*," said Sandra gaily, and rang off.

Bunny duly arrived at six o'clock on the dot looking very smooth and a trifle self-conscious. Robin mixed him a drink, and we sat about talking with rather overdone casualness until Eloise appeared carrying a small suitcase and her work bag. Bunny sprang to his feet, took them from her, and went out to put them in the car. When he came back there was some further strained conversation until, unable to bear it any more, I suggested tactfully that they had better go because Robin and I had to change for Hali Alani's cocktail party. Bunny agreed with alacrity, but I was pleased to note a slightly petulant expression on Eloise's face. Robin and I went out with them to the car and waved benevolently as they drove away into the sunset. We looked at each other rather guiltily for a moment without speaking, then Robin shrugged his shoulders.

"An expense of spirit in a waste of shame," he said, and we went silently upstairs to dress.

SEVENTEEN

Hali Alani's house is high up in the mountains not far from the Lailanu Pass. The road to it, particularly the last part, is scarifying but it's well worth it when you get there. The house, originally an old Samolan planter's cottage, was built round about 1830, and although since then it has undergone many changes and been modernized rather haphazardly it still retains a great deal of charm. It is built of Pareanda wood which Time has mellowed into a gentle, greyish-green colour, and Hali has had the good taste to leave it unpainted. The terrace, which is rough-paved and has in the centre an ancient banyan tree, the lower branches of which are festooned with small cyclamen-coloured orchids, commands one of the most spectacular views on the island. In daylight you can see as far as Noonaeo when it is clear, and several of the other islands also, lying like little clouds on the horizon. At night it is even more sensational. Far away on the left you can see the revolving light on Paiana Head flashing out regularly every few seconds over the dark sea. Directly in front of you and two thousand feet below is spread the whole twinkling panorama of the town of Pendarla, and away on the right is the wide crescent sweep of Narouchi Beach backed by the descending range of the Lailanu Mountains which end in the gaunt cliffs of Pounakoyia. Behind the house is a rambling garden sloping upwards to a higher terrace, on which there is a dramatic, palm-fringed swimming pool fed by a waterfall.

Robin and I left the car at the lower end of the drive and walked through a pimento grove up some stone steps onto the terrace. Hali, wearing a scarlet sarong, a white silk shirt, and a multi-coloured scarf, came forward to meet us. He took us both by the arm and led us up to Sandra and George, who were standing under the banyan tree sipping Kala-Kala fizzes. This flustered me because I knew I should have to tell my prepared lie about Eloise with Sandra listening gleefully to every word. However, I pulled myself together and took the plunge. I couldn't very well say what I had originally intended to say about Eloise being exhausted by her three hectic days at Government House, so I floundered about and ended up with a not very convincing story of her suddenly developing a violent "migraine" and having to take to her bed.

"How very strange!" said Sandra wickedly when I had finished. "She was as merry as a grig at lunch."

I shot her a baleful look. "Well, she certainly isn't now. She's lying flat on her back, exhausted."

"Already?" Sandra looked me straight in the eye and giggled.

"What, please, is a 'grig'?" asked Hali, masking his obvious disappointment with a charming smile.

"I'm never quite sure," said Sandra. "It's either a small eel or a grasshopper. I'll look it up in *Chambers* and let you know."

"It is truly sad that the duchess should be in her bed," said Hali. "I was heartily looking forward to welcoming her to my humble dwelling."

"As dwellings go," said Sandra, "I must say I've seen humbler."

Hali laughed. "Lady A. is mocking at my bad English, and when she does that it makes me delighted because I know that she is in a tiptop cheery mood."

"Dear Hali." Sandra gave his arm an affectionate little pat. "I love your bad English, we all do, although I am not at all sure that you don't rehearse it painstakingly every morning."

"My father is forever chiding me about it, but then for him it is easy because he had the privilege of attending Eton school and Oxford college."

"That's more than I ever did," said H.E. "I was educated at the Huddersfield Grammar School."

"Now then, darling, none of that," said Sandra. "We know you're a man-of-the-people. But you really mustn't keep on about it, because it sounds so snobbish."

"I could never in my most wild dreams accuse His Excellency of the snobbery," said Hali. "He is the most free and easy of good fellows."

"Nonsense," said Sandra. "He's an absolute rouser—aren't you, darling?" She slipped her arm through H.E.'s and laughed. "But it's the inverse sort. Actually I'm quite convinced that in his deep heart he thinks he married beneath him."

"I don't think it," said H.E. dryly. "I know it."

When Sir George Shotter first arrived in Samolo there had been a good deal of muttering and head-shaking. His predecessor, Sir Hilary Blaise, had been, outwardly at least, all that a colonial governor should be. Aristocratic, distinguished-looking, and true-blue conversative to the core, he had moved with stately dignity through his term of office looking steadfastly to the right and so completely ignoring the left that Buddha had once irreverently remarked that he must be suffering from a chronic stiff neck. This Edwardian aloofness from the changing values of a changing world, although picturesque, had masked an administrative ineffectiveness which, in a less easy going and more politically minded colony than Samolo, might have been disastrous. Sir George was another cup of tea entirely. He was known to have been an ardent socialist during his early political years, in addition to which there was no getting away from the fact that he was the son of a grocer in Huddersfield. True, this inadvertent social error had been mitigated to a certain degree by his having married a duke's daughter, but even so his appointment was viewed with grave suspicion by the Ra stone, old Sir Albert, Mrs. Innes-Glendower, and various other island die-hards.

His first startling innovation was a complete reversal of Government House policy with regard to the Samolans themselves. Under the Blaise regime even the most prominent native citizens were seldom invited to Government House except on special official occasions such as the King's birthday garden party and the state reception following the opening of Parliament. Actually it was Sandra who delivered the first body blow to established precedent. Only a few days after her arrival, even before she had had time to change the loose covers in the drawing room, she gave an informal cocktail party to all the wives of the Legislative Committee and the House of Representatives plus the wives of the more eminent tradesmen in Pendarla and the leading lights of the Women's Federation. This free-for-all at which I duly assisted was a sensational success and was proudly referred to for months afterwards as "The Hen Scoop."

From then on, from the point of view of the die-hards, things went from bad to worse. No longer could Government House be regarded as a cosy stronghold of upper middle-class chauvinism. The doors were wide open and the barriers down. And when it was announced in *The Reaper* that His Excellency the Governor and Lady Alexandra had attended a Sunday night buffet supper at the house of Koga Swalu, the head of the Samolan Socialist National Party and leader of the opposition, it was considered to be the beginning of the end. Exactly what it was supposed to be the beginning of the end of was never clearly specified; however, after a few months, during which the popularity of George and Sandra steadily increased both socially and politically, the prophecies of doom gradually died away and even the dark forebodings of old Sir Albert and Mrs. Innes-Glendower were finally silenced.

On looking over the guests Hali had invited I realized how far we had progressed since the old "Blaise" regime. In those days such a casual, mixed bag would have been unthinkable. In the first place Sir Hilary and Lady B., even if they had consented to be present at all, which in itself was unlikely, would have been dressed to the nines and carefully protected from any intimate contact with the common herd by a comptroller and at least two A.D.C.s. In the second place they would have stood rooted to one spot waiting for various people to be led up to converse with them, after which they would have made a regal good-bye tour, saying a few appropriate words to everyone, and driven away in their Daimler while the assembled company stood respectfully to attention.

I observed that Hali had mixed his sheep and goats with a gay disregard of racial discrimination. There was poor Fritzi Witherspoon, who had been running the Narouchi Beach Guest House at a dead loss for several years; Sir Noka Grualugi, the retired president of the Samolan Cement Company, and his wife Ninette, who looked like an ochre-coloured marmoset after an intensive course of Elizabeth Arden beauty treatments; Lucy and Bimbo Chalmers; Alma Peacock, wearing a sort of feathered coronet which one expected to take wing at any moment and perch on one of the pimento trees; both the Fumbasi brothers, who owned the Empire Hardware Store in King Street and who, although twins, couldn't have been less alike. Kuna, the elder by seven minutes, was tall, languid and willowy, and, surprisingly, an ardent athlete; indeed he had won so many silver trophies by his prowess at tennis, cricket, football, and golf that his flat overlooking the harbour was known locally as Mappin and Webb. Nilo, the younger, was darker in colour, thick-set, robust, and a collector of Chinese jade. All they had in common visually were rows of exquisite teeth which they bared with enthusiasm when George and Sandra and Robin and I came over to join the group. We subsided into long chairs, were given long iced drinks, and the conversation was general for a little while until Ivy Poland arrived accompanied by Esmond Templar, Peter Glades, Kerry Stirling, and Inky Blumenthal; then inevitably, as soon as preliminary courtesies had been exchanged and they had been served with drinks, we found ourselves up to our necks in the water pageant.

"Ivy's had a *sensational* idea," cried Esmond. "We've been discussing it all the way here in the car."

"What is it?" enquired Alma with a suspicious note in her voice. Although the pageant had been Ivy's idea in the first place, she obviously had no intention of allowing her to become uppish.

"Go on, dear," said Peter to Ivy. "Give! I know that Alma will be just as thrilled with it as we are."

Ivy took a sip of her drink and leant forward confidentially. "It's not all that remarkable," she said with a self-deprecatory simper. "The boys are exaggerating. But I do think it might work."

"I hope that whatever it is it doesn't involve any change in the running order," said Alma. "At this stage that would be quite out of the question."

"Go ON, Ivy," said Esmond, wriggling with impatience. "The suspense is absolutely killing absolutely everybody."

"It's only a tentative suggestion," said Ivy. "But I *have* been mulling it over and over in my mind for several days. The whole production is turning out to be much larger and more ambitious than we originally intended, and I do think that we oughtn't to run the risk of letting the Queen and Prince Philip see it before we ourselves have had some idea of audience reaction. Therefore I propose that we give a sort of public dress rehearsal two nights before they arrive, so that we shall still have time to correct anything that may be wrong. I also thought"—she added, aware of Alma's glacial stare—"that if Their Excellencies would be gracious enough to attend, we could charge fairly high prices for the tickets and give the proceeds to our own fund—and believe me we are sadly in need of a little help—or perhaps divide them among some specified charities. *Do* say that you think the idea is remotely feasible!" She finished with rather a rush and looked anxiously first at George and Sandra and then at Alma, who had pursed her lips and was frowning. There was an uneasy silence for a moment during which I observed Sandra fumbling hurriedly in her bag for her handkerchief and knew that she was on the verge of giggling. When Alma finally spoke it was with the pained calm of a field marshal who has suddenly been offered some gratuitous advice on high strategy by an overeager subaltern.

"I am afraid," she said, "that the idea is *not* remotely feasible."

"Oh, *Alma!*" wailed Esmond. "Don't be so stuffy. Why ever not?"

"For the simple reason that we couldn't possibly be ready in time."

"Both Kerry and Inky think it could be done," said Peter, and turned to them appealingly. "You do, don't you?"

"As far as we are concerned, yes." Inky nodded portentously. "The orchestration may not be quite complete, but enough of them will be there to make a reasonably pleasant noise, I hope." He gave a little snigger and lapsed into silence.

"My girls are ready," cried Ivy. "They've been working away like slaves."

"Your girls are always ready," replied Alma crushingly. "But unfortunately that is not quite enough. In addition to which there are the Royal Shropshires to be considered."

"I telephoned to Colonel Shelton at lunchtime," said Ivy. "And he positively welcomed the idea. He said it would give his chaps an opportunity to get accustomed to the drill."

Alma glanced skywards for a moment as though seeking divine assistance. "I really do think, Ivy dear," she said with a dreadful smile, "that it would not only have been wiser, but more ethical, to have consulted me before discussing the matter with Colonel Shelton."

"I'm very sorry, I'm sure," said Ivy with spirit, "but if you must know I also talked to Mrs. Garinuaga about the church choir and to Finch and Faber about the construction of the grandstands and seats, and they all assured me that it would be perfectly all right as far as they were concerned."

Alma rose majestically. "It is not very polite to inflict this sort of argument on our host and his distinguished guests," she said, rallying her forces and still captain of her soul. "I suggest, therefore, that we postpone any further discussion of the matter until our next committee meeting."

"But the next committee meeting isn't until Friday," said Esmond. "And days will be wasted when we really might be getting on with everything. I really do feel, Alma dear, that you are being just a teeny bit obstructive. After all the whole thing was Ivy's idea in the first place. Personally I think we ought to put it to the vote here and now. There are enough of the committee present to make a quorum." He turned eagerly to George. "What do *you* think, sir? Please say you agree!"

"I fear," said George with a slight gleam in his eye, "that both my wife and I are unable to give an unprejudiced opinion. Technically I am forced to agree with Alma that the behaviour of Ivy, although resolute, has been highly unethical. This judgment, however, may be somewhat clouded by the realization that if your side wins, we shall be obliged to sit through the whole damned performance twice." At this, both the Fumbasi brothers and Hali Alani went off into gales of laughter. George smiled at Alma, shrugged his shoulders, and lit a cigarette. From then on the conversation degenerated into a general wrangle with everyone talking at once. Poor Alma, like an animal at bay with the acrid stench of imminent defeat in her nostrils, sat down again heavily and was immediately given a strong whisky and soda by Hali. Sandra grabbed Robin by the arm and disappeared into the shadows, and I could tell from her back that the *fou-rire* that had been threatening her for some time had finally caught up with her. At long last, after everyone had been served with fresh drinks and the general din had subsided a little, Esmond and Peter darted over and knelt, one on each side of Alma's chair, like anxious courtiers at the feet of some distraught monarch. I watched them out of the corner of my eye hissing and gesticulating. Ivy remained aloof and embarked, with tremendous social poise, on a conversation with Sir

Noka Grualugi and Ninette about the recent activities of the Women's Federation. Hali, who had been talking to Fritzi and Bimbo and Lucy, left them and came over to me.

"Sir George," he whispered confidentially, "is in my opinion the very devil of a humourous fellow. If he had not spoken with such lightness and fun my humble party might have been the scene of a wicked drama."

"I quite agree. But the danger isn't quite over." I nodded in the direction of Alma, who was listening stonily to the urgent pleadings of Esmond and Peter.

"Alma and Ivy are both splendid ladies," went on Hali. "And I admire most heartily their great works for the theatre, but I feel that beneath them there is a certain scratchiness."

I laughed. "There is indeed, and after this there will be a great deal more."

"You think it will be a beneficial thing for Her Majesty and His Royal Highness to see this water pageant?"

"I haven't the faintest idea. I only know that personally I can't wait."

"Is it true that my friend Keela Alioa will appear naked in the royal presence?"

"Not quite. He'll have an Aqua Lung, I believe."

"He is very worried and telephones to me constantly. He would rather, I think, if you could use your influence, be in a frog suit. He is after all a large fellow and fears dreadfully to expose himself. You will perhaps at the next meeting make the suggestion of the frog suit?"

"I'll do my best," I replied helplessly. "But I don't really think the Spirit of the Island should strike such a utilitarian note."

"I am not understanding what is a utilitarian note."

"Never mind, Hali. As I said before I'll do my best, but it really isn't my department."

At this moment Sandra came back with Robin. Her face looked a little ravaged, but she was quite calm.

"I feel better now," she said. "But it was ghastly while it lasted. Has the burning issue been put to the vote yet?"

"No. And I don't think it will be. The worst is over. Look." I pointed to Alma, who, accompanied on each side by Esmond and Peter, was moving with stately mien towards Ivy. The conversation in the immediate vicinity died down and there was an expectant hush. Ivy turned from Sir Noka and Ninette and met Alma face to face; her mouth was twitching a little at the side, but there was a look of defiance in her eye and it was obvious that she was prepared to fight to the death if need be.

Alma spoke gravely in a voice pregnant with resigned magnanimity. "There is no necessity to put anything to the vote, Ivy dear," she said. "Esmond and Peter have persuaded me, a little against my will, I admit, to agree to your suggestion. I think, however, that we should call an emergency committee meeting tomorrow afternoon to discuss the matter in detail. It will, I fear, entail a tremendous amount of extra work, but we must all be prepared to put our shoulders to the wheel and pull together."

Ivy, conscious of victory but not to be outdone in grace, changed her expression swiftly from defiance to humble admiration and seized both Alma's hands in hers. "I had no right to do what I did," she said. "I have been thoughtless and inconsiderate, but I would like to say here and now that the Samolan Amateur Dramatic Society would not be what it is without the inspiration and generosity of a great leader!" With this she kissed Alma firmly on both cheeks and turned away abruptly, obviously in the grip of deep emotion. Alma permitted herself a weary smile and Esmond clapped his hands ecstatically.

"Hurray!" he cried. "Little birds in their nests agree!"

Ivy tossed her head. "Really, Esmond," she said. "You are too ridiculous."

Later on, when Sandra, George, Robin, and I had said goodbyes and were strolling down through the lower garden to find our cars, Sandra slipped her arm through mine.

"You must be out of your mind to grumble about being on that committee," she said. "I envy you with every fibre of my being!"

EIGHTEEN

Át about half past eleven that same night Robin was sitting up in bed reading aloud extracts from *Time* magazine while I rubbed cold cream onto my face, wondering bleakly whether or not it was worth the effort.

"You will be interested to hear," he said, "that balding, fifty-two-year-old Kendrick Claybourn has divorced forty-year-old, vivacious ex-model Claudia Blake for mental cruelty."

"I'm more than interested. I'm appalled."

"It was his fourth marriage and her third," Robin went on. "And what is more she left the court on the arm of her eldest son by her first marriage to forty-eight-year-old Bandleader Zippy (Hi-Fi) Jackson weeping uncontrollably."

"Poor thing," I said, leaving my face for better or worse and getting into bed. "What *will* become of her?"

"You may also like to know that a seven-pound daughter has been born to ageing movie star Coop Haggerty by his fifth wife, twenty-one-year-old-ex-Warner Brothers starlet, at their home in San Bernardino Valley. Coop, the father of six sons by his former three marriages, was jubilant on hearing the news. 'I've always wanted a girl,' he said. 'And now by golly I've got one!'"

"Which just goes to prove that dogged perseverance always succeeds in the long run."

"Died," said Robin, still reading, "eighty-four-year-old, one-time Cleveland gangster Ricky (Hot Fingers) Pinolo at his luxury home in Trenton, New Jersey, of double pneumonia. His wife and family were at his bedside."

"Don't tell me any more," I said. "I shan't sleep a wink."

At this moment the telephone rang. I reached over to take up the receiver.

"Let it ring," said Robin. "Nobody who rings up at this time of night deserves an answer."

"I can't let it ring, it'll drive us mad." I lifted the receiver to my ear and said sharply, "Hallo—who is it?" Then my heart sank because it was Bunny's voice and I knew by his tone of controlled urgency that there was trouble again.

"I'm sorry if I've wakened you up," he said. "But I couldn't think of anything else to do."

"What's the matter?"

"It's Eloise. She's ill. I've just taken her temperature, and it's over a hundred and two."

"Oh, Bunny—this is too much." I suddenly felt too tired to make the effort of keeping the irritation out of my voice.

"For God's sake don't be cross. I need help."

"Has she broken out in spots yet?"

"No," he replied gloomily. "But she probably will soon. What am I to do?"

I looked hopelessly across at Robin and then answered as calmly as I could. "You'd better bring her back here at once."

"I can't," said Bunny. "My bloody battery's run down, the car won't budge. I've been trying to crank it for the last hour."

"You mean you want us to come over and fetch her?"

"I can't think of any other solution. I could ring the Royal Samolan and ask them to send a taxi, but if I did that the whole thing would be all round the island by the morning."

"It will anyhow," I said flatly. "Don't let's any of us fool ourselves."

"Please come. I really can't cope with this by myself."

I looked across at Robin again, who was making frantic signs of disapproval, and shook my head.

"It's no use," I said, covering the telephone with my hand. "One of us will have to go. Eloise is ill and Bunny's car has broken down." I spoke into the telephone again. "I'll be over as soon as I can," I said, and hung up.

Ten minutes later Robin and I, with coats on over our pyjamas and armed with three blankets and a pillow, were driving along the coast road again in the station wagon. Robin sat grimly at the wheel and curtly refused a cigarette when I offered him one. I didn't blame him for being in a bad temper, but I did wish ardently that he had let me come by myself as I wanted to instead of being chivalrous and insisting on coming with me. We drove along the dark road in heavy silence while I sorted out miserably in my mind the problems that this new development entailed. In the first place I decided to send the children away with Nanny the first thing in the morning. Even though they had all had chicken pox I couldn't possibly take the risk of them catching it again, which they might well do, with Eloise in the house blazing with it. I knew that medical science pooh-poohed the idea of anyone's having the disease twice, but I steadfastly refused to believe that anything followed the normal, logical course when it pertained to Eloise.

I did for a moment toy with the idea of us driving her straight to the Pendarla Hospital and leaving her there, but I knew for a fact that all the private rooms were full and I really hadn't the heart to deposit her ruthlessly in the quarantine ward. Overwhelmed by the irritation of the situation and on the verge of tears, I shakily lit another cigarette.

"You smoke far too much," said Robin. "You'll be suffering from nicotine poisoning the next thing we know."

"I should welcome it."

"I expect the inside of your lungs is coated with dark brown fur at this very minute."

"I can't be bothered about the inside of my lungs now. I've too many other things to think of. I wouldn't care if they were covered with bulrushes."

"Do you think she really has got chicken pox?"

"Of course. What else could it be?"

"It just might be something lighter, like flu."

"Or something darker like the black plague," I said snappily. "But I'm willing to take a running bet that it's chicken pox. In which case we shall have to send the children away immediately."

"Why should we? They've already had it."

"I'm just not going to take the risk of them having it again."

"You're being thoroughly hysterical."

"And you're being thoroughly disagreeable, so we both know where we are, don't we?"

Robin gave a grunt and patted my knee. "Light me a cigarette," he said. "Don't just sit there bellyaching."

I lit a cigarette and handed it to him in silence. We lurched heavily over a particularly large bump.

"This road's a sod," he said conversationally. "Bunny ought to do something about it."

"It isn't his to do anything about."

"If he had the faintest sense of civic responsibility he'd write to the town council."

"We can discuss it later," I said. "While we are all wrapping Eloise up in the blankets."

At this moment we turned into Bunny's drive and swerved round to the front door where we found him waiting for us wearing a shirt and slacks and holding in his hand a very dark whisky and soda.

"I've taken to thé bottle," he said by way of greeting. "I intend to drink myself to death as soon as I possibly can."

"First things first," I said sternly. "Where is she?"

"Lying on the bed moaning. I've wrapped her in blankets and given her a hot-water bottle."

"Good. We've brought some extra blankets as well, they're in the back of the car. I'd better go in to her."

"Have a drink first," said Bunny. "I've got them all ready on the verandah. We've got to talk things over."

"There doesn't seem to me to be much to talk over. Eloise has obviously got chicken pox, and the only thing to do is to get her home and into a less compromising bed as soon as we can."

"Do you think I ought to have sent for Dr. Bowman?"

"No," I said wearily. "It's much better that you didn't. I'll telephone him first thing in the morning."

"Please have one little drink with me," Bunny pleaded. "I'm feeling so bloody miserable."

I sighed and looked at Robin, who nodded, and we followed Bunny silently through the house and onto the verandah. The sea was flat calm, and the hibiscus hedge just above the beach was ablaze with fireflies. Bunny poured us each a whisky and soda and then perched himself on the verandah rail with his back to the view.

"It's no use me saying how sorry I am to have let you in for all this, is it?" he said.

"No use at all," I replied briskly. "And waste of time into the bargain."

"Nor how deeply grateful I am to you both for standing by me?"

"Write us a letter," I said. "And we'll read it aloud to each other later on when we are old and grey and full of sleep."

"Personally," said Robin, "I'm feeling old and grey and full of sleep now."

"I've been thinking things over." Bunny drummed his heels against the verandah rail and looked at us gloomily. "And I've come to the conclusion that I've made a cracking idiot of myself. The whole business has been doomed from the outset."

"Cheer up. The course of true love is well known to be a bit bumpy."

"That's just the trouble." Bunny stopped drumming his heels and took a swig of his drink. "I'm beginning to suspect that it isn't true love at all and probably never was."

"Good," I said heartlessly. "You're making giant strides. What happened? Did you have a row?"

"Yes." Bunny hung his head. "A real rip-snorting upper and downer."

"What about?"

"Everything really. It started over dinner."

"My sympathies so far are with Eloise. What did you give her?"

"Some delicious black bean soup, then curry, and then guava jelly."

"What sort of curry? Chicken, mutton, or goat?"

"I'm not sure. It seemed all right to me."

"If I know Cynthia, it was goat."

"What's the matter with goat curry?"

"As made by Cynthia, practically everything."

"It's one of the principal delicacies of the island."

"As made by Cynthia it's lethal. I've tried it."

"I wish you'd shut up about Cynthia. She did her best."

"Cynthia's best is not enough. You must have been out of your mind to have tried to stage a passionate reunion on Cynthia's goat curry. Why on earth didn't you give Eloise something plain and unprovocative like cold beef and salad?"

"Because there wasn't any. Anyhow it wasn't anything to do with the food really, that was only an excuse. She was determined to be bloody-minded from the start, I sensed it in the car. She kept on about how upset Hali Alani would be because she hadn't gone to his damned cocktail party." Bunny got off the rail and mixed himself another drink. "Then when she got here she knocked back two martinis and started grumbling about the house. She said it looked like a drill hall."

"She was quite right," I said. "Except for all those dusty shells, it does."

"This isn't getting us anywhere," said Robin testily. "Hadn't we better wrap up the corpse and take it home?"

"Go on a little bit more about the row," I said to Bunny, conscious of an unworthy enjoyment of the situation mixed with a genuine sense of relief. If he really was disillusioned and the scales really had dropped from his eyes, the future was rosier than I had dared to hope.

"Oh, it was just one of those things," said Bunny, retiring a little into his shell. "We wrangled for about three hours and said a lot of things to one another that we never should have said."

"Such as? . . ."

"Stop cross-examining me, Grizel." He looked at me accusingly. "You're enjoying this a little too much and giving yourself away."

"Quite right," I said firmly. "If you really have come to your senses at last, I couldn't be more delighted. How did it end?"

"It didn't end in any way decisively. She went on a lot about wishing she'd never come out here and being tired of all the furtiveness and hiding behind other people, then I said that as we neither of us were seeing any future in it at the moment the best thing would be for me to drive her back to you. Then I went out to get the car and the bloody thing wouldn't start and when I came back she was lying on the sofa crying and saying that she never wanted to clap eyes on me again and that she'd been sick."

"That was probably the curry," interposed Robin. "Vomiting isn't a recognized symptom of chicken pox."

"For Christ's sake will you shut up about the Goddamned curry!" shouted Bunny, losing his temper.

"Don't bellow," said Robin equably. "You'll wake the patient."

"Come on," I said rising to my feet. "We'd better take her home. Go and get the blankets from the car, Robin."

Robin, with alacrity, ran down the verandah steps and disappeared in the direction of the drive while Bunny and I walked into the house and into the bedroom. Poor Eloise was lying on the bed with her eyes closed. Her face was very flushed, and she had kicked off the blankets. I was glad to see that she was fully dressed, which at least relieved us of the necessity of getting her into her clothes. I bent over her and felt her forehead, which was blazing hot. She opened her eyes and gave a little moan.

"It's all right, dear," I said. "Robin and I have come to take you home."

"You're angels," she murmured huskily. "You really are."

"Do you think you can sit up?"

"No," she said, "but I'll try."

I helped her into a sitting posture on the side of the bed. She swayed a little and put her hand to her head.

"I'm afraid I'm going to be sick again."

"Hold on to me," I said. "And we'll go into the bathroom." With an effort she got to her feet and, leaning heavily on my arm, managed to get into the bathroom in the nick of time. When that was all over I took a face towel, which seemed to be made of cardboard, soaked it in cold water, and dabbed her head and neck with it. When we got back into the bedroom Robin had returned with the extra blankets and, between us, we wrapped her up in them and half led, half carried her out to the car. Bunny followed us helplessly, carrying the hot-water bottle, which was already tepid.

"That's no use any more," I said irritably. "Go and refill it with boiling water."

"I can't," he said. "I burned the bottom out of the kettle last time."

Having tucked Eloise into a sort of nest of pillows and cushions on the back seat, we got into the front and Robin started the engine. Bunny, forlorn on the front step, waved the hot-water bottle halfheartedly at us and we drove away into the darkness.

NINETEEN

The next day was unmitigated hell and a fitting prelude to the three weeks that followed it. The first thing in the morning I telephoned to Dr. Bowman, who, as I suspected, diagnosed chicken pox although in a mild form, wrote out prescriptions for calamine lotion and other médicaments, and announced firmly that Eloise must have a professional nurse for the first few days at least. He also said that the children should be out of the house by midday. When he had gone I rang up Juanita, who said that Kelly's Tavern was full up but that she would manage something and that I wasn't to worry. At ten-thirty while I was helping Nanny to pack and the children, entranced at not having to go to school, were jumping about and shrieking like engine whistles, Tahali came in and said I was wanted urgently on the telephone. I went irritably downstairs, lifted the receiver, and was greeted by Keela Alioa's voice.

"Forgive me for disturbing you," he said, "but I have been speaking to Hali Alani, who said he had been speaking to you about me not being naked in front of Her Majesty."

"You must forgive me, Keela," I said, controlling my impatience as well as I could. "But at the moment I am too involved in my own domestic problems to care whether you wear pink chiffon or a raccoon coat in front of Her Majesty."

"What, please, is a raccoon coat?"

"I will explain it to you at the next committee meeting."

"That then will be this afternoon?"

"Oh my God, so it will. I had completely forgotten."

"I have caught you at a bad moment?"

237

"Yes, dear Keela, you certainly have. My house is on fire and my children are gone, or at least, nearly gone."

Keela laughed appreciatively. "You are always making the jokes, Mrs. Craigie. I will be seeing you then in quite a small while."

"Yes. If I'm still alive, you will."

"You will not forget what Hali Alani told you about my idea of wearing a frog suit?"

"I think you'd look ghastly in a frog suit, and I'm quite sure the Queen would hate it."

"But what am I to *do?*" His voice rose desperately.

"We'll discuss the whole thing at the meeting, that is, if we are allowed to get a word in edgeways, but not *now*."

"I am very very worried about this matter. I have not slept all night."

"Neither have I," I said wildly. "And speaking for myself, I should like to squeeze myself into a frog suit at this very moment and retire to the bottom of the sea for several years."

"You are making the jokes again," he said reproachfully. "And when I am most unhappy that is not kind."

"Never mind, Keela. It will all be all right on the night." I hung up abruptly and went back to Nanny and the children.

At half past eleven when damp swimming suits had been collected, missing toys retrieved, and the bags all packed, Nanny, resigned and disapproving, drove off with them in the Austin and I retired onto the back verandah for a short breather. I kicked off my shoes, lay flat on the swing seat, and closed my eyes. I was not, however, permitted to relax for long because Tahali appeared almost immediately and said that the nurse had arrived from the hospital and would like to speak to me. I sat up wearily, put on my shoes again, and lit a cigarette.

"You'd better show her out here," I said. "She's not the same one that Mr. Bunny had, is she?"

"No, no." Tahali smiled. "This is a large white lady with a voice that is most strange. I will fetch her now." He bowed and left me, returning after a moment or two followed by a vast, cheerful woman of about fifty, with piercing blue eyes and a wild bird's nest of grey hair with a tiny white cap perched on the top of it.

"Good morning to you," she said in a thick Irish brogue, depositing a small brown bag on the swing seat and shaking my hand forcefully. "I thought it best to have a few words with you before taking stock of the patient. I've always found it pays in private cases to get meself acquainted with the lay of the land, as you might say, as soon as possible. It's liable to save a great deal of blather and misunderstanding afterwards. My name's Duffy, Maureen Duffy."

"How do you do?" I said, and added rather inadequately, "It was so kind of you to come."

"Not a bit of it," she said. "I go where I'm told to go and stay until the job's done." She fished in her pocket and produced a small notebook and pencil. "I'd be much obliged if you'd be kind enough to answer a few questions."

"By all means." I motioned her to a chair. "Please sit down."

"Thanks." She ignored the chair and sat on the swing seat. "This contraption could do with a drop of oil, couldn't it?"

"It certainly could. I've been meaning to see to it for ages." I sat down again myself and waited while she fished in another pocket for her glasses. She perched them on her nose and opened her notebook.

"I understand from the doctor that the poor soul's got chicken pox?"

"Yes. I'm afraid she has."

"Are there any children in the house?"

"There were, but there aren't any more. I've sent them to Kelly's Tavern."

"Holy Mother of God! That's no place for kiddies." She looked at me over her spectacles. "They'll be getting themselves caught up with all kinds of riffraff."

"Mrs. Kelly is an old friend of mine," I said coldly. "She most kindly offered to take them in at a moment's notice, and I'm very grateful to her."

"She's a warmhearted creature, I grant you, but her language is enough to freeze the marrow in your bones. I once nursed her through influenza and, believe me, I know what I'm talking about."

"My children are unlikely to be nursing her through anything, so their marrows will probably remain at a normal temperature."

"I like that," she said, laughing heartily. "You've got a sense of humour, and I always say a sense of humour is half the battle. Now then let's get down to brass tacks. How's she taking it?"

"How is who taking what?"

"The patient of course. How's she reacting to her symptoms? Morose, languid, hysterical? I like to know these things in advance so that I can decide on what line to take."

"I'm afraid I can't tell you. I haven't seen her this morning. I've been too busy getting the children off."

"So be it. No doubt I'll find out soon enough." She paused and looked at me searchingly. "You've had chicken pox yourself?"

"Yes," I said firmly, refusing to be intimidated by her piercing stare. "I had it when I was a child. I also had measles, whooping cough, croup, scarlet fever, and mumps, and I was bitten in the calf by a collie when I was five."

"Collies can be unreliable," she said scribbling in her notebook. "But they're not nearly so treacherous as Alsatians. You never know where you are with an Alsatian. Now then about my meals. Where am I to have them?"

"Wherever you like. The house is fairly large."

"Is there a room next to the patient?"

"Yes. But it's a lavatory. I think you'd be happier in the nursery, which is just along the passage."

"I have to have me meals regular as clockwork on account of being a diabetic."

"A diabetic!" I stared at her blankly.

"There's nothing to worry about." She gave a merry laugh. "Just so long as there's always some sugar handy. I've been a diabetic for twenty-odd years. One gets used to everything. I have to inject meself with insulin every blessed day. I've got all the paraphernalia here in me bag in case of emergencies."

"I'm so glad."

"The only thing I have to be careful of"—she went on cheerfully —"is going off into a coma."

"Is that liable to happen often?"

"Only every now and again when I'm overtired and haven't eaten regularly. All you have to do is to force some sugar into my mouth and I'm right as a trivet in a couple of shakes."

"What happens if nobody's about and there isn't any sugar?"

"Thanks be to God there always has been so far—touch wood.

You'd better warn your staff to be on the *qui vive* just in case."

"Thank you," I said. "I'll make a point of it."

"I'm likely to fight a bit just at first, we diabetics are stubborn as mules, but tell them to pay no attention and carry on. If my teeth happen to be clenched and I won't take the sugar, a cup of very sweet coffee will do the trick."

"You've never found that this—this disability affects your professional work in any way?"

"God bless you, no, not in the least. On the contrary sometimes it's turned out to be very useful with fractious patients. It gives them something to think about over and above their own troubles, poor souls."

Feeling that our cosy little chat had lasted long enough I got up from my chair. "I'll give all the necessary instructions to the servants," I said. "Do you require anything special in the way of diet?"

"Apart from starches"—she rose too and gathered up her bag— "I'll take anything that comes. I eat like a horse."

"I'll tell them that too," I said, and led her upstairs to Eloise's room.

Robin came back from the plantation in time for lunch, and we had it on the back verandah as we usually do when we are alone. Tahali served us, and I could see from his expression that he was in a state of repressed giggles. A little earlier on I had collected him and Clementine and Eulalie in the kitchen and explained carefully that for the next few days they were never to be without lumps of sugar in their pockets. This, not unnaturally, bewildered them, and when I went on to explain the reason for it, as well as I could remember, they all three went off into such gales of laughter that I had to close the kitchen door hurriedly for fear the noise would penetrate to the sickroom upstairs.

"What's the matter with him?" asked Robin when Tahali, having caught my eye, vanished, snorting, in the direction of the kitchen.

"It's the new nurse. She's got a strong Irish brogue and diabetes."

"Good God!" said Robin, looking startled. "Isn't that rather unsuitable?"

"I don't know," I replied. "She looks hale and hearty enough and seems to take it in her stride. She's had it for twenty years and is quite used to it, she says. The only thing is that we all have to have sugar handy and watch her like lynxes in case she suddenly goes off into a coma."

"Does Eloise know?"

"She's almost sure to by now. Reticence is not Nurse Duffy's strong point."

"Isn't it rather casual of Bowman to send diabetic nurses into strange houses without so much as a by-your-leave?"

"There's only one of her, and I must say she seems thoroughly efficient. I expect she was the only one available. The hospital's crammed to overflowing. At all events I'd rather have her than that beast who looked after Bunny. She's at least cheerful and well disposed."

"Has Bunny been over?"

"No. He telephoned. He said he was in the grip of a monumental hangover, was going on a fishing trip to the outer islands, and would review the whole miserable situation when he got back."

"There's nothing like packing up your troubles in your old kit bag and handing it to other people."

"I don't suppose Eloise sees herself as an old kit bag, exactly."

"You know what I mean," said Robin. "What are we going to do now?"

"There's nothing very much we can do, except wait until she recovers. We're landed with her."

"Don't you think we'd better play down the fact that she's got chicken pox? I mean if that gets round the island people are liable to start putting two and two together."

"They will anyhow," I said. "In any case if we have to embark on any more complicated lies I shall go mad."

"Why couldn't we pretend that she's laid up with a bad cold, or flu, or a minor nervous breakdown? So far nobody knows what she's really got except Bunny and us."

"And Dr. Bowman and Nurse Duffy and the servants. I expect Tahali's friend in the valley is discussing her symptoms at this very moment."

"We might start a whispering campaign about her having got ptomaine poisoning from the goat curry."

"Who are we going to whisper it to? And anyhow that wouldn't explain why we've had to send the children to Kelly's Tavern."

"We could say they looked peaky and run-down and we thought they needed a breath of fresh sea air."

"Don't be silly. In the first place the air up here is far fresher than on the coast, and in the second place the children look about as peaky as all-in wrestlers."

"You're giving in," said Robin reproachfully. "And throwing up the sponge."

"I'm giving *up* and throwing *in* the sponge."

"Sponge or no sponge we'll have to think of something. It's not like you to weaken in a moment of crisis."

"This crisis has been going on for far too long and I'm sick to death of it."

"Why not say that she's contracted some weird tropical virus that nobody knows anything about and that she's being kept under observation?"

"I don't think it's exactly tactful to spread the rumour that the island is riddled with obscure diseases three weeks before the royal visit."

"At all costs," said Robin, getting up, "it must *not* be known that she's got chicken pox. You'd better take Dr. Bowman into your confidence and cook up something between you. We've got ourselves thoroughly involved in this intrigue, and we must do everything in our power to see it through successfully." He kissed me lightly and disappeared into the house.

I lit a cigarette and moved over to the swing seat while Tahali cleared the table. He had recovered his outward composure, but he kept shooting me sidelong glances and I could see by his expression that he was thoroughly enjoying the situation.

"It is very sad about the duchess, is it not?" he said, coming to a standstill in front of me and balancing a loaded tray negligently on his right hand.

"Very," I replied laconically.

"Has she the chicken disease like Mr. Bunny?"

"No, Tahali." I met his eye unflinchingly. "It's something quite different. It's a weird tropical virus that nobody knows anything about."

"What, if you please, is a weird tropical virus?"

"A virus is much smaller than a germ or a microbe, in fact it's so small that you can't even see it with a microscope and it gets into your bloodstream and gives you a fever. That is why Dr. Bowman is so worried and is keeping her under observation until he finds out what it is."

"Oh." Tahali looked at me sceptically and shifted the tray to his left hand.

"So if anyone asks you any questions just you say exactly what I've just told you."

"Cynthia told the cousin of Eulalie that the duchess and Mr. Bunny had high words last night and shouted at each other very loud."

"Well, you tell Eulalie to tell her cousin to tell Cynthia that her cooking is enough to make anybody shout very loud."

"Cynthia is most lazy and ramshackle," said Tahali with a broad grin. "She used to work at the Narouchi Guest House, but Mistress Witherspoon sent her away."

"Where on earth did you pick up 'ramshackle'?"

Tahali looked alarmed. "It is not an evil or filthy word?"

"No. But I would just like to know where you heard it."

"It was you, mistress, who said it to Jock when you were angry about the garden."

"If I did it was an understatement. Go away now, Tahali, because you're wasting my time and I have a great deal to do. And don't forget what I told you about the tropical virus. You might begin by whispering it to your friend in the valley. I'm sure he'll be fascinated."

Tahali bowed politely and went off with the tray.

Before going to the committee meeting I went to Eloise's room for a moment. She was lying back on the pillows still looking flushed and with her eyes closed. Nurse Duffy was sitting by the bed knitting industriously and humming under her breath. She looked up when I came in and gave me a cheerful nod, and I was just about to tiptoe out again when Eloise opened her eyes.

"Don't go," she said weakly. "I wasn't asleep, just dozing."

"How are you feeling?"

"Itchy. They've begun to come out on my back. I suppose I shall be covered from head to foot by tomorrow."

"Now now now," said Nurse Duffy briskly. "We don't want any of that downhearted talk. You'll be worse before you're better, but there's no sense in worrying your head about it."

"How can I help worrying my head about it?" said Eloise petulantly, "when I know I'm going to be blazing with hideous red spots for weeks and probably be disfigured for life!"

"You won't be any such thing." Nurse Duffy put down her knitting, got up, and started very gently to rearrange the pillows. "You've only got a mild attack, the doctor told you so himself, and your temperature's down two points already. All you've got to do is to be philosophical about it and keep your pecker up." She turned to me. "If you'll just excuse me for a few minutes," she said, "I'll be popping downstairs for some fresh barley water. The more fluid she drinks the better she'll be." She went out purposefully, closing the door behind her.

"She's an angel really," said Eloise wearily. "But she has diabetes."

"I know. She told me before lunch."

"It isn't catching; is it?"

"Of course not."

"She has a hypodermic syringe in that beastly little bag. She showed it to me this morning. It gave me the shudders."

"Never mind. Try not to think about it."

"What am I to do if she suddenly has an attack and falls down or something?"

"Just ring the bell," I said soothingly. "All the servants are fully primed and bulging with sugar."

"I'll never never forgive myself for giving you and Robin all this trouble. I wish I were dead."

"Don't," I replied. "Because that would give us a great deal more trouble. Funerals on this island are terribly complicated on account of having to be done in a flash because of the climate."

Eloise gave a wan smile. "You do put things funnily, Grizel, you really do." She reached out and took a cigarette from a box on the bedside table. "I know I really oughtn't to smoke really and it tastes awful but it *is* something to do."

"Would you like some more books?" I asked, lighting it for her. "Or a *Times* crossword or anything?"

"No, thank you. I don't seem able to concentrate on reading for more than a few minutes and I've never done a crossword puzzle in my life. I can't make head nor tail of them. I'll be all right if only these damned spots don't spread to my face. You don't see any signs yet, do you?"

"No," I said, scrutinizing her carefully. "Not a blemish. But even if one or two do appear you mustn't be too depressed about it. They clear up quite quickly."

"It's all been a miserable failure, hasn't it?"

"Never mind about that now."

"I must have been mad to have come out here in the first place. I ought to have known."

"What ought you to have known?" I tried valiantly to keep a note of exultance out of my voice.

"That there was no future in it," she sighed. "Bunny's a darling in many ways and madly attractive, but it wouldn't really *do*. I mean I don't think we could ever be permanently happy together, do you?"

"It's not for me to say," I replied warily. "I quite see that your tastes are very different and that you haven't apparently very much in common apart from—well, apart from being in love. But one can never tell about other people, can one?"

"We had an awful row last night. We've had a few squabbles before, of course, but nothing like that. I'd no idea he had such a violent temper. I thought at one moment that he was going to hit me."

"Good heavens!" I said, and added hypocritically: "What started it?"

"I don't really remember," she said, watching the smoke of her cigarette with half-closed eyes. "We sat in that dreary barrack of a room for ages before dinner was ready, sort of bickering about this and that. And then when at last the dinner came it was simply disgusting and I could hardly eat any of it. I suppose I was already beginning to feel ill really. And then he started off about me being far too luxury-loving and thoroughly spoilt and said that I couldn't expect always to be stuffed with caviar and ortolans and pink champagne and that the simple, healthy things of life were much better for me, and it was just then that the maid slouched in with that ghastly grey curry that looked like chinchilla and—— Oh, I don't know—I just felt suddenly miserable and sick of the whole thing and said I wished I'd never come and that I wanted to go home. Then he began shouting at me and the row went on from there until he stamped out of the house and couldn't start the car. I expect I was to blame in the first place, really, for allowing myself to be rushed over there when I didn't feel in the mood. You know how agonizing it is to have a thing with somebody when you're not feeling in the mood. At any rate it all showed me a side of his character that I never knew existed, so I suppose that's something gained?"

"Wait until you're feeling better before you make any final decisions," I said, with what I hoped was sympathetic conviction. "Perhaps the old black magic will come surging back when you're hale and hearty again. At all events don't worry about any of it at the moment. Bunny's gone off on a fishing trip anyhow."

"Oh he has, has he?" She looked at me sharply. "He can go right round the world in a rowing boat for all I care."

"I've got to leave you now," I said. "There's been a special committee meeting called to discuss giving a public dress rehearsal of the water pageant."

"I do admire you, Grizel, honestly I do. You're always so occupied and cheerful and full of 'go.' I don't know how you do it, really I don't. I never seem to do anything but just sort of sit about. I'm like one of those awful thingumajigs that cling to rocks."

"Limpets?"

"No, darling, prettier than that. I think I mean sea anemones."

"Well, you just be a sensible sea anemone and do what Nurse Duffy tells you and try not to worry about anything and you'll be up and about again in no time."

"If I were a really sensible sea anemone I should find a good solid rock to cling to and not go drifting here and there with the tide," she said pensively. "I've been an absolute idiot over all this, and now I'm being paid out and it serves me right."

"There's no sense in giving way to self-recrimination." I gave her what I hoped was a comforting smile and went to the door. "It's merely waste of energy and will probably send your temperature up. Is there anything I can get you in the town?"

"No, I don't think so, unless you just happened to see some cyclamen-coloured wool. I've only got half a skein left."

"Cyclamen-coloured wool is not the sort of thing one *happens* to see in Pendarla, but I'll pop into Carianeega's and see what they've got. Hadn't I better take a bit with me so that I can match it?"

"You're an angel," Eloise said mechanically. "My work bag's over there on the chair by the dressing table."

I went over to her work bag, rummaged in it, found the colour she wanted, and left her. She waved wistfully to me as I went out of the room.

The committee meeting was hot, boring, and uneventful. Alma and Ivy, obviously having agreed to a private truce, were almost overpoweringly polite to each other. Cuckoo Honey, not having been told about the public dress rehearsal scheme in advance, decided to oppose the whole idea and made a series of sharp little speeches most of which started with "But I don't really *see . . .*" However, she was finally overruled and reduced to muttering under her breath and scribbling little notes on a pad. The question of whether Keela should be naked, half dressed, or completely swathed in some sort of rubber substance was discussed hotly for nearly three quarters of an hour until I could bear it no longer and crept out unobtrusively in order to get to Carianeega's for Eloise's wool before it closed.

Shopping in Pendarla in the late afternoon is fairly chaotic, particularly downtown near the harbour where most of the best shops are and where the streets are narrow and congested. I knew that to attempt to park my car in any of the usual parking places was doomed to failure, so I drove directly to the Royal Samolan, told the doorman to put it where he liked, and set off on foot. It was as well that I did so because King Street, which meanders for about half a mile from the Royal Samolan to the Customs House and the Bakhua Ferry building, was chockablock with almost stationary traffic from end to end. To add to the confusion certain areas of it had been blocked off for the erection of grandstands for the royal visit. Indeed the consciousness of this event seemed to have infected the whole town with hysteria. The results of this infection, to anyone accustomed to Samolan lassitude, were startling. Even the traffic policemen standing on their little platforms under striped umbrellas, who as a rule are lethargic to the point of inanition, were flailing their arms and blowing their whistles with such abandon that occasionally groups of cheerful passers-by stopped dead in their tracks and broke into delighted applause.

I fought my way along the crowded pavements and finally managed to edge myself into Carianeega's American-style store. Carianeega's American-style store is Samolo's pride and joy, but to me it is unbridled hell and has been ever since three years ago when it first opened its dreadful automatic doors. In the first place it is air-conditioned to freezing point so that going into it is almost as violent a shock to the system as coming out of it. In the second place its—presumably—true-blue American technique of salesmanship makes it impossible to buy so much as a toothbrush in less than a half hour. In the third place, owing to a preponderance of chromium, hard floors, and ceaselessly grinding escalators, it is far noisier than a steel mill.

The general din is enhanced by the gramophone and radio department's being in the middle of the ground floor. The escalators are on each side of the building: Up on the right and Down on the left. These the Samolans adore and frequently ride gleefully up and down on them for hours without the slightest intention of buying anything.

Having finally achieved the drapery department, which is on the third floor, I spent an exhausting ten minutes shrieking at a beautiful but abstracted Samolan salesgirl and waving Eloise's cyclamen-coloured wool in her face. After burrowing about languidly in a number of cardboard boxes she eventually produced the colour I wanted and I steeled myself for the inevitable half an hour's wait while she laboriously wrote out a bill, took the money I gave her, squeezed it and the bill into a little wooden ball which, with a twitch of the wrist, she sent rolling off on a wire chute and slowly, very slowly, proceeded to wrap up the parcel. Fortunately I found a vacant chair a little way off and sat down on it. I lit a cigarette, closed my eyes briefly, and imagined I was in Harrods with cold, grey weather outside and the less shrill sound of London traffic rumbling along the Brompton Road. Living permanently in the tropics is apt to induce these sudden bouts of nostalgia. Both Lucy and Dusty are addicted to them. In fact only the other day Lucy was standing on the steps of the post office lost in a vivid, S.W.L. reverie, when a stranger accosted her and asked her if she felt all right, whereupon she opened her eyes with a start and said she felt fine and was merely waiting for a Number Nineteen bus.

It isn't that one doesn't enjoy living in a far-flung outpost of Empire, especially when it is as enchanting as Samolo, but in the British there is an inherent capacity for summoning up remembrance of things past at the most irrelevant moments. I am not so insular as to assume that the British have a monopoly of homesickness. I am sure that Frenchmen in Guadeloupe, Belgians in Léopoldville, Italians in Tripolitania, and even Russians in Earl's Court are frequently smitten with sudden yearnings for Notre Dame, the Brussels Opera House, the Leaning Tower of Pisa, or the Kremlin. It is all tied up with atavism and roots and deep, subconscious divine discontent and the good old human failing of always wanting to be somewhere quite different from where one is at the moment. On rereading the above paragraph I have a feeling that the late Mr. Henry James would be far from happy with it, but as there are a great number of his paragraphs that I am far from happy with, I shall let it stay. As a matter of fact, I believe that it is smell more than anything else that can carry one most swiftly over the hills and far away. It must have been some sudden, reminiscent twitch of the olfactory nerve that whisked me in a split second across the whole wide world from Carianeega's in Pendarla to Harrods in Knightsbridge. Harrods anyhow is a paradise of variegated smells ranging from the heady fragrance of the scent department, through the appetizing food and groceries to the Ronuk-y pungence of the modern and antique furniture. I don't remember that the china and glassware exude much, and I don't suppose that the ladies' and gents' clothing and drapery departments smell very differently from those of Selfridges, Barker's, or even Fortnum & Mason's. But I do know that if I were suddenly transported blindfolded from the farthermost corner of the earth and deposited in any part of Harrods, I should know where I was in an instant. Carianeega's has no particularly individual tang. It smells much the same as all the other shops in Samolo: a general miasma of heat, humanity, sweat, and dust, with, underlying it all, the pervasive sickliness of copra wafting up from the harbour.

Presently the salesgirl finished wrapping up my wool and stood staring at it, pensively scratching her ear with a yellow pencil. She was remarkably pretty, with honey-coloured skin and blue-black hair, and I wondered what she was thinking about standing there so still and staring so vacantly at a pink paper package. Unaware of my scrutiny, she took a small hand mirror from the pocket of her skirt, stretched her mouth into a wide grimace, and looked searchingly at her teeth, at which moment there was a whirr and a click and the little wooden ball bounced back with my change. I got up, collected it, picked up my parcel, and left her. When I looked back just before springing onto the Down escalator, she was still examining her teeth.

I walked back along King Street to the Royal Samolan and, feeling hot and dusty, decided to have some iced tea before getting the car and driving home. I found an empty table on the inner terrace, ordered my tea, and looked out over the garden to the sea. There was a Blue Funnel Line freighter steaming in slowly across the bay with a little pilot boat fussing along in front of it like a terrier: I almost expected to hear it bark. Presently the boy brought me my tea and I was just settling down to enjoy it when, to my dismay, Cuckoo Honey appeared festooned with parcels and plumped herself down onto a chair opposite to me.

"I thought it was you," she said breathlessly. "I recognized your hat from right across the other side of the terrace."

"I didn't think it was all that flamboyant."

She laughed skittishly. "It's divine," she said, depositing her parcels on the chair beside her. "I had one rather like it last year only it was black instead of red. Is that iced tea?"

"Yes, it is."

"I shall have some too, my throat's as dry as a bone. . . . Boy!" She clapped her hands so loudly that some people at a nearby table turned round in surprise. When the waiter had appeared and taken her order she leant across the table and stared at me intently. "You look tired," she said. "I noticed it at the meeting."

Knowing from experience that the only way to deal with Cuckoo was to hit back immediately, I said, "So do you. Absolutely exhausted. There isn't anything wrong with you, is there?"

"Good heavens no. I never have anything the matter with me, not so much as a head cold from one year's end to another."

"Then it must be the heat," I said relentlessly. "It makes all of us look a bit sallow."

"I shall be glad when the royal visit's over and done with," she said, changing the subject abruptly. "It's upsetting the whole island. You know that Harbour Street is closed to traffic for a whole week while they put up those stands and flagstaffs?"

"Yes. I saw it in the paper."

"Personally"—she went on—"I think the itinerary for the official drive round the island has been very foolishly planned. I thought of saying something to Sandra about it, but she's been getting more and more touchy these last few weeks and snaps one's head off at the least thing."

"She has a good deal on her mind."

"I can't bear to see things *mismanaged*," Cuckoo went on. "I mean I think it's simply *insane* for them to start at eight-thirty and go through the Lailanu Pass in the morning when everyone knows it's bound to be cloudy and almost never gets *really* clear until the afternoon. Then for the royal party to lunch with *Juanita*, of all people!"

"Kelly's Tavern has far and away the best food on the island," I said. "And Juanita will organize everything beautifully."

"I know you and I don't see eye to eye about Juanita." Cuckoo gave a supercilious sniff. "I'm sure she runs the hotel very efficiently and is supposed to be terribly amusing, but personally I find her appallingly vulgar. I mean one never knows what she's going to say next. You must admit that she has the most uncontrollable temper and is always flying at people."

"I think she's unlikely to lose her temper and fly at the Queen and Prince Philip."

"Of course she won't. I didn't mean *that*. But I *do* think the whole arrangement isn't very *suitable*. It would have been much better if H.E. and Sandra had stuck to their original plan and let them lunch with old Sir Albert at Bingall's Bay."

"I don't agree," I said flatly. "Old Sir Albert is a pompous bore. In addition to which he's deaf as an adder and his house is a nightmare."

"How can you say things like that, Grizel! He's one of the most distinguished figures in Samolo and at least he is English through and through, whereas everyone knows that Juanita has a strong touch of the tarbrush."

"I suspect," I said evenly, "that when the Queen embarks on tours of her dominions and colonies that she is fully prepared to meet touches of the tarbrush here and there. . . . Here's your

252

iced tea," I added, as the boy came up with it. "You'd better drink some immediately, it's very soothing and will calm you down."

Cuckoo sniffed again and proceeded to pour her tea into the glass of ice. Obtuse as she was, she had obviously noted the red gleam of danger in my eye and so for the next few minutes the subject of the royal visit was dropped and we devoted ourselves to the sort of questions-and-answers small talk that so frequently occurs between people who haven't very much to say to each other.

"How are the children?"

"Splendid. Except for Michael. He has a touch of earache, poor little chap."

"Probably from diving."

"It can't be. He's too small to dive."

"You ought to scour his ears with surgical spirit every time he's been in the water." ·

"I've tried that, but he screams the place down."

"What does Dr. Bowman say?"

"I don't trust Dr. Bowman. He's too pleased with himself. We have old Dr. Radcliffe."

"Isn't he a bit gaga? He's well over eighty."

"He's solid and reliable and he's at least a gentleman," said Cuckoo defensively. "And he was wonderful to Cynthia when she had those swollen glands under her arms at Christmas, poor little mite. How are yours?"

"Glands or children?"

"Children of course."

"They're bright as buttons. They're having a little holiday by the sea because I thought, with Eloise ill, they'd be better out of the way."

Cuckoo's expression brightened perceptibly, and I could have bitten my tongue out. "Eloise ill?" She leaned forward eagerly. "What's the matter with her?"

"Nobody seems to know exactly. Dr. Bowman says it may be some weird tropical virus. He's taking all sorts of tests and keeping her under observation," I added recklessly.

"Good heavens!" Cuckoo quivered with anticipatory excitement like one of Dr. Pavlov's dogs when a sudden bell announces to their conditioned reflexes that food is imminent. "Whatever can it be, do you think?"

"Nothing very serious, I'm sure. She has only a slight temperature."

"Well! . . ." Cuckoo lit a cigarette and looked inscrutable. "At least it will keep her out of mischief."

I laughed. "Mischief! Really, Cuckoo, what *can* you mean by that?"

She gave a little frown as though she were debating with herself whether to speak or forever hold her peace. Being Cuckoo, of course she spoke.

"I've been wondering whether or not I ought to tell you something. It's been on my mind for some time, but I haven't seen much of you lately except at the meetings and I'm never quite sure how you're going to take things. You're rather like Sandra in that . . ." She gave a little titter. "Unpredictable!" I raised my eyebrows at this and she went on hurriedly. "I mean you're both liable to fly off the handle if someone says something you don't like."

"Surely that's a fairly normal failing? What do *you* do when someone says something *you* don't like?"

She bridled. "I believe in being absolutely frank and saying what I think straight out," she replied firmly. "I know it upsets people sometimes, but it's better, in the long run, to be honest. Don't you agree?"

"I'm never quite sure," I said. "Too much honesty applied at the wrong moment can wreak considerable damage. What's on your mind?"

"It's about Eloise."

"Yes. I gathered that."

"I don't know how much you know and how much you don't know, but I do feel, as an old friend, that it is my duty to warn you about something."

"All right, Cuckoo." I glanced ostentatiously at my wrist watch. "Warn away, only stop being mysterious. I've got to go in a minute."

"I had a letter ten days ago from my sister Veronica."

"Is that the divorced one or the one in the Isle of Wight?"

"The divorced one. She travels a great deal, you know."

"I didn't. But I think it's very sensible of her. There's no point in sitting at home and just brooding."

"She met Eloise in Capri last summer at a dinner party on somebody's yacht. She was with Bunny Colville!"

I smiled blandly. "I don't blame Veronica in the least," I said. "Bunny is a very attractive man."

Cuckoo pressed on heavily. "It was *Eloise* who was with Bunny. She was having an affair with him quite openly."

"Do you mean that they were committing a public nuisance?"

"It's all very fine to be flippant, but it really is serious. Apparently it's been going on for over a year." She paused. "And if you ask me I believe that that's the real reason she came out here, so as to be with him. I don't mean to imply that she isn't fond of you and Robin, I know you're old friends from the M.T.C. days, but I *do* think you ought to know what the real situation is underneath."

"Thank you, Cuckoo," I said. "I'm most grateful to you for tipping me the wink."

"Do you think it's true?"

"I haven't the faintest idea." I rose to my feet and signalled to the boy to bring the bill. "It may have been true in Capri, but I haven't noticed any signs of it here. She's only met Bunny once or twice since she arrived."

"But he's had chicken pox."

"Even so, if she were that mad about him she would at least have visited and taken him some fruit or flowers or something. Actually she hasn't clapped eyes on him for weeks, and now he's gone off on a fishing trip to the outer islands."

"Oh." Cuckoo looked disappointed, then she brightened. "You don't suppose that this mysterious illness of hers is chicken pox too and that she caught it from him?"

"Really, Cuckoo, you're incorrigible!" I laughed convincingly. "You may not care for Dr. Bowman, but you must admit he's bright enough to recognize chicken pox when he sees it."

"Veronica said it was an open scandal in London and that everyone was talking about it. Not that it's any business of mine really. I mean I'm not in the least prudish and I don't mind *what* people do. But it did just cross my mind that for the Duchess of Fowey to be carrying on an illicit affair just when the Queen and Prince Philip are arriving really wouldn't be quite the thing. I mean it might put us all in the most embarrassing position, mightn't it?"

"Absolutely ghastly," I said cheerfully. "We should never be able to hold our heads up again." I gathered up the parcel of Eloise's wool. "Now I really must fly because I promised to be home by six-thirty to see Dr. Bowman and hear the results of poor Eloise's blood tests."

"Thank you for the iced tea," Cuckoo said in a flat voice. "I didn't mean you to pay for both of us."

"Don't give it another thought. It's been lovely seeing you, and I've adored our little gossip. We really ought to do it more often, oughtn't we?" I blew her a kiss and went hurriedly away to retrieve my car, leaving her sitting at the table looking pensively at her empty glass and biting her lip.

When I got home I put the car in the garage, noting by the absence of the station wagon that Robin wasn't back yet, and went quietly upstairs to lie down for a few minutes. I felt hot and dusty and tired, and by now, irritable as well. I kicked off my shoes, took off my coat and skirt, slipped into my dressing gown, and lay down on the bed; and, resolutely pushing out of my mind the image of Cuckoo with her pale, slightly protuberant eyes and her uncanny knack of infuriating me to madness, I tried to relax completely and compose myself for forty winks. Just as I was succeeding and becoming aware of that lovely tingling sensation which starts at the feet and, if you remain still enough, works its way slowly upwards until the next thing you know is that you are waking up, warm and cosy and refreshed after half an hour's semioblivion, I heard a loud crash followed by a muffled scream coming from the direction of the spare room. I started up from my beautiful trance as though someone had lobbed a hand grenade through the window and ran barefoot along the passage. The door of Eloise's room was open, and when I rushed in I found her sitting up in bed wide-eyed and emitting little moans of fright while her right hand jabbed violently at the electric bell. Scattered over the floor were the remains of my best tea service. The milk jug was broken in half, and the teapot lay on its side with a river of Earl Grey pouring out of it and soaking into the blue carpet. Among this devastation was stretched Nurse Duffy with her head resting in a cut-glass jam dish, breathing stertorously and looking like something from Madame Tussaud's. Taking in the situation at a glance, as the heroine of a novel would say, I knelt down on some bread and butter and shook her gently. But she only grunted, and her head lolled out of the jam dish onto the floor.

"Sugar!" I cried. "Sugar—quickly."

"I don't think there is any," said Eloise tremulously. "I suppose Saxin wouldn't do?"

"Of course it wouldn't." I got up from the floor, dashed out of the room, and ran downstairs. At the foot of them I met Tahali charging out of the service door followed by Eulalie and Clementine. "Sugar!" I screamed at them. "Bring some sugar immediately!"

Tahali produced some rather grey-looking lump sugar from the pocket of his house coat.

"I don't think that's any good," I said frantically. "We shall never be able to get it into her mouth." I turned to Eulalie and Clementine. "Get some icing sugar or castor sugar or brown sugar and bring it upstairs, and make some strong black coffee as soon as you possibly can." They rushed back through the service door while I bounded upstairs again, followed by Tahali. We knelt down by Nurse Duffy, and Tahali held her head up while I tried to force a lump of sugar into her mouth, but her gleaming false teeth were tightly clenched and she merely gave an angry snort and knocked it out of my hand.

"Try some raspberry jam," said Eloise, who had crawled to the end of the bed to see what was going on. "It might be better than nothing."

I seized a teaspoon, filled it with jam, and rammed it between Nurse Duffy's lips. She gave a little growl and seemed to swallow some of it. I refilled the spoon and repeated the process, at which moment Eulalie and Clementine appeared bearing two bowls heaped with sugar.

"Quickly . . ." I said. "Dissolve as much as you can in half a glass of water."

Eulalie ambled into the bathroom and returned with a tooth mug half full of water. She and Clementine stirred into it a large amount of sugar with a nail file which Eloise handed them from the bed table, then, with the exception of Eloise, we all settled down on the floor round Nurse Duffy as though we were about to participate in some curious religious rite. Tahali held her head up while I poured the sugar concoction into her mouth. Most of it ran out again down the front of her dress, but we persevered until we became very sticky indeed. At this moment Robin came in carrying a small bunch of emerald-green bananas and a riding crop.

"What on earth's happening?" he queried.

"Nothing at the moment," I replied irritably. "But, as you can see, a great deal has."

Suddenly Nurse Duffy opened her eyes and sat bolt upright. "Holy Mother of God!" she exclaimed. "The place looks a shambles!"

"I'm afraid it does rather," I said, staring hopelessly at the broken china, the scattered bits of bread and butter, the over-turned teapot, and the stained carpet.

"It's all my own silly fault and I could kick meself and that's a fact." She made an effort to get up, but I restrained her.

"I think you'd better stay where you are for a few minutes." I turned to Tahali. "Bring over that chair for Nurse Duffy to lean against."

Tahali did so, and I sent Eulalie and Clementine downstairs to fetch the coffee. Meanwhile Nurse Duffy leant against the chair still breathing heavily but otherwise apparently normal.

"Give me a spoonful of that brown sugar," she said. "And I'll be as right as rain in two shakes of a duck's tail." She turned to me after I had given her the sugar and made a clucking noise with her tongue. "I apologize," she said. "And I can't say more than that, can I now? I overslept this morning and was out of the house like a scalded cat without having enough breakfast, then when lunch came I only picked at it on account of me stomach being troubled with the wind. I'm mortally ashamed of meself for me own damned carelessness and irresponsibility."

"Do you feel all right now?"

"Fit as a fiddle, apart from being a bit dizzy." She scrambled to her feet. "I'll clear up this mess with me own two hands," she said briskly. "It's the least I can do for making such a blithering fool of meself."

Half an hour later when Nurse Duffy had had her coffee, the room had been tidied up and poor Eloise had been resettled, exhausted, against the pillows, I went down to the back verandah with Robin and had a mild attack of hysterics.

TWENTY

The weeks following the first uncomfortable day of Eloise's illness seem in retrospect to have a "film montage" quality about them. Everything seemed to be happening on different levels at the same time. Preparations for the royal visit which up to then had consisted mostly of meetings and discussions suddenly gathered momentum and appeared to dominate every aspect of our existence. Even Sandra, whose energy was inexhaustible, wilted a little under the strain. Government House itself became virtually untenable, owing to the entire first floor having to be repainted, repapered, and, in parts, reconstructed, while in the gardens a bandstand was erected and two enormous marquees put up in case malignant fate organized a downpour in the middle of the garden party.

It was first of all decided that the much-discussed presentations should take place in a red-cord-enclosed space on the lower terrace. This idea was abandoned, however, when Sandra pointed out that those who were presented would be unable to curtsey and back away without falling head over heels down three stone steps. It was then suggested that the presenting should be done at various strategic points during the Queen's and Prince Philip's progress through the grounds. This entailed the forming of a subcommittee, headed by Cuckoo, whose job it would be to organize the favoured citizens into small groups and see to it that they were at specified places on the lawn at given moments so that they could we winkled out of the crowd, presented, and swallowed up again without undue waste of time. Needless to say, Cuckoo, with her usual uncanny skill, managed to offend everyone on the committee at the first meeting and the whole enterprise collapsed in chaos. It was finally decreed therefore that the organization of the presentations should be put in the hands of four officers of the Royal Shropshires plus Chris Mortlock and two extra A.D.C.s.

In the meantime rehearsals for the water pageant were proceeding convulsively through a series of crises. One of Ivy Poland's principal sprites stepped on a sting ray while flitting archly through the shallows and had to be carted off to hospital. Keela Alioa nearly drowned, owing to his Aqua Lung going wrong, and his first entrance had to be entirely restaged. Alma, Ivy, Kerry Stirling, and Inky Blumenthal had a blazing four-fold row in course of which each one accused the others of deliberately sabotaging the production from motives of personal jealousy. The repercussions of this brought everything to a stalemate and I took it upon myself to appeal privately to Sandra, who suddenly appeared at a rehearsal, like an avenging goddess, gathered Alma, Ivy, Kerry, and Inky round her in a sullen group, and delivered a stinging and admirably phrased lecture to them in front of the assembled company. The gist of this was that if they wasted any more time squabbling among themselves, not getting on with the job, and indulging their own petty feelings at the expense of their patriotic duty, the whole production would be cancelled then and there, and that she herself would see to it that their individual invitations to the royal garden party would be officially and publicly withdrawn. At the end of this Alma burst into violent sobs and was led off into a coconut grove by Ivy, a few of the minor members of the company gave a half-fledged cheer and subsided, while Sandra, without so much as a glance in my direction, turned on her heel, walked briskly through the sand to her car, and drove away. Half an hour later when the rehearsal, in an atmosphere of oppressive gloom, was under way again, I crept unobserved to my own car and followed her.

Meanwhile my own house, owing to Eloise's flamboyant convalescence, was becoming practically uninhabitable. After her first week in bed and when her temperature had dropped she was allowed by Dr. Bowman to come downstairs for a few hours each day and ensconce herself firmly on the back verandah. Fortunately her mild rash had erupted mostly on her back and chest and there were only very few spots on the lower part of her face and neck. These she camouflaged ingeniously by wrapping her head in a hyacinth-blue scarf which she arranged in the form of a yashmak, over which her lovely eyes looked sorrowfully and mysteriously. She lay on a chaise longue, which Tahali had carried down from her bedroom, under a patterned Chinese silk coverlet that Robin had brought me from Honolulu years ago. The effect, I need hardly say, was stunning.

The fiction was successfully maintained that she was suffering from a mild but obscure tropical malaise. I had primed Dr. Bowman, who had looked at me rather whimsically, I thought, but agreed to play up. Every afternoon between the hours of four and seven she received a stream of callers. Principal among these were Chris Mortlock, who stared at her yearningly; Hali Alani, who came less regularly but gaped with equal ardour; Lucy and Bimbo, Dusty and Buddha, Colonel Shelton and several officers from the Royal Shropshires who arrived with leis and immense bouquets and baskets of fruit; and both the Fumbasi brothers, bearing gifts of jade and alabaster. All this naturally upset the routine running of the house. The servants rose to the occasion magnificently, and Tahali, although overworked to the point of collapse, managed to remain calm, efficient, and almost miraculously good-humoured. Not so Robin, however, who took an increasingly embittered view of the situation. I had to admit that I saw his point. For a breadwinner to arrive home every evening tired and hot after a long day's work on the plantation and find a sort of cocktail marathon taking place on his own back porch was irritating, to say the least of it. After the first day or two when he faced up to the fact that there was going to be no letup and that the number of callers would probably increase rather than diminish, I arranged a small drink tray on our bedroom verandah so that we could enjoy our "sundowners" in comparative peace. The peace was only comparative, however, because the verandah looked over the front drive, and we were continually forced to cower well back in order not to be seen by Eloise's arriving and departing guests.

Every morning, from the first day of Eloise's illness onwards, there arrived punctually on the dot of nine-thirty a young Samolan boy on a bicycle who delivered a single gardenia wrapped in cellophane and pedalled away again. There was no card or message with these daily tributes, and finally, consumed with curiosity, I asked Eloise about them. She went rather pink and gave an embarrassed little cough.

"They're from Daphne and Lydia," she said. "It really is angelic of them, isn't it?"

"Most thoughtful," I replied, repressing a desire to burst out laughing. "Nobody can deny that your personal impact on this island has been considerable all the way round."

"I must say everyone has been terribly sweet to me." She smiled wanly, then her expression hardened. "Everyone, that is, except Bunny. I haven't had a sign from him of any sort."

"He's away on a fishing trip."

"Even so he might at least have sent a telegram or something."

"It's difficult to send telegrams from remote coral atolls."

"The whole wretched business is all his fault anyhow," she said petulantly.

"How much do you really mind—about Bunny?"

"I don't know." She turned her head away. "I feel miserable about him at moments and wish everything was lovely and gay and romantic like it was in Capri last year. Then when I think of that awful house and how beastly he was to me I feel sort of numb inside and don't care if I never set eyes on him again. In any case I've decided to go home as soon as I'm well enough. I've imposed on you and Robin for far too long as it is."

"Nonsense," I said. "It's been lovely having you, you've cheered up the whole place."

"Angel!" she murmured weakly, blowing me a kiss and closing her eyes. I went quietly out of the room.

One morning about a week after this conversation I was preparing to go over to Kelly's Tavern and have a picnic lunch with the children when Daphne drove up to the front door at breakneck speed in an M.G. convertible. She was wearing scarlet pants, a white shirt, and a bandana handkerchief tied rakishly round her head. All she needed were gold earrings and a green macaw on her shoulder for her resemblance to a weather-beaten pirate with unusually large hips to be complete.

After she had crushed my hand in a hearty grip I led her through the house out onto the back verandah, feeling that I ought to shout "yo ho ho" and offer her a noggin of rum. However, she settled, surprisingly enough, for a tomato juice and sat on the verandah rail swinging her legs.

"I thought I'd just pop over and see how the invalid was," she said. "Has anyone found out exactly what's the matter with her yet?"

"Oh yes." I smiled confidingly. "It's a rather rare virus infection with a peculiar name. Dr. Bowman told it to me yesterday, but it's gone clean out of my head. Fortunately Eloise's case is an extremely mild one and she's recuperating by leaps and bounds. Would you like to go up and see her?"

"Not before I've talked to you first." She got off the rail and stood looking out over the garden for a moment, whistling nonchalantly through her teeth. "You must have been having a pretty bloody time what with one thing and another. It's not much cop having someone ill in the house anyway, is it?"

"No. Hardly any cop at all."

"How's the epileptic nurse?"

"She's gone, and it wasn't epilepsy she had but diabetes."

"Pretty bad show for a nurse to have either, if you ask me."

"I quite agree. But she was very good about it. She only had one attack, poor thing."

"I know. Eloise told me all about it on the telephone." She paused. "What I really came over to suggest is this . . ." She paused again and cleared her throat. "Would it be any help to you if Eloise came to Fisherman's Hole for a bit? I didn't want to ask her definitely without consulting you first, but I do feel that being right on the sea would be a change for her and probably perk her up a bit. What do you think?"

"If she agrees I think it's a splendid idea," I replied, trying to keep too much enthusiasm out of my voice. "And it really is most kind of you. Have you discussed it with her at all?"

"Well, I sort of hinted at it." Daphne looked down almost demurely. "And she didn't sound dead against it. But of course I don't want to shove my oar in where it's not wanted, after all she is your house guest, I merely thought that . . ." She cleared her throat again. "With all you've got on your hands at the moment it might be a bit of a relief to have your house to yourself for a little."

"How does Lydia feel about it?" I asked, and immediately wished I hadn't because it sounded impertinent and overintimate.

However, I needn't have worried, for Daphne gave a hearty laugh.

"Oh, Lydia's all for it. You see, we've got old Ursula stuck with us for another two weeks at least, and between you and me she's beginning to get us down a bit. She is inclined to be rather intense, you know."

"Yes," I replied feelingly. "I did notice that tendency."

"And if Eloise is in the house," Daphne went on, "it will sort of lighten the atmosphere, if you know what I mean."

"I certainly do. Eloise is a splendid atmosphere lightener. However, I think you'd better be prepared for followers. The rush hours are generally from four to seven."

"We can cope all right." Daphne laughed again. "She doesn't have to have any particular medical treatment, does she?"

"Oh no," I said without thinking. "The scabs are all off now, and the whole thing's disappearing rapidly."

"Scabs?"

"From Dr. Bowman's injections," I went on hurriedly. "He treated her with some special serum which made two little scars on her arm—rather like vaccination, you know, when it takes. But they've nearly cleared up, and in a day or two they should be gone entirely."

"Good show!" said Daphne. "Let's go up and pop the question."

Two days later Daphne reappeared in the M.G. and bore Eloise away, waving gracefully, in a cloud of dust. When they had gone I wandered from room to room like Madame Ranevsky in *The Cherry Orchard*, except that she was bidding farewell to her house and I seemed to be meeting mine again after a long absence.

Robin and I lunched blissfully and alone on the back verandah, and in the afternoon, when he had gone back to the plantation, Tahali and I resolutely stripped the swing seat of its awning and cushions and oiled it within an inch of its life. This took quite a time, but when it was done and the various pools of oil on the floor had been wiped up and the awning and cushions replaced, Tahali retired, grinning triumphantly, to the kitchen while I lay back, swinging myself soundlessly with one foot and staring up at the pattern of trees against the sky.

At four-thirty Nanny returned with the children, who were burnt black and in a state of high excitement. We had a "family reunion" tea under the Pareanda tree on the lawn, during which they regaled me shrilly with accounts of their adventures by the sea. They had been taken out in a speedboat by an American gentleman who wore a shirt with pineapples on it: Simon had been taught by Kokoano, Juanita's head beach boy, how to do a jack-knife dive: Cokey and Janet, while building a sand castle, had found a gold cigarette case with "To Baba now and forever" written on it in diamonds. This, on Nanny's insistence, they had handed in at the desk whereupon the owner, presumably "Baba," a Mrs. Garsch from Omaha, Nebraska, had, on identifying the case, uttered a great cry, burst into sobs, and crushed Cokey and Janet to her bosom. Later on when her emotion had subsided she had appeared suddenly in their bungalow while they were having their supper, smothered them both in kisses, and given them each a large box of chocolate peppermints. In addition to all this excitement Juanita had organized a moonlight picnic for them and some other children staying in the hotel. This had taken place in a cove a few miles away, and they had lit a bonfire and roasted popcorn and Simon had been sick. At the end of the recital Tahali cleared away the tea things, and we played "Grandmother's Steps" up-roariously until it was time for them to go up and have their baths.

I returned, exhausted but happy, to the silent swing seat and glanced through the evening post which Eulalie had left on the table. There were three bills, one receipt, a post card for Robin from his sister in Scotland, and a letter from Mother. When I opened this a newspaper cutting fell out of it onto the floor. I picked it up and read the headline with a sinking heart. "Duchess Stricken in Tropical Paradise." The article under it was brief and to the point. "The Duchess of Fowey, at present visiting friends in the Samolan Islands, has been struck down by a virulent but obscure tropical disease. Local specialists have as yet been unable to identify its exact nature and are keeping her under the closest observation. The Duke of Fowey, on being telephoned to at Kemberton, his ancestral home in Cornwall, expressed surprise at the news. 'It's the first I've heard of it,' he said. When asked if there was any truth in the rumours that he and the duchess were planning a separation, he refused to make any comment." I put down the cutting with a trembling hand and turned to Mother's letter.

My Darling Grizel,

What *on earth* is happening? Jeannie found this piece in the paper this morning so I cut it out and am sending it to you *immediately*. I *cannot* believe you wouldn't have cabled me if things were *really* serious but I must admit I am very worried. Are you and the children all right? How tiresome of that silly woman to get a tropical disease in the first place and how *idiotic* of the doctors out there not to know what it is. I expect they're all lazy and behind the times like that dreadful Indian with a high voice that poor Lavinia had in Ceylon who gave her nothing but rice and garlic and nearly killed her. Cynthia came to lunch last Tuesday and told me a lot about the Foweys. She apparently knows them quite well and says that *she*, your Eloise, has always been a great one for the men and that for the last year she has been carrying on with a Bunny Something-or-other who lives in SAMOLO! This all sounds very fishy to me and I can only hope darling that you haven't allowed yourself to become *involved* in any way. You know how easily persuaded you are. I shall never forget how you encouraged that foolish Gladys Hokeby to go rushing off to Kenya with Bluey Duckworth, and look at them now! Stuck out there without a penny to their name and surrounded by Mau-Maus. I know you probably think I'm a stupid old woman and belong to another generation, but I can only say that *I'm glad I do* when I see how people are behaving nowadays. Ellen Fennel came up to London from Exeter for a week and we had a high old time. She really is wonderfully cheerful considering everything. We went to the cinema twice and also to a matinee of the Royal Ballet at Covent Garden which was *thrilling*. As for that Margot Fonteyn I could just eat her up! No more news now. Please write the *moment* you receive this. I shan't have a minute's peace until I know that everything is all right. Fondest love to Robin and the children and lots of hugs, from your loving,

Mother.

P.S. Jeannie went to spend the day with her married niece at Chislehurst and my dear, all the children were in bed with chicken pox! Fortunately grown-ups can't get it otherwise I should have been *very* worried!

TWENTY-ONE

The next few days, as far as my own household was concerned, were comfortingly uneventful, although as far as the island of Samolo was concerned, they were very eventful indeed.

Two enormous cruise ships arrived and dropped anchor in the harbour and disgorged upon the already palpitating city of Pendarla hundreds of eager American tourists who crammed the hotels, restaurants, and beaches, photographed everything within reach, including each other, and, as Buddha had predicted, sent all the prices in the shops soaring to astronomical heights. "Hinchcliffe's Samolan Tours" had very astutely imported a large number of vast Cadillacs and Chevrolets from Honolulu several weeks before, and these, bulging with perspiring sight-seers, swirled in clouds of dust along the once quiet roads, making the air hideous with the din of their klaxons and adding considerably to the mounting frenzy and confusion which was pervading the whole island. Also, as Buddha had predicted, journalists of all sorts and descriptions swarmed out of the air from all corners of the world. These not only overran the hotels, restaurants, and beaches, but forced their way into various houses, extorting interviews and "real life" stories from the startled inmates which they reported back to their editors in London, Paris, New York, and Hollywood, thereby completely disrupting the local postal, telegraph, and telephone services and reducing the ordinary business routines of the colony to a state of chaos and frustration.

Sandra and H.E., with loathing in their hearts but welcoming smiles on their faces, gave an official press reception in the ballroom of Government House. Robin and I, Dusty and Buddha, Lucy and Bimbo, Hali Alani and about thirty others were asked in to help, so we all assembled early to greet the invading hordes. The whole thing was admirably organized with a series of buffet tables set on the patio and the Royal Shropshire's band blowing away at Gilbert and Sullivan on the newly erected bandstand. The guests were a motley collection, but they all seemed to be enjoying themselves.

At one point, having disengaged myself tactfully from an intense American lady with double-lens rimless glasses who had been questioning me relentlessly about child welfare in Samolo, I forced my way through the milling throng and went out onto the patio for a breather. I found a vacant chair behind a pillar, sank into it gratefully, and lit a cigarette. My peace, however, was short-lived, for I was immediately assailed by a sharp-eyed young man wearing a Guard's tie and a crumpled tussore suit, accompanied by a dusty-looking girl in green.

"You are Mrs. Craigie?" He spoke with an inadequately camouflaged cockney accent.

"Yes." I nodded amiably.

"I represent the *Daily Express*," he said. "My name is Hodge. This is my colleague, Miss Beeker, *Evening Standard.*"

I rose and shook hands with them both. Mr. Hodge produced a notebook from his breast pocket.

"I hope you don't mind if I ask you a few questions?"

"Not in the least." I sat down again. "What would you like to know?"

"I understand you are a resident of Samolo?"

"Yes. My husband owns a banana plantation."

"How much does that bring in per year?" He looked at me searchingly.

"I cannot believe that the readers of the *Daily Express* could possibly be interested in my husband's financial status." I smiled as convincingly as I could. "In any case it would be difficult to assess it exactly. The yearly income depends on the crops, the crops depend on the weather, and the weather depends on the Almighty."

"That's good," he said, scribbling in his book. "That's very good indeed."

"I understand that you are one of the island's most prominent hostesses?" interposed Miss Beeker.

"Then you have been misinformed," I replied. "We entertain rarely and on a very small scale."

"Is it true that the Duchess of Fowey is your house guest?"

"Quite true."

"She has been seriously ill, hasn't she?"

"No." I shook my head. "She had a mild fever for a few days, but she is now quite well again."

"Is there any truth in the rumour that she and the duke are planning to divorce?"

"As far as I know, none whatsoever."

"If it was true that would make her position here rather difficult, wouldn't it?"

"Why should it?"

"I mean with the Queen and Philip arriving."

"Philip who?" I enquired blandly.

Mr. Hodge looked surprised. "The Duke of Edinburgh, of course."

"Oh, I see." I lapsed into silence and, assuming a vague expression, stared beyond him at the garden. The daylight had nearly gone and the bandsmen were packing up their instruments.

Aware of a certain frigidity in the atmosphere, Mr. Hodge smiled ingratiatingly and changed the subject.

"Would it be correct to say that the colour problem in this colony is practically nonexistent?"

"Quite correct."

"There is no underlying feeling of resentment among the natives?"

"No. As far as I know, there isn't anything for them to resent."

"I was actually thinking of the royal visit."

"We all are," I said enthusiastically. "We're looking forward to it enormously."

"There have never, in your experience, been any race riots, for instance?"

"Occasionally," I said.

"Oh!" Mr. Hodge's eyes brightened.

"But only among the American tourists. And then only on gala nights in the larger hotels."

"Now you're pulling my leg." He sniggered.

"I believe," said Miss Beeker, "that Mr. Bunny Colville is a close neighbour of yours."

"Indeed yes. He has a delightful house, right on the edge of the sea. He's a keen skindiver, you know."

"It is rumoured in Fleet Street that he and the Duchess of Fowey are intimate friends." She gave a refined little cough before the word "intimate."

"Is it really?" I met her eye coldly.

"Is there any truth in it?"

"He's away on a fishing trip at the moment," I said, rising to my feet. "When he comes back I suggest you ask him; his telephone number is in the book." I shook hands with them both. "Please forgive me if I leave you now, but I must go and find my husband. Good-bye. I do hope you both enjoy your stay in Samolo." I bowed to them and walked back into the ballroom.

It was now about seven-thirty, and the ladies and gentlemen of the press had shed what little initial shyness they may have had and were beginning to get rowdy. At eight o'clock Sandra and H.E., still with smiles pinned onto their faces, retired helpless upstairs to their private apartments. Shortly after they'd gone I collected Robin and we sneaked out, got into the car which we'd left by the stables, and drove home.

On the morning following the press reception my garden-party dress arrived from Madame Alice and, assisted by Eulalie and Clementine, who were in transports of excitement, I tried it on immediately, together with the gloves and hat belonging to it. Taken all round the effect was agreeably surprising. The hat was rather larger than I remembered it to be when I had tried it on in the shop; it was also a little big in the crown and inclined to wobble, but we soon fixed this by padding the inside with some cotton wool. I walked slowly downstairs, intending to practise a few curtseys on the back verandah, and was met by Tahali, emerging from the service door. He clapped his hands delightedly and cried, "Beautiful! Beautiful! Mistress look most smashing!" Eulalie and Clementine, who were following me downstairs, joined in the applause and Jock, who was cutting back the hibiscus hedge by the verandah rail, gave a husky cheer. Heartened by this, I curtseyed gracefully to an imaginary monarch and her consort and went over to the swing seat to look at the morning post. Eulalie and Clementine disappeared into the kitchen, Jock went on with the hedge, and Tahali went off to answer the front-door bell. I was just opening a parcel containing two *Spectators* and one *Time and Tide* when he reappeared. I knew, by his whole demeanour and the glint of repressed excitement in his eye, that he was the bearer of startling news.

"There is a gentleman to see you, mistress."

"Gentleman? Who is it?"

"He wished me to say that he is the Duke of Fowey."

I rose hurriedly, bumping my head against the awning of the swing seat and knocking my hat on one side.

"Ask him to come in," I said in a strangled voice, adjusting my hat and trying to tear off my gloves at the same time. Tahali retired and returned in a flash, announcing rather more loudly than was strictly necessary, "The Duke of Fowey." He stepped aside with a low bow, and Droopy walked out of the house wearing a beige-coloured Palm Beach suit and carrying a Panama hat. He looked rather nervous.

"I'm most awfully sorry to burst in on you like this without any warning," he said. "I meant to send a cable but there wasn't time; I only just caught the plane by the skin of my teeth as it was."

I managed to wrench off my right glove in time to shake hands with him.

"What a lovely surprise!" I said, a little breathlessly. "I'm delighted to see you. Do sit down and have some coffee or a drink or something; you must be exhausted."

"It's a bit early for a drink," he said, "but I wouldn't say no to a whisky and soda." I nodded to Tahali, who bowed again and retired. The duke sat down and put his Panama hat on the table.

"It was a bit bumpy coming in to land," he said. "I expect it was the mountains."

"Yes," I said, laughing merrily for no reason whatsoever. "I expect it was." He looked at me with an expression of faint bewilderment and I went on quickly, "I must explain that I don't usually dress like this in the mornings. I was only having a sort of private rehearsal for the royal garden party. As you may know, we're expecting the Queen and the Duke of Edinburgh the day after tomorrow, and we're all in rather a frizz." I took off my hat, flung it onto a chair, and pushed my hair into place.

271

"I was a bit worried about Eloise," he said. "How is the old girl?"

"Completely recovered. There really isn't anything to worry about at all."

"Is she here?"

"Well, as a matter of fact she isn't at the moment." I tried, not very successfully, to keep a note of embarrassment out of my voice. "She's staying at a place called Fisherman's Hole, on the coast."

"Is that Bunny Colville's place?" I could detect no emotion in his voice, and he looked me straight in the eye.

"No. It belongs to Daphne Gilpin. She and Eloise were in the M.T.C. at the beginning of the war. I was too. That's where we first met."

At this moment Tahali returned with a whisky and soda which he handed to the duke, and looked at me enquiringly.

"Yes, Tahali," I said, feeling as if I were drowning, "I should like one too." I sat down on the swing seat, and Droopy and I looked at each other in silence for a moment. We had never actually met before, although I had seen photographs of him occasionally in the *Tatler* and the *Sketch*. He had thinning fair hair which was turning grey; his deep-set eyes were blue and looked vulnerable and his figure was impeccable. His weakest feature was his chin, which, although not actually receding, looked as though it might begin to at any minute. I was aware, sitting there face to face with him, of an overwhelming sense of guilt. I must, I reflected, appear in his eyes to be a thoroughly shoddy character. I cursed Bunny bitterly in my heart for having landed me in this hideously unattractive position, but I cursed myself even more for having been such a weak-minded idiot in the first place. From the very outset I had had vague premonitions of scandal and divorce, but I had envisaged it all in general terms, more or less remote from myself. Never, in my worst moments of uneasiness over the whole affair, had I foreseen that a day would come when I would be confronted with the victim, the injured party, a perfectly polite and agreeable man at whose betrayal I had so shamelessly connived. It was intolerable, and I felt myself blushing to the roots of my hair. Perhaps some of my inner turmoil communicated itself to the duke, for he looked at me over the edge of his glass and said, with a glint in his eye, "Cheer up."

"I'm afraid I don't know what you mean." I gave what I knew to be a glassy smile. "I'm perfectly cheerful, only a little hot." I put my hand up to my flushed face and wished the ground would open and swallow me.

"I'm feeling a bit hot too," he said. "Would you mind terribly if I took off my coat?"

"Of course not. Please do by all means." He rose to his feet, took off his coat, hung it carefully over the back of his chair, and sat down again.

"A cousin of mine, Jennifer Trout, used to be rather thick with Daphne Gilpin," he said. "Did you ever run across her?"

"No, I'm afraid I didn't." I offered him a cigarette from a dreadful bamboo box that the plantation workers had given Robin on his last birthday, and noticed that my hand was trembling. "What a peculiar name."

"She was a peculiar gal," said the duke, taking one. "Went about everywhere in jodhpurs and rode a motor bike. Used to be known in the family as Gunga Din."

"Oh!" I said weakly, and started to laugh.

"I don't know what's become of her now." The duke lit a cigarette and settled back in his chair. "The last we heard of her was that she was clambering up a mountain somewhere or other with a Mexican lady novelist. What's this Daphne Gilpin like? I never actually met her myself."

"She's quite fun in a way. She has a very fast speedboat," I added fatuously.

The duke lifted one eyebrow at me. "One of the boys, I presume?"

"Well . . ." I hesitated. "She has got the reputation for being a little eccentric. She and Lydia French have been living out here together for some years. Their house is quite lovely; it's built on the rocks overhanging the sea. Robin and I took Eloise there to dine a short while ago and Eloise absolutely fell in love with the place, and so, of course, when Daphne very kindly suggested that she should go there for a few days to convalesce, she naturally jumped at the opportunity." I finished with rather a rush and met his eye boldly.

"How ill was she actually?"

"Not very. She had some weird sort of tropical virus that sent her temperature up, but the doctor soon got it down again."

"Good." The duke smiled affably and sipped his drink. "I think it's been uncommonly nice of you and your husband to have looked after her for all this time."

"We've loved having her," I said. "She's been an angel."

"Oh God!" said the duke, and laughed.

At this moment Tahali appeared with my whisky and soda. I took it and turned to the duke.

"Would you care for something to eat? A sandwich for instance. It wouldn't take a minute."

"No, thank you. I had a sort of cardboard breakfast on the plane." Tahali bowed and withdrew. The duke lifted his glass. "Here's to your very good health," he said.

I murmured a rather strangled "thank you," lifted my own glass, and took a large gulp from it. My brain was racing. How much did he really know about Eloise and Bunny, and how much was he guessing? When I had told him that Eloise was at Fisherman's Hole, he had said, "Is that Bunny Colville's place?" so nonchalantly, as though he took it for granted that she would be there. Why had he flown out here so suddenly? Was it because he was really concerned over Eloise's illness? Or had he pounced down out of the sky unexpectedly so as to catch the guilty lovers red-handed? He appeared to be completely composed, sitting there opposite to me, and the expression in his eyes was devoid of suspicion, merely mildly humourous. But how was I to know whether or not this apparent composure was only a façade masking an inner ferment of outraged pride, jealousy, and an implacable desire to avenge his honour at any cost? I had to admit, looking at him, that if this were the case he must be a consummate actor, for he seemed to be utterly relaxed and without a care in the world. He looked out over the garden at the view appreciatively. The banana leaves on the other side of the ravine were vivid in the morning sunlight, and the far away mountains were misty blue against a cloudless, eggshell sky.

"This is certainly a beautiful place," he said. "I've never been to the real tropics before. You can't really count Madeira, can you?"

"No," I said, still distracted and struggling to make up my mind what line to take. "I don't suppose you can."

"What's that enormous tree covered in red flowers?"

"A flamboyant, or a poinciana, whichever you like. There are always several names for everything out here. The Samolans call it 'raki tali,' red tree. When it's not in blossom it's covered with large brown pods which look rather like bedroom slippers."

"I expect you're wondering why I suddenly appeared like this, so abruptly and without any warning?" he said, disconcertingly.

"Well," I replied with a slight gulp, "as a matter of fact I was, rather."

"Do you think you could give me a brief résumé of the situation as you see it at the moment?" he asked gently.

"Situation?" I met his eye and felt myself flushing again.

"That is, of course, without betraying too many confidences." He smiled a trifle absently and sipped his drink.

"At the present time almost anything anybody asks me seems to entail betraying confidences," I answered. "It's becoming rather a strain."

"I expect you know that there have been rumours in the press about Eloise and me divorcing?"

"Yes, I do. I had a letter from my mother. She mentioned having seen it in the *Daily Express*." I evaded his steady gaze and lit a cigarette with as much casualness as I could muster. "I hope there's no truth in it?"

"Well, in a way there is and in a way there isn't. What I really mean is that it's up to Eloise actually. I'm not particularly keen on the idea myself on account of being fond of the old girl. But I can't go on letting her go bashing about indefinitely and imagining I don't know anything about it, can I? It makes me look such a bloody fool." He sighed without rancour and went on. "You see, I've known about the Bunny Colville business for a long time, ever since it began really. I knew when she said she was coming out here to stay with you that the whole thing was a bit of a put-up job and that she was really coming out to be with him. I half intended to have it out on the mat before she left, and then I decided that it would be better to wait and see how things turned out. It's no use arguing with somebody when they've worked themselves up into a 'thing' about somebody else, is it? I mean it only leads to scenes, and I loathe scenes."

"That applies to most people." Feeling suddenly irritated, I put my glass down rather more heavily than I intended and looked him squarely in the eye. "But if I may say so I think that a few well-timed scenes in the earlier years of your married life might have prevented this present situation happening at all."

"I had enough well-timed scenes with my first wife. She revelled in them. She once threw a soup plate at me in Claridge's," the duke said reminiscently. "If it hadn't been for the two boys I'd have got rid of her long before I did. However, she finally bounded off to Cairo with a trombone player, and so everything turned out for the best."

"What on earth would a trombone player want to go to Cairo for?"

"To play his bloody trombone, I suppose," replied the duke. "He was an Arab anyhow."

"I presume you got the custody of the children."

"Oh Lord, yes. David, the younger one, is still at Eton, and making a little beast of himself if all I hear is true. The older one, Nigel, is at Oxford. He'll be twenty-one next month. I'm going to give a 'do' for him at Kemberton. You know, trestle tables and tenants and all that sort of lark. I'm hoping Eloise will be back in time for it. Nigel will be damned disappointed if she isn't. He adores her."

"And what about you?"

He lifted an eyebrow at me. "How do you mean?"

"Do you adore her?"

The duke pursed his lips, blew a smoke ring through them, and watched it spiralling up into the air. "I think that would be putting it a bit strongly," he said. "When we were first married in 1946 I was potty about her, of course, but that wore off in time, as it usually does. The trouble with Eloise is that she's so damned decorative. I mean you can't see the wood for the trees."

"You must know what the wood's like by now."

"Yes, I suppose I do," he chuckled. "It isn't even a wood really; it's nothing but a pretty little copse. At times rather a shady little copse!" he added, and chuckled again.

"Do you really mind whether she comes back to you or not?"

"Yes, of course I do. As I said before, I'm genuinely fond of her. I know she's as vain as a peacock and a terrible fathead over a lot of things, but when she's at her best and not mooning about over some new heartthrob or other, she can be damned good value and gay company."

"With her looks and charm, do you think that just being damned good value and gay company is enough to satisfy her?"

"Perhaps not. But a time will come when it will have to be. She's no chicken, you know."

"We none of us are." I laughed suddenly.

"Why are you laughing?"

"I don't know. I think it's relief more than anything else."

"Where is Bunny at the moment?"

"He's away on a fishing trip. We haven't heard a word from him for two weeks."

"Oh." The duke looked thoughtful.

"I suppose you know him?"

"Oh Lord, yes. I've known him on and off for years. We often play backgammon together at White's."

"Do you like him?"

"Of course." The duke looked surprised. "He's a very attractive chap."

"How do you feel about him now? I mean since you've found out about him and Eloise?"

"I'm not sure really. Much the same, I suppose. Naturally there have been moments when I've felt pretty bitter, but there's not much sense in that. After all I can't very well blame him for falling in love with Eloise. Lots of people do. I faced up to that when I married her. I never seriously imagined that I should be able to keep her to myself for long."

"Wasn't that rather a defeatist attitude?"

"It seemed to me to be plain horse sense at the time. As a matter of fact it still does."

"Oh dear!" I felt at a loss for words.

"I expect it sounds a bit spineless to you," the duke continued. "I suppose I just don't happen to be the jealous type, that's all. In any case, Bunny isn't the only one she's had a flip around with, only I think perhaps that this is a bit more serious than the others. That, of course, is the real reason I flew out here. I wanted to find out whether this was the final crack-up or not."

"I see." I stared at him helplessly, wondering how much of his clinical detachment was real, or how much of it was assumed in order to deceive others and, possibly, himself.

"I married Eloise fourteen years ago," he said quietly. "She was one of the most sought after and alluring young women in England. The first few years were fine, absolutely nothing wrong with them at all. Then things inevitably began to change. I should have been a fool not to have expected them to. From then on I've merely proceeded to adjust myself as well as I could. The process hasn't been entirely painless, of course, but certainly not so bad as it might have been if I had worked myself into jealous frenzies and made scenes and broken everything to pieces. I am no longer in love with Eloise, but I'm proud of her and fond of her and I have a feeling that, in the long run, she'll be happier with me than with anyone else. She's not nearly so amorous and promiscuous as she pretends to be, you know. She just loves being adored and wanted. And one man isn't enough." He paused and leaned forward with a pleading look in his eyes. "You haven't yet done what I asked you to do a little while ago."

"You mean give you a brief résumé of the situation as I see it at the moment?"

"Yes. I would like to know. Honestly I would."

"As a matter of fact," I said gently, "things are definitely looking up, from your point of view I mean. The situation isn't as bad as you think. Owing to a number of quite unforeseen circumstances, the huge cloudy symbols of Eloise's high romance have dwindled considerably."

"How do you mean?" he asked, his eyes brightening.

"It's a long saga, and fraught with incident, and I promise you that later on I will tell it to you in detail. Actually, I assure you I can hardly wait because by doing so I shall be able to purge my conscience, and, believe me, my conscience has been going through a sticky time during these last few weeks. But it is all really far too complicated to explain at the moment. I have a thousand things to do, including getting out of these idiotic clothes and attending a committee meeting at eleven o'clock. Where are you staying?"

"I'm not staying anywhere," he replied forlornly. "I tried four hotels on the way here, but they were all crammed to the gunwales."

"Where's your baggage?"

"I've only got one case. It's in the taxi outside."

"Good heavens! Do you mean to say you've kept a taxi ticking up all this time?"

"I told him to switch off his engine," said the duke apologetically. "I wasn't quite sure if you would be at home or how long I was going to be here or anything."

"You'll have to stay here for a night or two at any rate. There's no chance of your getting into a hotel until after the royal visit."

"It's most awfully kind of you, but I really can't impose on you to that extent."

"Nonsense. There's nowhere else for you to go, and you can't sleep on the beach. You can have Eloise's room. And when she comes back you'll have to share it."

"She may not want to."

"Eloise must learn to take the rough with the smooth," I said firmly. "Anyhow, it's a vast bed so you needn't get in each other's way. Incidentally, have you had chicken pox?"

"Chicken pox?" The duke looked startled. "Yes, I suppose so, when I was a kid. Why?"

"I'll explain later," I said. "It's all part of the saga. In the meantime, you pay off the taxi and I'll tell Tahali to take your bag up. Please relax and make yourself comfortable. You might have a dip in the pool if you feel like it. Tahali will show you where it is. It doesn't look very attractive, I'm afraid, because of the frogs, but it's clean as a whistle and lovely and cool. I shan't be gone more than an hour and a half. If Robin, my husband, gets back for lunch before I do, just tell him who you are and watch his reaction. It might be enjoyable. I really must go and change now."

He took my hand and shook it warmly. "I can never thank you enough," he said, "for being so welcoming, and so understanding."

"My dear duke . . ." I began, feeling rather flurried again, but he interrupted me.

"I am known to my friends as 'Droopy,'" he said. "It was a nickname I had when I was young and very thin indeed, and it sort of stuck."

"Dear Droopy," I said, gratefully aware that an enormous weight had been lifted from my mind, and restraining an impulse to fling my arms round him and hug him, "Welcome to Samolo!"

I left him and went hurriedly upstairs.

TWENTY-TWO

The committee meeting at first was uneventful and dealt mainly with the allocation of seats for the public dress rehearsal. The demand for these had been disappointing because, naturally enough, most people wanted to attend the gala itself when the royal party would be present. It was decided after a certain amount of argument to invite fifty working members of the Women's Federation with one husband or relative each, to fill up the back rows. Alma and Ivy, with the memory of Sandra's tirade still quivering in their minds, cooed at each other like turtledoves. However, Cuckoo, bristling with moral indignation, decided, for reasons best known to herself, to bring up a subject that we had all tacitly agreed to ignore and which was known as "The Problem." The "problem" was that after a recent evening rehearsal, a Sergeant Hancock of the Royal Shropshires had been discovered in a state of considerable undress behind the grandstand with one of Ivy Poland's sprites. The sprite concerned was a lush Samolan girl well over the age of consent whose reputation for casual dalliance with the young bucks of Pendarla had been firmly established for some time. Cuckoo's shrill insistence that "Something Must Be Done," that the girl should be summarily de-sprited and the wretched sergeant arraigned before his commanding officer and confined to barracks, was received coldly. In the first place the girl was one of the leading dancers and much admired locally, and her dismissal would entail a great deal of extra rehearsal for which there was no time. In the second place Sergeant Hancock had already proved himself invaluable as a dashing pirate chief, and his replacement, at this late stage, would cause grave confusion and throw one of the principal scenes in the first half out of balance. Neither of these very practical considerations, however, deflected Cuckoo from her chosen path of moral righteousness. We sat round the table, glum with exasperation, while she expounded her arguments in a spate of clichés, growing rather pink in the face as she did so, until Esmond Templar, unable to bear it any longer, sprang to his feet and flew at her. "Pipe down, dear, for God's sake!" he cried. "You're wasting your own time and everybody else's. We all know that you're the wife of the colonial secretary, but that doesn't mean that you have the right to go on yakking at us like Aimee Semple McPherson. We all know that Tauhua Tali and dear Albert Hancock *shouldn't* have been having a boozle behind the grandstand and that the whole thing is *wicked* and *immoral* and *antisocial* and beyond the pale! But we also know that boys will be boys and girls will be girls and that sex is here to stay and that all the high-flown bellyaching in the world isn't going to make the slightest difference. In addition to which this particular incident isn't any of your business or any of ours either, if it comes to that. If Albert Hancock and Tauhua Tali like to bounce about in the sand till the cows come home that's entirely their affair, providing they don't do it during the performance, and they're unlikely to do that because Inky hasn't written any suitable music for it. So once and for all let's stop all this nonsense and get on with the job." He sat down abruptly and Peter, who was sitting next to him, said "hear hear" loudly.

Cuckoo rose to her feet, white with fury. "How dare you speak to me like that?" she cried, trembling. "How *dare* you?"

"Order, please. Order, everybody!" Alma whacked the table with her hammer.

"Order indeed! I like that, I must say." Cuckoo's voice had risen to a shrill squeak, and she glared balefully at Alma. "You, Alma, as chairman, have the effrontery to say 'order, please' when you have sat there silently and allowed me to be insulted before the entire committee! I have no alternative but to resign here and now and I hereby do so. I have nothing further to say." She pushed back her chair with such force that it fell over with a crash, picked up her bag, and stalked from the room, slamming the door behind her.

There was a dead silence following her exit until Alma, tight-lipped and with a face of stone, whacked her hammer on the table again and declared, in a flat voice, that the meeting was adjourned.

This scene, having protracted the meeting well beyond its ordinary limits, caused me to arrive home a good deal later than I had intended. Instead of putting the car away as usual I left it outside the front door and walked straight through to the back verandah where I found Robin and Droopy comfortably relaxed and drinking bloody Marys. Droopy was attired in a pair of Robin's shorts, a yellow polo shirt, and a pair of faded pink *espadrilles*. They both sprang to their feet politely when I appeared, and I subsided onto the swing seat while Robin mixed me a drink.

"You're very late," he said. "We were beginning to think you'd been involved in a ghastly accident."

"The idea doesn't seem to have disturbed you very much," I observed mildly. "Is lunch ready?"

"Lunch has been ready for at least three quarters of an hour," said Robin. "It is now completely ruined."

"It can't be, because it's only cold beef and salad." I turned to Droopy. "How have you been getting on?" I asked. "Was Robin suitably flustered at finding you here?"

"He doesn't know who I am yet," said Droopy. "I didn't want to spoil your fun, so I told him my name was Mullion and that I had come with a letter of introduction from your mother."

"What on earth made you think of Mullion?"

"It's a cove in Cornwall where I used to go for picnics when I was a boy."

"What on earth are you talking about?" Robin handed me my drink and looked at us both sharply.

"This is the Duke of Fowey, dear," I said. "He just popped over to see how Eloise was getting on."

"Good God!" Robin's jaw dropped and he stared at Droopy incredulously.

"That's an entirely satisfactory reaction," I said. "But you can relax now and banish all craven fear and dissembling because *He Knows All.*"

Robin sat down rather heavily. "The hell he does!"

"Well, perhaps not *quite* all. That is, not the exact details. Because I hadn't time to tell him before I went out. But he has a firm grasp of the essentials."

"I'm sorry about Mullion," interposed Droopy conciliatingly. "It was just a little joke. Your wife and I had quite a long talk this morning, and I think we understand each other."

"Well, I'll be damned!" Robin still looked a bit bewildered. "How about Eloise? Does she know you're here?"

"Not yet," said Droopy. "I thought I'd telephone her later on." He turned to me. "I suppose this Fisherman's—thing has a telephone?"

"Hole," I said. "And it has. 5032."

At this moment Tahali appeared and announced lunch so the three of us went into the dining room, taking our drinks with us. During the meal we obeyed the *pas devant les domestiques* rule and discussed the royal visit, mutual friends, and other general topics. It was not until afterwards, when we had settled ourselves comfortably under the Pareanda tree on the lawn and Tahali had served us our coffee and retired, that I explained to Droopy everything that had happened from the very first morning when Bunny had arrived and persuaded me to have Eloise to stay. Robin interpolated a few comments here and there as I went along, and Droopy listened attentively to the whole saga without changing his expression and without the faintest display of emotion of any sort. I tactfully avoided the temptation to dwell on some of the more comical aspects of the situation because my instincts told me that although he was obviously not lacking in humour, his deeper feelings were a great deal more involved than he would have us believe. When I had finished there was a long silence. Droopy lit a cigarette, lay back in his chair, and gazed thoughtfully at Westinghouse, who was darting in and out of the hibiscus hedge chasing lizards.

Personally I felt an overwhelming sense of relief. I still had an inner feeling of guilt and wished fervently that I had never had anything to do with any of it, but at least now I was free of any further responsibility to Bunny or Eloise. I need no longer torment myself with visions of discovery and public scandal and fears of what new dreadful complications the next day might bring forth. Droopy was here now, and it was up to him and them to settle the situation as they saw fit. I was also fairly certain that, owing to one thing and another, there really wasn't much of a situation left to settle. I glanced at Droopy out of the corner of my eye. He

283

was still puffing away at his cigarette and staring into space. Robin fidgeted uneasily in his chair and coughed.

"I would like to add," he said, obviously feeling that the silence was becoming oppressive, "that Grizel and I feel none too comfortable about our own behaviour over all this." He cleared his throat again. "It all started because Bunny happens to be an old chum of ours and we didn't want to let him down. Later on of course when Eloise arrived and things began to get tricky we realized that we'd got ourselves a good deal more involved than we had ever intended to be. Naturally enough we didn't take your point of view into account very much because you were thousands of miles away and we had neither of us even met you. I know it's a bit late now to say we are sorry, but as a matter of fact we are, damned sorry. And all I can say is that I hope it all turns out all right, for you and Eloise, I mean, and that whichever way it goes you won't feel too bitterly about us." Robin lapsed into silence and went rather red in the face.

"There's no need to apologize, really there isn't." Droopy looked at us both with a wry smile. "I'm not blaming you, either of you, in the least. I expect I'd have done exactly the same if I'd been in your place. Actually I'm not blaming anybody, except perhaps myself, but that's my lookout, isn't it?" He shrugged his shoulders and threw away his cigarette. "The only thing now is to decide what to do. I would welcome any suggestions."

"Would you like me to go and telephone to Eloise?" I said. "Or we could go over and fetch her if you like?"

"I don't quite know." He heaved a sigh. "I'm feeling a bit weak-kneed at the moment. The gunpowder is running out of the heels of my boots."

"I really think I'd better telephone her and tell her you're here," I said, getting up purposefully. "I'll break it to her gently."

"All right. Anything you say." He smiled again, but his eyes looked troubled and I suddenly felt deeply sorry for him. Leaving him and Robin under the tree I walked across the lawn and into the house. As I went into the library the telephone rang and I lifted the receiver irritably, thinking it was probably Lucy or Dusty prepared for a nice gossip or Esmond or Peter wanting to discuss the morning's meeting and Cuckoo's resignation. However, it was neither Lucy, Dusty, Esmond, nor Peter. It was Lydia French, and she was obviously in a state of high hysteria.

"Grizel!" she cried. "Oh, Grizel, is that you?"

"Yes," I replied with a sinking heart. "Of course it is."

"Are you alone?"

"Quite alone. What on earth's the matter?"

"Is Eloise there?"

"Of course she isn't. I understood she was with you."

"Oh God!" Lydia burst into racking sobs.

"Pull yourself together," I said with an edge in my voice. "And tell me what's happened."

There was a slight pause, and then she said in strangled tones, "There's been a terrible scene and I hit Daphne!"

"Fair's fair," I replied unfeelingly. "She's hit you often enough. What did you hit her with?"

"A bottle of crème de menthe." Lydia started to sob again. "And now she's got concussion and Ursula has sent for Dr. Bowman."

"What happened to Eloise?"

"I hit her too," Lydia wailed. "And she ran out of the house."

"I'm glad to hear she was able to," I said furiously. "And I think it's high time you and Daphne learnt a little self-control. To carry on like a couple of elderly Teddy boys at your age is absolutely idiotic and you ought to be ashamed of yourselves!"

"I *am!*" cried Lydia. "Dreadfully ashamed. That's why I rang up—to tell Eloise I was sorry and ask her to forgive me. But now you say she isn't with you there's no knowing what's happened to her. She might have got concussion too and fallen down somewhere, and it's all my fault."

"Don't be so silly," I said. "If she was well enough to run out of the house it's unlikely that she'd suddenly fall down later. However, if she has we shall just have to wait until she gets up again, shan't we? In the meantime I suggest that you take three aspirin, write her a letter of apology, and stop being hysterical. Good-bye."

I hung up the receiver and went into the hall, at which moment there was a screaming of brakes and Daphne's M.G. drew up within a foot of the front door. Eloise switched off the engine, waved cheerfully to me, and uncoiled herself from the driving seat. She was wearing lime-green slacks and a bright pink shirt and looked radiant.

"I'd have got here sooner," she said, giving me a peck on the cheek. "But the traffic on the sea road is ghastly. Just like Derby Day."

"Are you all right?" I enquired anxiously.

"Perfectly," she replied. "But I've learnt a sharp lesson. Those sort of people really aren't my dish, and it's no use pretending they are. I'm sorry to bounce back on you like this without warning, but I really couldn't bear it any longer. That ass Lydia hit me with a bottle!" she added. "Just imagine!"

"I know she did," I said, leading her into the library. "She just called up in a frenzy."

"Fortunately I ducked and she only got me on the shoulder." Eloise took a cigarette from a box, lit it, and sat down on the sofa. "But I thought the time had come to leave, so I took Daphne's car out of the garage and here I am. I suppose we shall have to get it back to her somehow."

"She can send for it," I said coldly. "And serve her right."

"Poor Daphne," Eloise gave a slight giggle. "I really can't help feeling rather sorry for her. She's out for six at the moment. Lydia gave her a terrific bash, and she went down like a sack of potatoes. Fortunately the bottle didn't break."

"What started it all in the first place?"

"Me—I suppose, really." Eloise sighed pensively. "But it's been working up for quite a time, ever since I got there. You see Daphne got a sort of 'thing' about me and kept on taking me out in the Chris-Craft, and of course Lydia got crosser and crosser until to-day at lunch it came to a head and they started screaming at each other. They'd had three stingers each and a lot of red wine. Then we all went into the living room for coffee because the verandah was scorching, and the moment the boy had served it and gone out, the row broke out again and the bullfighter intervened and tried to make peace and Daphne flew at *her* and told her to mind her own bloody business. Then there was a moment of calm and I thought I'd nip upstairs to my room and lie down, but Lydia saw me out of the corner of her eye and suddenly went berserk and started yelling at me. Then chaos set in. Daphne sprang to my defence and slapped Lydia in the face. Lydia seized the bottle of crème de menthe and socked her with it. The bullfighter gave a loud scream and tried to get the bottle away from Lydia, but she evaded her, bashed me with it, and I left." Eloise looked at me with an appealing expression in her lovely eyes. "I don't want you to think that I encouraged Daphne in any way because honestly and truly I didn't. But one can't be absolutely beastly when people are absolutely besotted about one, can one?"

"No," I said dryly. "I suppose one can't."

"Last night after dinner we went off for a spin in the Chris-Craft and things got a bit hectic." Eloise sighed again and her forehead puckered alluringly. "So I just had to tell her straight out that that sort of thing wasn't really my idea of fun and games and never had been. And she really was awfully sweet about it."

"Good for her," I said. "I'm very glad you came back, because I've got a surprise for you."

"Surprise?" She looked at me suspiciously. "It isn't anything to do with Bunny, is it?"

"No," I said. "It isn't anything to do with Bunny at all."

"Is he back?"

"Not that I know of."

Eloise looked relieved. "I'm glad," she said. "I really don't feel I could face any more scenes. I've been thinking a lot lately about the whole business, and I've decided I'd rather not see him again for a while. I thought I'd fly home in a day or two. It ought to be quite easy to get a plane reservation while the royal visit's going on. What do you think?"

"Quite easy. If that's what you really want to do."

"I could cable Droopy to come up to London to meet me. He's sure to be at Kemberton."

"I shouldn't bank on it."

"What do you mean?" She stared at me in astonishment.

"I mean," I said very gently, "I think it's a mistake to take anything or anyone too much for granted."

"Oh." She bit her lip thoughtfully and looked suddenly depressed. "I expect you're right. What's this surprise you were talking about?"

"I'll go and prepare it," I said, getting up.

"Prepare it? It isn't anything to eat, is it?"

"No. It isn't anything to eat." I smiled reassuringly. "If you'll just stay here quietly without moving for two minutes, I'll send it in to you."

"You haven't gone and bought me a present?"

"I haven't bought you anything. But it is a present in a way. A sort of 'going home' present," I added.

"You are an angel, Grizel," said Eloise. "You really and truly are."

I went quietly out of the room and closed the door behind me.

TWENTY-THREE

The public dress rehearsal of the water pageant was due to begin at eight o'clock, so Droopy, Eloise, Robin, and I left the Royal Samolan punctually at seven-thirty. Droopy had insisted on giving us a slap-up farewell dinner party and had gone to a great deal of trouble about it. He and Robin had had a long conference with Siggy Rubia in the morning, and the result was, for the Royal Samolan, ambrosial. We started off with vodka and caviar and then went on to "Cocomaneya," which is one of the few really succulent Samolan specialities. It consists of green coconuts, scraped out and refilled with chicken fricassee, sweet corn, chopped bacon, onions, garlic, and the coconut flesh, then sealed up again with flour paste, baked in a hot oven, and served, steaming dramatically, with dry white rice and chutney. This was followed by the usual array of exotic Samolan fruits and papaya ice cream, all of which, accompanied by a great deal of delicious pink champagne, had put us into a good mood to say the least of it, and we piled into the station wagon and set off, giggling happily and prepared for anything.

Sandra, very sweetly, had sent round in the afternoon four large pink tickets which not only gave us the right to sit with her and H.E. in the Royal Stand but allowed us the additional privilege of driving right into the cove itself instead of having to leave the wagon in the car park and go down on foot.

Cobb's Cove, in its own untrammelled state, is one of the show places of the island. It is a perfectly symmetrical crescent of white coral sand, only a few hundred yards in diameter, enclosed by two rocky headlands, the sides of which drop sheer into the deep water beyond the line of the incoming waves. The real surf of

289

course is a mile out to sea and thunders perpetually on the reef with a muffled roar . . . a sound so familiar to all of us who live here that when we go away we miss it and are suddenly startled and think there's something wrong with our ears.

Behind the beach a coconut grove slopes gradually towards the road, and on the left-hand side a deep, clear stream of cool fresh water slides into the warm sea.

Finch and Faber, assisted by the Fumbasi brothers and the Pendarla Electrical Company, having been labouring for weeks, had certainly made a remarkable job of the seating arrangements and lighting, but the intrinsic magic of the place had, not unnaturally, evaporated considerably in the process. Sandra and H.E. hadn't yet arrived, and we settled ourselves in the front of the box where the royal party, poor dears, would be compelled to sit in a few days' time. There was a great deal of activity going on. The rows of seats to the right and left of the grandstand were filling up rapidly, and from a large bamboo and banana-mesh enclosure on the right, presumably a dressing room, came the sound of giggling interspersed occasionally by shrill screams. As is usual in all Samolan public entertainments, there were children all over the place who were continually scampering out onto the sand and being shooed back to their relatives by half a dozen smartly uniformed policemen who had been placed at strategic points along the beach to keep order. On the tier immediately below where we were sitting the cream of Pendarla society, dressed to the nines, were assembling. The appearance of Eloise, ravishing in a plain white Dior dress with a black chiffon scarf, caused a mild sensation. Led by Hali Alani, who kissed her hand passionately over the rail, her island admirers crowded round and enquired ardently about her health. Droopy, obviously well accustomed to this sort of procedure, beamed complacently and with a gleam of possessive pride in his eye.

Presently, when the excitement had died down a little, the band of the Royal Shropshires, which was huddled, a trifle insecurely, I thought, on a wooden rostrum under an umbrella of wild almond trees, began to tune up with little irrelevant trills and glissandi on the trumpets and wood winds and intermittent bangings on the drums. Ever since I was taken to my first pantomime at the age of nine this particular sound has enchanted me. It evokes nostalgic memories of warmth and plush and gold: of squeezing sixpences into slots to release tiny pairs of opera glasses: of sudden, thrilling darkness followed by footlights glowing on red velvet curtains: of feverish anticipation, excited wriggling, and chocolates in silver paper. I have never outgrown this special joy, although the present-day theatres of our welfare state with either no music at all or a panatrope scratching away in an empty orchestra pit concealed by dusty greenery have dampened it considerably and provide little prelude to glamour. However, I managed to recapture a small whiff of it sitting there looking out over the dark sea with the band tuning up and the lights glimmering in the trees.

Eloise, having been "receiving" at the rail for at least ten minutes, finally sat down and adjusted her scarf. "You must admit, darling," she said to Droopy with an almost tremulous smile, "the people here simply couldn't be sweeter. They've been absolutely wonderful to me, really they have."

"I don't blame them," said Droopy. "You look smashing!"

At this moment a programme seller came up and presented her with a single gardenia wrapped in cellophane and a card attached to it with a pin. Eloise read the card. "Oh dear!" she said with an apologetic expression, and handed it to me. I recognized the handwriting immediately. It was neat and firm and had a masculine flourish. The message was brief and to the point. "Farewell! Thou art too dear for my possessing." There was no signature. I handed it back to her. "Why didst thou promise such a beauteous day," I said. "And make her travel forth without her cloak?"

"Darling!" Eloise looked at me wide-eyed. "What on earth are you talking about?"

Suddenly there was a long roll of drums from the bandstand and six trumpeters sprang to their feet and blew a rather untidy fanfare.

"I'll explain later," I said, rising. "Here comes His Excellency the Governor."

We all stood up, and after a minute or two's pause H.E. and Sandra came into the box followed by Chris Mortlock and a handsome young man who had been co-opted from the Royal Shropshires as an extra A.D.C.

"We ran over an idiotic hen," Sandra hissed to me. "And had to stop and apologize and pay for it. That's what's made us late. The whole business has unnerved me." She hurriedly greeted Robin and Eloise and Droopy and moved, with H.E., to the front of the box. The audience rose and applauded and we stood to attention while the band played the National Anthem. When it was over Sandra beckoned to Droopy to sit on her right and placed Eloise on George's left. Robin and I and the A.D.C.s sat immediately behind. The audience reseated themselves on their chairs and benches amid a babble of conversation which was drowned out by the band embarking briskly on a selection from *The Pirates of Penzance*.

"The dear Royal Shropshires," said Sandra. "They're always right up-to-the-minute, aren't they?"

"Inky Blumenthal's overture isn't orchestrated yet," I said, leaning forward. "The only alternatives to this were *The Indian Love Lyrics*, *The Gondoliers*, and *William Tell*."

"We shall probably get the lot before the evening's over." Sandra produced her glasses from her bag and studied the programme. "I'm afraid it's going to be a long job."

At the end of the overture the lights in the trees went out all except one which stayed on, resolutely pinpointing Mrs. Innes-Glendower, who was sitting in the front row wearing a multi-coloured Chinese coat and a glittering Spanish comb embedded in her bright blue hair. She fidgeted unhappily in the glare and shaded her eyes with her hand. There were some muffled shouts, and Alma's voice rang out authoritatively from the darkness. "If it won't go out by itself somebody must climb up and *turn* it out!" There was a short pause and the sound of further argument until a small boy dashed out onto the sand, shinnied up the tree like a monkey, and wrestled valiantly with the lamp. He managed to shift it slowly round so that it illuminated each of the occupants of the front row in turn, including old Sir Albert, who shrank back in his seat and placed a handkerchief over his head. Finally the poor boy, obviously in the grip of mounting panic, shook the lamp violently with the result that it broke away from its moorings and fell with a dull thud onto the beach where it was pounced upon by two policemen who staggered away with it into the shadows. The little boy slid down the tree to vociferous applause and the band struck up the opening bars of Inky Blumenthal's water music.

While this was going on, Captain Gedge and Lieutenant Proctor of the Royal Shropshires, both of whom had had previous experience of Military Tattoos at Aldershot, switched on two searchlights from each side of the cove and Keela Alioa was discovered standing facing the sea with his back to us with his arms outstretched to the stars. The small waves were breaking over his feet and he turned slowly, with exquisite grace, and walked out of the sea towards us. He was wearing a short silver tunic, and in the bright light his dark skin shone like polished mahogany. He began to speak, but his first words were lost in a spontaneous burst of applause. We were all well used to Keela's good looks, but the picture of this handsome young Samolan standing there against the night was suddenly breath-taking.

"Well," said Sandra, clapping vigorously. "It's started with a nice sexy bang at any rate, hasn't it?"

Keela certainly spoke the prologue resonantly and well but alas, the lines themselves fell a good way below his rendering of them. Kerry Stirling, although he was Samolo's literary lion and had written a number of successful novels reeking with local atmosphere, obviously had no more than a nodding acquaintance with the poetic muse. His verse, hovering uneasily between Scott, Macaulay, and Ella Wheeler Wilcox, was at its best merely serviceable and at its worst almost excruciatingly banal. There was a great deal of heavy-handed allegory interspersed with flowery rhyming couplets such as:

> "Long long ago in Time's primaeval dawn
> This island paradise, in fire, was born
> And fire and water, striving hand in hand
> Wrought, on this desolate, small coral strand
> Strange music where, as yet, no birds had sung
> And whilst the ancient universe, still young,
> Gazed down upon a sea of azure blue
> Amazed to see a miracle come true,
> Far out, beyond the breaker's thundrous boom,
> Other small islets born of Neptune's womb
> Rose up like jewels from the deeps below
> Thus to create our archipelago."

"Fancy Neptune having a womb!" whispered Sandra. "I always saw him as rather a hearty type."

When the prologue ended, Keela, with his arms still raised in a gesture of invocation, turned slowly, walked into the sea, and with a graceful dive disappeared from view. The lights went out, and in a silence after the applause had died away we distinctly heard Alma's voice say "now!" in a piercing whisper. There was the sound of whispering and scuffling in the darkness; the lights came on again, and from down the gangways on each side of the grandstand Ivy Poland's sprites bounded onto the beach where they arranged themselves, a little breathlessly, into a stylized tableau. They were dressed in diaphanous sea-green chiffon, long flowing green wigs to represent seaweed, and necklaces of coral-pink shells. They held the tableau gallantly for a long time, occasionally shooting anxious glances at the band, which remained discouragingly mute. Finally, after some audible hissing in the direction of the bandstand, the music began and they started their dance. It was a pretty enough dance although not startlingly original and they executed it charmingly, but it didn't really come to life until Tauhua Tali suddenly appeared from the outer darkness glittering like a dragonfly in peacock blue and did a quite enchanting *pas de deux* partnered by Kokoano, Juanita's head beach boy, who wore nothing but gilded bathing trunks and looked like a dusky Greek god who had been touched up by Gauguin. This brought forth storms of applause and they were recalled over and over again.

"If I were Sergeant Hancock," said Sandra, "I'd marry them both and take them straight to Ninette de Valois."

"How did you know about Sergeant Hancock?"

"My spies are everywhere," she replied, and turned back to the performance.

One of the principal difficulties in the original planning of the pageant was the almost monotonous tranquility of Samolan history. Whereas other Pacific islands had had their full quota of wars, invasions, human sacrifices, and bloodshed, the Samolan archipelago had basked peacefully and cheerfully in its eternal sunshine for centuries. True, there had been a gentle whisper of incipient revolution in 1791 when it had been considered advisable to ask King Kopalalua III to abdicate, but this had been swiftly hushed by the willing co-operation of Kopalalua himself, who, after a feast lasting for three days and nights, made a public announcement to his subjects. This announcement stated candidly and with dignity that, as he found no personal satisfaction in intercourse with the opposite sex and could therefore contribute little to the future of the dynasty, he thought it wiser to retire with his private entourage to the island of Tunaike and leave the ruling of Samolo to his nephew, young Prince Kefumalani, who, although still in his teens, had already proved that his procreative capabilities were beyond question. Esmond Templar and Peter Glades had enthusiastically voted that this historical incident should be included in the pageant but had been sharply overruled by the rest of the committee.

As it was, the pageant had been divided into two parts, the first of which dealt mainly with fantasy and the ancient legends, including the famous eruption of FumFumBolo. This, although technically complicated, went smoothly and was most effective. Tauhua Tali and Kókoano played FumFum the goddess of fire and Bolo the god of water, respectively. An enormous raft with the volcano built onto it was towed, under cover of darkness, from behind the left headland and, when suddenly illuminated by searchlights, erupted entirely satisfactorily. When the applause for this had died away the lights were swivelled back onto the beach again and the Royal Shropshires, dressed picturesquely as pirates, came whooping and shrieking down the two side gangways and engaged each other in a tremendous battle with pikes and cutlasses, eventually, as the lights faded, leaving many of each other for dead. This was enjoyed, not only by the audience, but very much indeed by the Royal Shropshires.

The finale of the first half was the historic landing of Captain Evangelus Cobb with his cargo of missionaries and their reception on the beach by King Kefumalani and his retinue. It had originally been intended to show the actual shipwreck with *The Good Samaritan* breaking up on the rocks. But this idea had been abandoned when Peter Glades had pointed out that for a ship to break up on rocks in perfectly calm water would not only be expensive and difficult to do, but would inevitably cast a slur on the heroic Captain Cobb's skill as a navigator. It had therefore been decided that the wreck must be *presumed* to have taken place out of sight behind the headland and that the survivors, battered and exhausted by a *presumed* tempest, should appear out of the darkness in one of the ship's boats.

All this went according to plan except that poor Letty Togstone, who had made a striking success last season as Mrs. Alving in *Ghosts*, was stricken down by malignant fate in what should have been her moment of triumph. As Mrs. Brunstock, the chief evangelist missionary, she had to spring onto the prow of the boat when it was only a few yards from shore, clad in a long white shift with a blood-stained bandage round her head, and declaim exultantly with arms outstretched:

"Land—Land! The Blessed Land at last.
The storm is over and the tempest past.
Thanks be to Thee, dear Lord, our faith sufficed
To carry to these isles the Word of Christ!"

This dramatic moment had been meticulously directed by Alma Peacock and, at the last few rehearsals with the band playing "Nearer My God to Thee" in the minor and Letty Togstone giving the full force of her voice, many onlookers, including Madame Alice and the Fumbasi brothers, had been reduced to tears. Tonight however, owing to nerves, perhaps, she miscalculated her leap onto the prow and teetered dangerously on the edge. Michael Tremlett, who was navigating the boat slowly from the stern with a muffled outboard motor, perceiving poor Letty's plight, suddenly, in a misguided effort to help, slammed the engine into reverse, whereupon she tumbled head foremost into the sea. Even then the situation might have been saved if she hadn't unfortunately repeated the word "Christ!" as she struck the water.

There was a horrified gasp from the audience and then, as she surfaced, an uncontrollable roar of laughter. She disregarded this with magnificent presence of mind, waded ashore, and sank gracefully at the feet of King Kefumalani, who, bending forward to lift her up, struck her sharply on the head as he did so. With a loud cry of pain she fell back onto the sand again and from that moment on the scene went to pieces. Michael Tremlett, unnerved by his previous error, switched the engine to full speed ahead and the boat shot forward and grounded on the beach with such force that Captain Cobb and the missionaries fell into a heap. The audience's laughter rose to a hysterical pitch, the band played a crashing chord, and all the lights went out. Unhappily they came on again a moment or two later disclosing the missionaries clambering out of the boat, Letty Togstone in floods of tears, and Alma Peacock in a gold lamé dress, up to her knees in water, gesticulating furiously at Michael Tremlett.

After this debacle there was a twenty minutes' interval during which we retired to the Anteroom behind the royal box. This, enclosed by red, white, and blue bunting and open to the sky, was furnished with some chairs and sofas and a trestle table on which were drinks and sandwiches. Sandra, whose control had been snapped by Letty Togstone's high dive, sank into a chair laughing convulsively.

"Pull yourself together, old girl," said H.E. sternly. "You really *must not* let anyone see you carrying on like that."

"I can't help it—poor Letty—oh dear!" She went off again.

"Have a drink quickly. They'll all be in in a minute." H.E. forced a glass of champagne into her hand.

Robin, Droopy, Eloise, and I formed a loyal screen round her while she did up her face and fought to regain her composure. Hali Alani came in, followed by Mrs. Innes-Glendower and old Sir Albert, Bimbo and Lucy, the Fumbasi brothers, Dusty and Buddha, and several others. Last of all Admiral Turling and the "Princess" appeared looking grave.

"Henry is worried." The "Princess" fastened a warm claw round my wrist. "Henry is very worried indeed."

"Why—what's the matter?"

The admiral, brick-red in a white dinner jacket, pointed significantly at the sky.

"Don't like the look of it," he said.

I glanced up and noticed that there were no longer any stars to be seen. I nudged Robin.

"The admiral's worried."

Robin looked up at the sky too and murmured, "Oh God!"

"I warned them." The admiral fixed me with a piercing blue eye. "I warned them weeks ago. This is a tricky time of the year, and the rains are overdue by about ten days."

The admiral's weather forecasts were, as a general rule, uncannily accurate, and my heart sank.

297

"You don't think that they might hold off? Just for a little longer, long enough at least to cover the royal visit?"

The admiral grunted and put his head on one side as though he were in private commune with the elements.

"The glass is going down," he said. "I noticed it before we left the house. And the wind's freshening—listen."

I listened, and sure enough there was an ominous rustling in the trees. At this moment Dusty and Buddha came up.

"How long is the second part?" enquired Buddha. I detected an anxious note in his voice.

"Quite long. Another hour and a half at least."

He turned to Dusty. "What do you think? Shall we take a chance and stick it out?"

"Some lovely things have happened so far," said Dusty. "I couldn't bear to miss anything. And if we leave now Ivy will never speak to us again. She's been sitting on that stool under the bandstand and watching us like a lynx."

"If we don't leave now she may never have to speak to us again because we shall probably get soaked to the skin and catch double pneumonia."

Dusty slipped her arm through his. "As a member of the committee," she said, "I must obey the call of duty and stick to my post."

"As a member of the committee," said Buddha, "you ought to be shot for having encouraged the production of this water-logged nightmare in the first place."

"You're a member of the committee too, dear, and you encouraged it just as much as I did. Come along now and don't be fractious. You don't want to miss the church choir, do you?"

"Yes," said Buddha, as they moved away. "I most emphatically do."

Presently the lights flickered on and off, there was a long roll of drums from the band, and we all returned to our seats. I looked over my shoulder as we went, and observed the admiral and the "Princess" disappearing furtively in the direction of the car park.

Before the lights went down I became aware of a general restlessness among the audience. I noticed several people looking up at the dark sky and whispering to each other. The air was perceptibly cooler, and the sound of the wind in the trees was growing louder by the minute.

"As a rule," said Sandra, "I find the weather as a subject extremely boring, but at this particular moment I must admit that it's absorbing me. Are you thinking what I'm thinking?"

"Yes," I replied. "I've also had a disturbing little chat with the admiral. He and the 'Princess' have just made tracks for the car park. I saw them out of the corner of my eye."

"I still maintain," said Sandra, "that as a member of the committee you ought to have discouraged the whole idea of this ghastly entertainment in the first place."

"You are the governor's lady," I hissed. "And I am your guest. Both of these circumstances make it impossible for me to reply as frankly I should like to."

"Hold on to your hats," said Sandra. "We're off again."

The lights dimmed and went out and suddenly, from the two headlands, the little bay was brilliantly illuminated. In the middle of it, a few yards from shore, was moored the raft that earlier on had held the erupting volcano. It now held the Ladies' Church Choir in full strength. The singers were arranged in three tiers and stood immobile, staring fixedly at their leader, Mrs. Lamont, who, vast in black satin, was standing, baton raised, in a small flat-bottomed dinghy just below their eye line. The dinghy was kept in position by two Samolan boys, one in the bow and one in the stern, each clasping an oar.

Owing to a slight miscalculation the Royal Shropshires hadn't quite finished playing the *William Tell* "Overture" when the lights came on. Realizing this, the band leader, Sergeant Major Brocklehurst, increased the tempo violently, but there was still an appreciable time lag before the music crashed to an untidy conclusion, during which Mrs. Lamont shot baleful looks over her shoulder at the bandstand.

To Mrs. Lamont the Ladies' Church Choir was the be-all and end-all of existence, the sum total of her dreams and the golden apple of her eye. She rehearsed it interminably year in year out; fought tigerishly in defence of its rights and monotonously insisted on its appearance at any and every public function where it could conceivably be appropriate. For this occasion Alma Peacock had suggested that the choir's routine costumes of plain white Mother

Hubbards banded with red, blue, and violet ribbons to distinguish the sopranos, mezzos, and contraltos, should be abandoned in favour of native dress. But Mrs. Lamont, deaf to all entreaty, had stood firm. Vainly had Alma and Ivy pleaded that as the scene represented the first burgeoning of Christianity on the island which took place early in the nineteenth century, the coloured sarongs and gay brassières of the period would not only be effective but a great deal more accurate from the point of view of atmosphere, but Mrs. Lamont had remained obdurate. The Ladies' Church Choir was primarily a religious body, she argued, and as such could not be expected to jettison the insignia by which it was so justly famed and impair its high dignity by romping about in the wanton apparel of a pagan age. Finally, after much heated discussion and a lot of acrimonious correspondence, Alma and Ivy were forced to give in and Mrs. Lamont won the day. So here they were, those serried ranks of white covered bosoms and exalted brown faces, looking as they had always looked and standing as they had always stood, except that on this occasion a slightly ambulant raft had been substituted for the more familiar terra firma of the Town Hall.

At the long-awaited end of the overture there was a short pause, Mrs. Lamont raised her baton still higher, Sandra gave an audible groan, and the Ladies' Church Choir burst forth.

The oratorio, "Blessed the Hearts That Suddenly See," was, in Inky Blumenthal's opinion at least, the high spot of his musical score. He had worked over it laboriously for weeks, and poor Kerry Stirling had been driven to the verge of a nervous breakdown by having to rewrite the verses no less than eleven times. Not that he need have bothered, because the Ladies' Church Choir in all their years of triumph had never been known to enunciate a single word that was even remotely comprehensible. However, the sounds they made were generally considered to be of high quality, and when they all opened their mouths together and let fly, as they were required to do in the opening bars of Inky's opus, the impact was considerable.

There was no escaping the fact that "Blessed the Hearts That Suddenly See," musically speaking, was a pretentious hash-up of Handel, Elgar, and Verdi with, alas, none of the melodic quality of any of them. It was also far far too long. We sat there battered into a state of hypnotic resignation watching glumly the rows of bosoms rising and falling, the numberless mouths opening and shutting, and Mrs. Lamont flailing the air with her arms and rocking the dinghy dangerously with her feet. After a while I closed my eyes and tried to shut my ears and my mind to what was going on and concentrate on something entirely different. Suddenly, however, I became conscious of an extra sound over and above the incessant booming and trilling. A queer, metallic whining noise that seemed to be growing in volume. I opened my eyes again and saw that the raft was rocking alarmingly. At this moment, with a shriek and a roar, the storm struck. There were a few screams from the audience and a panic-stricken rush for the exits. The skies opened and a curtain of rain, shining like glass spears in the searchlights, crashed down onto the sea obliterating completely the raft, the choir, Mrs. Lamont, and even the palm trees a few feet away from us. We all instinctively rose from our seats and crowded up into the back of the grandstand to get as much cover as we could, but it was of little avail because the wind was blowing straight into the cove and within a few seconds we were all drenched to the bone.

"This," said Sandra through chattering teeth, "comes under the heading of 'An Act of God,' and I must say I'm on His side."

"We'd better make a dash for the car, sir," said Chris Mortlock. "It's just outside."

"We'll stay where we are for the moment." H.E.'s voice was resigned. "We can't sit in the car while everybody else is getting soaked. Here, darling." He took off his coat and wrapped it round Sandra's shoulders. Droopy and Robin did the same for Eloise and me, and there we stood, huddled into a sodden little group waiting for the first violence of the storm to die down. After what seemed an age there was indeed a slight lull. The force of the wind lessened and the density of the rain thinned out.

"Oh Lord!" cried Sandra. "Look at the church choir!"

We all looked, and the sight that met our eyes will be emblazoned on my memory forever and a day. On the first impact of the storm the raft had broken loose from its moorings and begun to drift away towards the open sea. At the same moment, apparently, the dinghy had capsized and was now floating upside down with Mrs. Lamont lying across it like a large black seal supported on each side by the two fisherboys. The choir itself, Samolan-born and -bred from the biggest contralto to the smallest soprano and therefore as at home in the water as on dry land, appeared, at the same moment to arrive at a unanimous decision. In almost perfect unison they tore off their coloured ribbons, whipped their white robes over their heads, and in varying states of nudity dived into the turbulent waves and struck out firmly for the shore. At this moment the wind struck again with a renewed shriek, and a fresh deluge of rain blotted the scene from view.

"If only they'd done that in the first place," said Sandra, "it would have brought the house down."

TWENTY-FOUR

During the whole of that night and the next day the sky lay on the island like a gun-metal blanket and the rain fell solidly and relentlessly without even a moment's letup. Mountain streams swelled into torrents and came crashing down from the high land, laying waste plantations and crops and flooding the roads. There was a heavy landslide in the Lailanu Pass and the bridge across the Grua-Bolo River was swept away, which caused all the traffic to the north coast to be suspended.

By some miracle the telephone service continued to function, and when I called the airport after breakfast to check as to whether or not the plane on which Droopy and Eloise were booked would take off I was told, to my surprise, that it would leave on schedule, and so at noon we set off in the station wagon and drove gingerly through the teeming downpour muffled in rain-coats. The airport, fortunately less crowded than usual, was breath-lessly hot and had a damp, steamy smell like the reptile house at the zoo. When Droopy and Eloise had checked their bags we set-tled ourselves in a row on the excruciating wooden chairs and lis-tened to the rain drumming thunderously onto the corrugated tin roof. The noise of this made conversation impossible, and so we sat in resigned silence, each, presumably, a prey to his or her pri-vate thoughts. Mine, I admit, were fairly kaleidoscopic. The dramas and crises of the last few weeks shuttled back and forth before my mind's eye in a series of disconnected scenes like an amateur film that had been spliced together too hurriedly by an inexperienced cutter. I saw Nurse Duffy lying like a cast sheep on the spare-room carpet; Robin and me driving interminably to and fro along the coast road in the middle of the night; Bunny lying on his bed covered in spots and swearing deliriously; Eloise, swathed in her hyacinth-coloured yashmak, "receiving" graciously on the back verandah, and the heart-sinking embarrassment of Droopy discovering me in full garden-party regalia at nine-thirty in the morning.

I glanced at Eloise, who was sitting blandly next to me, and wondered what was going on in her mind: whether she was happy or unhappy; whether or not the disintegration of her romantic adventure had left any lasting regrets; and what real hope there was that the resumption of her married life with Droopy would be satisfying enough to her ego to keep her wayward vanity within reasonable bounds. It would be a pity if it didn't. Droopy, although lacking in flamboyant sex-appeal, was obviously a gentle and affectionate man. The more I had grown to know Eloise since her arrival in Samolo, the more I had become convinced that sex, qua sex, was by no means the basic driving force of her casual infidelities. I suspected—correctly, I think—that the physical aspects of passionate love were a great deal less important to her than most people imagined. She was by nature placid and temperamentally more suited to the lilies and languors of virtue than the roses and raptures of vice. Her incontestable beauty, although superficially a dazzling asset was, and had been all her life, her principal stumbling block. Without it, or at least without quite so much of it, her whole existence might have been considerably less complicated and probably a great deal happier. On a sudden impulse I slipped my arm through hers and gave it an affectionate squeeze.

"Dear Eloise," I said. "I'm sad that you're leaving and I shall miss you a lot—really I will."

She returned my pressure and gave me a ravishing smile. "I shall never forget all you've done for me. You and Robin have been absolute——" She broke off suddenly and looked down. "I'm not going to say 'angels' because Droopy says I say it far too much and that it's high time I changed the record." She paused. "Perhaps I'd better say—very patient, very understanding, and most awfully awfully kind." She looked up again, and, to my surprise, I noticed that her eyes were glistening.

At this moment the departure of the plane was announced over the loudspeakers and we all got up and walked to the exit gate.

Robin and I waited, a trifle anxiously, to see the plane take off.

We watched it lumber away through the driving rain and disappear from view. After a few minutes' pause we heard the increased roar of its engines and suddenly it reappeared, whizzing along the runway amid fountains of spray. It rose into the air as gracefully as a heron, lingered for a moment in our sight, and then vanished for good into the grey clouds.

We walked silently back through the lounge and then made a sudden, violent dash through the wild weather to the station wagon. Robin started the engine.

"And so they stayed married," he said. "And lived happily ever after."

TWENTY-FIVE

The night before the day of the royal arrival Robin and I retired to bed in a state of abject depression. We talked spasmodically for a while and then turned out the light and lay sleeplessly in the dark listening to the rain thudding down.

It had been a ghastly day: the new young crop at the lower end of the plantation had been completely inundated and almost certainly ruined; under the Pareanda tree an ever-widening pond of beige-coloured water had spread over the lawn transforming it into a soggy marsh in which the garden chairs, stripped of their cushions, stood about like forsaken relics. Three leaks had appeared simultaneously in the roof of the back verandah, and the evening had been a nightmare of pails and mops and mounting exasperation. Sandra had rung up, and I knew from her voice that she was in despair. The gardens of Government House were a shambles and the grandstands erected round the harbour and along the royal route were not only waterlogged but one, opposite the Town Hall, which was destined to hold the members of the House of Representatives and their relations, had collapsed entirely and now lay, a sodden mass of wood and bunting, in a heap in Parliament Square. The water pageant had of course been cancelled. All the carefully planned itineraries had had to be rearranged provisionally. In fact the whole pattern of the royal visit, on which the entire island had been concentrating for months, had been reduced to chaos.

In the afternoon I had loyally fought my way through the deluge to attend an urgent committee meeting of the S.A.D.S. This had been a dismal affair conducted with resigned efficiency by poor Alma Peacock. Her face looked puffy, and a redness round her

306

eyes betrayed much recent weeping. Ivy Poland chain smoked, her hands shook, and she gave every indication of being on the verge of a nervous breakdown. Esmond Templar and Peter Glades, drained of their usual vivacity, sat with their chins resting on their hands and stared mutely at the rain streaming down the windowpanes. The others—Keela Alioa, Dusty, and Michael Tremlett—doodled on the white paper pads in front of them and listened to what was said abstractedly and without comment.

After about an hour's listless discussion it had been decided to requisition the Kebololali Cinema, which was the only one in the town with a large enough stage, and string together as much of the pageant as could be got onto it, bolstered up with two or three tried-and-true items from the Ivy Poland Dancers' repertoire and culminating in a grand finale consisting of the Ladies' Church Choir and the Royal Shropshires, en masse, singing "Abide with Me" and "Land of Hope and Glory." Fortunately the water pageant had originally been planned for the last evening of the royal visit in any case, so there were three days in hand in which to rehearse and organize the substitute entertainment. Finally Alma had adjourned the meeting with a spiritless whack of her hammer and a strangled sob, and we had all parted, with forced smiles glued onto our faces, and gone our ways.

I woke early, just after dawn, and tiptoed over to the window in order not to wake Robin, who was lying on his back and snoring rhythmically. I noticed in passing that there was another button missing from his pyjama jacket. I peeped out and suddenly, with a whoop of joy, dragged the curtains back with a clatter, flooding the room with sunshine. Robin woke with a grunt and said, "What the hell's happening?"

"Come and see for yourself," I cried exultantly. "Come quickly —quickly!"

He jumped out of bed and joined me at the window, and we stood there in silence staring unbelievingly at the miracle. The mountaintops were glowing pink in the early light and the pale, lovely sky was without a cloud. At this moment the telephone rang.

"Who the devil can be ringing up at this time of the morning?" Robin said testily.

I went over and lifted the receiver. It was Lydia and there was panic in her voice. "I'm terribly terribly sorry to wake you up at this unearthly hour, but I can't find the telephone book and I want Dr. Bowman's number urgently."

"What's wrong?"

"It's Daphne. She's running a temperature of a hundred and four. I thought at first it was the result of her concussion the other day, but she's come out in the most awful rash all over her back and chest and I can't imagine what it can be!"

"I can," I said. "It's chicken pox. Dr. Bowman's number is 5064."

She thanked me effusively and I hung up and climbed back into bed.

A few hours later Robin, Nanny, the children and I, dressed to the nines and tingling with anticipation, drove through the flag-bedecked, crowd-lined streets to the harbour and took our allotted places in the grandstand. The morning had remained glorious. The sea was flat calm with a sheen of lavender and blue on it, and the dramatic outline of Paiana Head looked as though it had been painted in purple onto the sky. Occasionally light gusts of wind started up and died down again, making sudden moving shadows on the placid surface of the water. A new jetty had been built out from the landing stage, enamelled white and covered with a scarlet carpet. Rows of handsome Samolan policemen wearing topees and tight navy-blue trousers with wide red stripes stood to attention in front of a line of wooden posts connected by crimson cords. Behind this line the Samolan people, eager and expectant, chattering like parakeets and dressed in every vivid colour imaginable, waited with mounting excitement for the moment when two young and handsome people, crowned with the symbolic majesty of many centuries, would set foot for the first time upon their gay, gentle, and enchanting island.